DINO M. DATTOLICO

SPECIAL
MEN

Also by Dennis Foley
Published by Ivy Books:

LONG RANGE PATROL

SPECIAL MEN
A LRP's
Recollections

Dennis Foley

IVY BOOKS • NEW YORK

This book is dedicated to the men of the Tiger Force.

Ivy Books
Published by Ballantine Books
Copyright © 1994 by Dennis Foley
Introduction copyright © 1994 by David Hackworth

ISBN 0-8041-0915-X

Manufactured in the United States of America

FOREWORD

•

I believe that men are neither destined nor born to great courage in battle. Rather, they are drawn to the higher challenges of combat and remarkable deeds by the camaraderie, inspiration, and encouragement of others.

What follows is a winding path that led me into the company of remarkable men—men whose most dominant qualities were then, and still are, loyalty, reliability, and tenacity.

It was my distinct privilege to be allowed to serve with such men in command of Airborne, Ranger, and Long Range Patrol units. Their dedication to their country and their sacrifices, in most cases, are known only to those who were near to them in battle and near to them in life.

In these pages I would like to remember them and describe the extraordinary deeds they performed and the pain that they suffered in answering their country's call. They make me proud to know them and to remember them.

INTRODUCTION

by David Hackworth

I can remember the day Dennis Foley reported in to my parachute battalion in Vietnam as clearly as I remember the day my first child was born. Dennis was a tall, lanky infantry second lieutenant with no special skills except that he was qualified as a 7-1542: Airborne infantry platoon leader. His service record indicated that he was just another untried lieutenant joining his first combat unit. Yet there was something about him. It wasn't his youthful eagerness—most shavetails are eager—or that he was the son of a distinguished combat officer—many of the officers in the battalion were warrior bred and reared—or that he had risen through the enlisted ranks and graduated from Fort Benning's tough infantry officer candidate school (OCS), which as a rule produced the most combat-ready platoon leaders. On the surface, there was nothing special about the twenty-one-year-old, but my sixth-sense antenna told me he was worth watching. I decided to keep him close at hand. I assigned Foley to the battalion's elite Airborne Ranger special operations unit, the Tiger Force.

Like most former sergeants, I had little use for second lieutenants. They could get a platoon in trouble faster than a stroll through a minefield. George Patton is reported to have said that an officer wasn't worth a pinch of salt until he'd been with troops for ten years, and I share the same view.

I never could figure out army logic. The leadership of an infantry platoon is the most demanding and dangerous job in the armed forces, yet the infantry platoon is commanded by the most inexperienced and least qualified guys in the military. I believed, and still do, that a lieutenant should serve in the infantry enlisted ranks for at least three years, and if he doesn't prove himself a leader by at least making buck sergeant, he should not go on to a commissioning school such as West Point, Annapolis, ROTC, or OCS. In sum, a lieutenant should shovel shit before he rides the horse. This approach will teach him to be streetwise and have respect for his men, because he will have been there and done that.

Over the bullet-splattered months that followed, my reading on Foley was proven to be dead on. He was an exception to the green-lieutenant rule. The something special my antenna picked up was his great heart, which pumped out a keen spirit; his extraordinary brightness, which allowed him to make complex things simple; his pit bull-like tenacity and unflinching loyalty to his troops and then to his bosses—in that order—which is the way it should be.

Foley was an up-front kind of leader and I frequently found myself on his flank sharing a foxhole in a hot firefight. There, at the bottom line of the soldiering business, I observed firsthand that he was capable, cool, and not afraid to take the high risks that came with his chosen life and death profession.

As is the way with old soldiers who see rare ability in young leaders, I became his mentor. He had the potential of becoming a senior officer and winning battles without taking hard lumps. I tried to pass on my knowledge and give him the assignments that would round him out.

He eventually commanded the Tigers after its skipper, Medal of Honor winner Jim Gardner, was shot down. Later, at Dak To, one of the most fierce, longest-running battles of the Vietnam War, he learned that skippering a battalion in combat is a flat-footed son of a bitch. I was my own operations officer, Foley was my assistant, and through twenty-one sleepless days and nights our battalion kicked the bejesus out of an enemy regiment that was four times bigger, but not one inch badder. Foley learned more there than he could have learned in two years at staff schools or skippering a battalion in peacetime. I believe that soldiers learn by doing, and by God he did a lot of doing in those three long weeks that saw our battalion lose almost half its officers and troopers while killing four times that number of North Vietnamese regulars.

After Dak To, on another battlefield with a different unit, one of my rifle companies needed a swift leadership transfusion. I put out the word, and with the power of my two-star boss, found Foley, who was about to be assigned as a starched briefing officer in some Disneyland east HQ and scooped him up. He quickly transformed a hard-luck company into a hard-core force and started kicking some mean Viet Cong ass.

Then one day I asked him and his tired unit to go that extra mile. They were due to go in reserve and rest after a grueling campaign. Just when they were about to be lifted out, hot intelligence targeted a

Viet Cong heavy-weapons outfit in his zone. After a heated argument in which Foley stood tall against going because his troops were too bushed, he launched; lieutenant colonels always win over captains. But it was a bad win on my part. Foley got blown out, and the hot intel target disappeared.

After our hitch in the hard-core battalion, we never served together again. But from the sidelines I watched him climb onward and upward toward the stars that blinked in the distance. And then . . . well, that's his story, which he tells beautifully in the following pages.

After Foley got shot up, I recorded the following notes about infantry lieutenants. Since little changes in infantry combat except how fast you go and how loud the bang, these observations are just as applicable today as they were back in 1969:

The average infantry lieutenant who joined my battalion was not prepared to lead a rifle platoon. He was not completely trained in the theory of combat in Vietnam; was extremely weak in soldier management, leadership, practical knowledge, small unit combat operations; and was almost devoid of actual field experience. The old saying, "Good judgment comes from experience and experience is gained from bad judgment" is certainly applicable here. Out of sixty-eight infantry lieutenants who joined the battalion, only two had ever stood in front of a TO & E platoon before. The rest were out of service schools, training centers, and other non-TO & E assignments. As a result of having no experience in the art of handling a platoon, these young and, on the average, well-meaning officers were completely lacking in self-confidence and were, with rare exception, almost valueless as platoon leaders without at least a thirty day OJT period with a "stud-type" platoon leader.

The biggest shortcomings of the young infantry leaders were their failure to be demanding and their reluctance to ensure that their men did the basic things which would keep them alive on the battlefield.

I believe one of the reasons for this deficiency is that many of the social values acquired as a civilian conflict diametrically with what is expected of a leader. A case in point is just one civilian-instilled value that drastically conflicts with combat leadership: popularity.

Great emphasis is placed in the American society to instill the "virtue" of being a popular fellow. The formal part of this training starts at kindergarten when the importance of socializing is first introduced and is thereafter never ending. The informal training begins even earlier, and hence, the young man, when first entering the army, has had about twenty years' indoctrination of "being a nice guy." After four years of college ROTC/military academy training or about a year of basic infantry and OCS training, he is supposed to be the well-prepared leader who always places the welfare of the troops just below the accomplishment of the mission. Wrong. The average leader has a virtual Pavlovian instinct toward being popular. He must be a good guy! Thus, he becomes a "joiner" instead of an "enforcer."

In Vietnam, good guys let their people smoke at night and take portable radios to the field, allowed night ambushes to set up in the abandoned hootch so they could have protection from the rain, and left only one guard by the door so everyone else could get a good night's rest. Good guys let their men leave their boots on for several days, resulting in inordinately severe immersion foot. Good guys didn't check to ensure that their men protected themselves against mosquitos or took the required malaria pills and salt pills. Good guys ended up killing their men with kindness.

The average young leader in my battalion generally knew what was required, but did not have the moral courage to enforce the rules. He preferred to turn his head and look the other way rather than make vigorous on-the-spot corrections. Deficiencies such as dirty ammunition and weapons, improperly safed weapons and grenades, incorrect camouflage techniques and the improper use of terrain (not using natural cover to provide protection from small-arms fire), and not staying alert to stay alive was common. The end result of this was that the soldiers' habits became sloppier and sloppier, and carelessness ran amuck. This resulted in casualties—casualties that could have been prevented had the leader checked and demanded the small things be done well.

My experience has been that soldiers in combat will only do what is required of them and, if under weak, nice-guy leadership, will try to get away with everything they can. This results in the violation of every basic rule in the book. As an aside, I believe that all the while they are placing their lives in jeopardy, they know they are wrong and will respond to the requirements of a positive, ass-kicking leader. Results: fewer casualties and greater respect for the leader who cares enough for his men to make them do it right.

I believe that another serious shortcoming is the failure to teach leaders the importance of supervision and the techniques of supervising. The average small unit leader seems to take for granted that what he wills will be done, so there is no need to check.

The nature of combat in Vietnam greatly extended this problem because small units normally operated on a widely decentralized basis in rugged terrain that restricted inspection visits from higher headquarters. These conditions generally prohibited the more experienced senior NCOs and officers from checking the platoon and passing along "tips of the trade." Without an experienced, demanding leader, a carelessly led platoon is headed for a violent collision. The infrequency of combat in Vietnam (as compared to World War II or Korea) and the seemingly good security of many areas had a tendency to lull soldiers and leaders into a false sense of safety. Consequently, alertness and security became relaxed and the likelihood of enemy attack increased proportionately. (Mao: "When the enemy is weak: attack.")

The leader must be inculcated with the burning need to keep his people alert and never let their guard down. The leader must be instilled with the need to supervise his people twenty-four hours a day. He must check: fighting position for adequacy; if soldiers know the mission, situation, and where the LPs are; if proper field sanitation is being practiced; if all battlefield debris is destroyed to deny the enemy a source of supply; if his people are all sleeping under cover and protected from "first-round bursts"; if his subordinate leaders are "heads up" and demanding that their men are alert and tightly controlled. A never-ending list of little things must be checked: magazines cleaned; weapons test-fired; LPs and claymores out; sectors of fire known; medics looking at feet, monitoring salt tablets, and malaria pills and watching out for "jungle rot"; stand-to being conducted, to name a few. But the main thing is the leader has to constantly check, following the adage: "The best fertilizer in the world is the boss's footsteps . . . they make things grow."

Small units must train not in the classroom, but in the bush. Here warriors must be taught the gut fundamentals of infantry combat. The basics must be drilled in employing the same instructional techniques as those used in Airborne training. Every block of instruction should be reduced to the salient "points of performance," and each soldier should be required to demonstrate his knowledge by ruthless practical examination. Rommel said, "The best form of welfare for the troops is first-class training, for this saves unnecessary casualties." First-class training means hard work and sacrifice. "The more sweat on the training field, the less blood on the battlefield" is an adage I have always followed, and I'm convinced it keeps the casualty list short.

Cadets and new leaders who show ineptitude should be eliminated and not "recycled," such as that atrocity, Lt. William Calley, who caused the massacre at My Lai. Calley was recycled three times after being found wanting in leadership. He was commissioned in order to show a "low attrition rate" to higher headquarters. The shame of My Lai, more than any major enemy victory, caused the American people to withdraw support for the war effort. They said, "Enough is enough."

Dennis Foley's story is an inside view of the United States Army from perhaps its finest pre-Vietnam hour to its darkest period when the Vietnam War almost destroyed it, to its slow post-war turnaround that set the stage for its magnificent performance in Desert Storm.

The army that Private Foley joined in 1962 was, in the vernacular of the day, STRAC—ready to go any time, any place, anywhere, and kick butt big time when it got there. Many of the senior NCOs who trained him wore the Perfect Attendance Badge (Combat Infantry Badge with one star—WWII and Korea) and most of these hard-core mothers, who are the steel backbone of any army, ran their outfits with total professionalism. These were the days before political correctness, "be kind," and "consideration for others" became the order of the day. These hard noncoms were straight out of *From Here to Eternity*. They soldiered hard, played and drank hard, and kept their units on their toes with tough love and tougher discipline. Their war experience taught them how to survive and win on the battlefield, and they passed this knowledge on to their young warriors and officers by making them do their soldier drills over and over again. "If you don't get it right in training, you won't get it right in combat and people will get killed," they barked. These were the days when few soldiers or junior officers were married. Soldiers lived in the barracks with their sergeants, and a duty day started at 0500 hours and frequently ended with the last notes of taps. It was a harsh life, but it prepared young Foley and his comrades for the harsher challenges of a distant battlefield, where too many of these wonderful noncoms were wasted in a war that only the people down in the rifle units understood; the generals and colonels who passed blindly through their units to get their tickets punched seldom asked these old pros.

So the brass, flying overhead in their choppers, went on failing to understand the nature of the war, and finally, three years after I first met Foley and he joined me in the Delta, there were few regular noncoms left. They were all dead or so shot up they weren't fit for regular infantry duty or, after having two or three wars under their pistol belts, hung up their rifles and joined the ranks of the retired army.

Foley graphically tells this story, which thousands of other young army and Marine officers painfully experienced in Vietnam. Many had to immediately pick up the chips without being able to be pulled along by an old pro sergeant who spoon-fed his new officer boss until he could eat by himself.

Foley's story is a good primer on how a leader develops after he leaves Fort Benning or Quantico with a head chock full of information and the back of his car even fuller with how-to-lead-and-fight books. And with all of this knowledge, how, when he gets on the killing field and the first bullet whizzes over his head, all electricity to his brain shuts off and fear takes over.

School cannot totally prepare a leader for this shock. But isolating the essentials can. If the basics, the fundamentals, are learned by rote, much like a boxer is drilled to counter punch, automatically reacting with a left cross, right hook or "the bomb" right down the middle without a conscious thought clicking through his brain, he'll get along just fine. And after each contact, the light will grow brighter as his experience level grows. It doesn't mean he won't be scared, but at least he won't be in the dark.

War is so simple, yet the military school system makes it so bloody complicated. The key to winning in battle is to sneak up on your opponent and belt the shit out of him from behind as hard and quickly as you can before he figures out you're in the neighborhood, and then scoot the hell out of there.

Besides having experienced noncoms to lead new small-unit officers through the minefields of a combat command, the best way for a new leader to get ready and learn his stuff is to read and reread books by combat warriors who have been there. Rommel's *Attacks*, Patton's *War as I Knew It*, Sajer's *The Forgotten Soldier*, and my book, *About Face*, are good starters. Don't bother with Clausewitz's convoluted double-talk, but make *The Art of War* by Sun Tzu your bible. It was written around 400 B.C., and his short and simple lessons of war are every bit as valuable today as they were then. I've been carrying Sun Tzu and reading it almost daily since I first picked it up in 1950. After some good OJT, the knowledge in these books and others will allow you to lead well, fight smart, and take care of your warriors.

A good knowledge of military history, like attending Airborne, Ranger, and Special Forces courses, is a confidence builder. In small-unit leaders, confidence, like fear, is contagious. Troopers can feel it, see it, smell it, and it will rub off on soldiers from a platoon to a division as quickly as a good rumor rumbles out of the latrine.

Confidence produces courage. Most leaders or warriors are not born with a double basic load of guts. Most leaders and warriors are as scared as the next guy in their first or 100th firefight, but if they are confident that they are tactically proficient and their unit is squared away and motivated by a strong sense of duty to accomplish the mission, the courage that is needed to do what many will view as impossible will be there. Mouths may be dry, guts may churn and hands shake, but when the slugs start snapping, the prepared leader will be as cool as Clint Eastwood on the outside and tell his boys, "Let's make somebody's day. Follow me." And no one will know who is scared out of their brain.

Besides being one hell of a job, leading men into battle is the ultimate responsibility. On the battlefield decisions are made in a split second, such as "go left" or "go right" or "go straight ahead," and right or wrong, good or bad, people get killed. Leaders carry the scars of those decisions for the rest of their lives. Later, battle scenes keep playing back. "Why didn't I wait?" "Why didn't I bring in more fire?" "Why didn't I go myself?" haunt the veteran day and night until he checks out of the net. Good preparation, hard training, and attention to detail keep nightmares to a minimum.

Dennis Foley's memoirs of his days as a small-unit combat leader give an excellent inside view of the United States Army during its troublesome Vietnam period, and you can almost feel, as you turn the pages, how a young combat leader grows from a scared, unsure-of-himself liability taking over his first platoon to an old pro company commander who has his shit together.

Foley's story is well told. Each page is alive with what soldiering is about: the relentless drill, excitement, boredom, the highs and lows and the brotherhood that, in the end, makes the whole journey a special trip among special men.

Dennis Foley served his country and men well, and the journey that unfolds in the following pages passes on his combat experience to present and future generations of infantry small-unit leaders.

To be a combat leader in the profession of arms is the most noble, deadly, and exciting occupation going. Its rewards are few, but if, at the end of the day, his men say, "He's a good man," those few words make a pretty good final epitaph for a war fighter.

As I look back on three decades of knowing the author, it's a pleasure to say Foley is a good man, and his primer on war fighting is an equally good read for warriors past, present, and future.

David Hackworth
Whitefish, MT

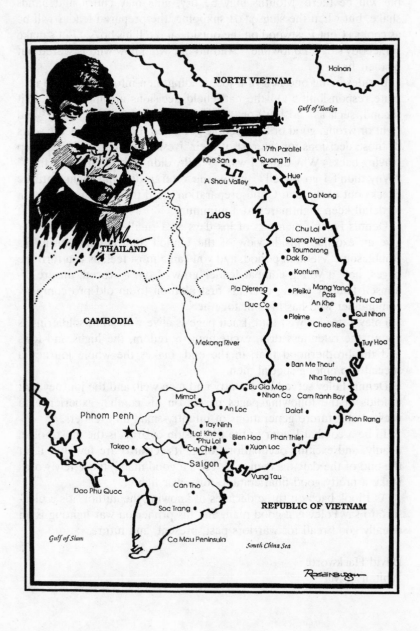

CHAPTER 1

·

I had the privilege of serving in three armies between 1962 and 1982: a post–World War II, atomic-age army; a Vietnam War army; and a post-Vietnam army. During that same span, the United States Army was a draft army for the first half of my years and a volunteer army for the second half.

Change was the only constant. The natural tendency for an organization to evolve and improve was sent into a tailspin by the Cuban Missile Crisis, the Berlin Wall, and the Vietnam War. The army's responses to these major world events took place during my first ten years in uniform.

My last ten were monopolized by the army's efforts to eliminate the draft; forget about Vietnam; adjust to the drawdown in manpower; deal with the impact of drug, racial, and disciplinary problems; and the reoriented general mission to defend Europe against a mechanized/armored force in a nuclear environment.

During two decades of service I never served in a unit, or at a post or service school that was not in the process of being organized, reorganized, or disbanded. I never served in a unit whose mission was the same when I left it as it was when I arrived. And I never served in a unit where my immediate superior or subordinate was the same when I left as when I arrived. Alice's Wonderland was sane, tame, and boring, by comparison.

I was just eighteen and only four days into basic training at Fort Dix, New Jersey, when my platoon was called out of our aging World War II barracks for the third formation of the morning. A cadreman, a young acting corporal, formed up the platoon with an uncharacteristic smirk on his face. Once he was satisfied that we were all there, had handed out a moderate number of pushups for various infractions that we didn't really understand, and once he had our attention, he told us that we were going to a briefing. He made sure that we understood it was a briefing we were not ready for, and one that the army was wasting time and money on.

He told us we were worthless, and that it was highly unlikely that we could hack it. In his opinion—formed in the six months he had been in the army—the army would be better off sending us to the regimental headquarters to police[1] the area.

We were joined by the other platoons, double-timed to a small battalion theater, and hustled into seats. My platoon was lucky to get seats in the front rows. None among us knew the subject of the briefing, and the late-June heat was almost unbearable in the tiny theater as we sat there waiting.

We waited for the longest time, reminded to sit still and be happy that we weren't out in the sun. In only a few minutes we were getting sleepy and the fight to stay awake was on. Getting caught dozing off would be worth an easy twenty pushups.

Finally, from the back of the room someone yelled, "On your feet!" and we jumped up, having learned the multiple-push-up penalties for anything less than an instant response. We couldn't see them, but two sets of boots clumped down the aisle, approaching the chin-high stage.

"Gentlemen, please take your seats," another voice said.

Gentlemen? It was the first time anyone had called us "gentlemen" since our arrival at the reception center on the other side of the post almost two weeks earlier. We'd not been in the army very long, but we knew something was up. And that something mounted the stage in the persona of two sergeants, one a sergeant first class and the other a master sergeant.[2]

Since our induction we had rarely seen NCOs of that rank. Our days had been controlled by privates first class (PFCs), acting corporals,[3] and an occasional three-stripe sergeant. A couple of times a day we would stand a formation led by our field first sergeant[4]—himself a sergeant first class.

But those two sergeants on the stage were nothing like the ser-

---

[1] A very old military expression meaning to clean up.

[2] The Army's enlisted rank system at this time went from recruit (pay grade E-1) to sergeant major (pay grade E-9). A sergeant first class or platoon sergeant (E-7) wore insignia of three chevrons over two rockers; master sergeant (E-8), three chevrons over three rockers. The other grades consisted of private (E-2), private first class (E-3), corporal (E-4), sergeant (E-5), and staff sergeant (E-6). Paralleling this was the specialist system for grades E-4 to E-7. Specialists were identified by a spread-eagle device (E-4) surmounted by arcs or rockers, one for E-5, two for E-6, and three for E-7.

[3] A temporary appointment carrying the rank and authority but not the pay of a given grade. Most commonly found in training units, acting grades are made for Corporal through Staff Sergeant.

[4] In training units, the NCO responsible for the troops while they are in the field or training, as opposed to the company first sergeant, who usually remains in the company area, attending to administrative duties.

geants we had all met in recruiting stations, induction centers, and the reception station. They were both tall, lean, and hard looking—yet they were younger than any NCOs we'd seen of comparable rank.

They radiated a sense of self-confidence that would have shown up on an X-ray. But most apparent were their uniforms: spit-shined paratrooper boots, bloused trousers with razor-sharp creases, highly polished brass, and badges that we would come to respect: parachute wings, the Ranger tab, and the Airborne tab over the Special Forces arrowhead patch. To us, they were truly men of iron.

They were there to recruit us into Airborne training and to set the hook for Special Forces. Before the briefing was over, we began to think of those men as much larger than we could ever be. As we listened to them tell us how difficult Airborne training was and how selective Special Forces was, we all were sure that the corporal was right. We were not made of the same stuff that those two soldiers were.

The two NCOs spoke with confidence and authority. Each word was carefully measured for its impact on us and each pause was well rehearsed to let the point that followed sink in.

They showed us a film about parachute training. We sat there in the dark watching soldiers—paratroopers—hurl themselves from aircraft at what seemed like incredible speeds and frightening heights.

No one spoke, and no one in the room missed any parachutes deploying from the pack trays of the jumpers, who seemed to us to be totally out of control as they exited the small doors of the large, silver C-119 Flying Boxcars.

A thought entered my mind for only a fleeting second, and then I quickly wished it away. Hell, I had never even *been* in an airplane. Stepping out of one at over twelve hundred feet above the ground was more than I could imagine, even though I was watching it happen in that steamy little theater.

The mass jumps were interspersed with scenes from training. It seemed every clip had one of three things in it: soldiers jumping from aircraft, soldiers running in formation, or soldiers practicing landings or exits. Nowhere in the film was there a moment where soldiers were sitting or listening or taking notes or relaxing.

It was very clear that anyone who volunteered for parachute training was in for a month of dawn-to-dusk PT, followed by an evening of spit shining and polishing.

While we were all impressed with the tales of derring-do and the promise of challenges and danger far beyond our imagination, not many of us were interested in falling out to the designated area to fill out the application forms to go to Airborne school at Fort Benning.

I walked out of that briefing unaware of how my life had been changed by the remote possibilities suggested by those two sergeants. Little did I know then that men like the two who had stood on that stage would be such a large part of my life—eventually finding a permanent place in my heart.

Joining the army or playing roulette with the draft had been a frequent topic of discussion among those in my high school class who had little or no hope of being accepted into a college. It was a subject of far less importance to us than it would become in the later half of the decade, after the large-scale commitment of American troops to Vietnam.

Our naïve notion of the gamble was that we could either volunteer and get military service out of the way, or leave it up to the Selective Service system to tell us when we would go. If we rolled the dice we could be pulled off a job, away from a new wife, or out of college with a simple letter from our local draft board. Our graduating class didn't have the widespread deferments that would suddenly appear during the Vietnam years. For us, being a student or being married were not automatic exemptions. So for us it was a crap shoot.

For those of us who were the sons of army personnel, there was a significant likelihood that we would be drafted before our civilian classmates, whose fathers were members of the community.

Like so many of my peers, I knew that one way or the other, the army was going to get some of my time. So volunteering seemed to be a chance (although slimmer than I would admit) for me to get into college—West Point—but before I could take the West Point Preparatory School exam, I had to be on active duty.

So I volunteered, and while at the reception station at Fort Dix, New Jersey, I got my notice to report for my induction physical. I had guessed right. That summer the army was going to get me anyway.

During basic training I was unable to shake the image of the two Airborne sergeants standing proud and tall on that stage in the stifling hot theater. While we were all sweating profusely, they were calm and cool. Their words faded, but that image never did. Though I had grown up the son of a career army man, I had never been close enough to my father's business to see images like those struck by the two Airborne recruiters.

* * *

I put all my extra energy into trying to convince my company cadre to let me take the West Point Prep School exam. At this point I have to explain that growing up as an army brat, moving frequently, and being a somewhat less than motivated student left me unprepared for college. I attended three high schools in my senior year alone, five in all since leaving junior high.

I never really got into the swing of high school, although I knew that my family expected me to go to college. Still I dragged my feet and found myself far below my classmates on the college-acceptability scale. All the while, I was sure that if I applied myself, I could make up for four years of bad study habits and low grades simply by joining the army and getting into the yearlong West Point Prep School, and then West Point.

Looking back, I am amazed at the response I got from the company cadre. They would have been well within their rights to recommend disapproval of my application. Had they, I'm sure I would never have seen the exam packet. But they didn't. My company first sergeant and commanding officer recommended approval, and the CO certified that he and other battalion officers would proctor the exam.

I was called in by the first sergeant who explained that I would *not* miss any training just to take the exams. So I took them at night, after the regular training day was over.

I regret that I never recognized the sacrifice that the company officers were taking for me by proctoring the exams, often from midnight to three A.M. They didn't have to do it, but they did, and it was one of the first of many small lessons in leadership.

But West Point never happened for me. I didn't score high enough on the competitive exams and the army felt that they could use me best as an electronics technician. I was sent to Fort Monmouth, New Jersey, for a yearlong school in advanced electronics—radar repair.

That was a real shock to me. I had been so cocky about just taking the exams and waltzing right into West Point without having laid the groundwork of a good high-school education. Like most teenagers, I had no idea how difficult it would be to get into the military academy. And on reflection, I'm sure now that I never would have made it to graduation if by some fluke I had gained admission.

Basic training was no smaller a shock to my teenage system than it was for the other 220 of my classmates. For the most part, we came from the eastern seaboard and New England. Our cadre consisted of young and inexperienced infantry officers, veteran Korean War senior

NCOs, and acting NCOs who hadn't been in the army much longer than we had.

During the first few days at Fort Dix I was singled out as one of the few among us who had had some ROTC training. This changed my status and got me off to a good start in the army.

I had attended a high school that offered Junior ROTC. A young combat veteran by the name of Charles T. Hamner was the professor of military science and technology at the high school ROTC detachment. He hit that place like a flying brick. Before Hamner it had been a boys' club that was all show and little go. Junior ROTC cadets wore ridiculously garish uniforms and did little in the way of studying military arts and sciences.

Hamner insisted that we learn the basic leadership and tactical skills that a mid-level NCO or a junior officer might master in the army. He immediately changed the curriculum to emphasize dismounted drill, leadership, map reading, customs and courtesies and military history.

He was also a stickler for treating subordinates with dignity and respect rather than the silly high-school hazing that had become a matter of course in the ROTC detachment. He treated each of us in a manner appropriate to our cadet rank. The higher our rank, the more he expected of us. It was a lesson taught, but for me not recognized for some years to come.

Though I only spent a short time in the detachment I learned a lot of the basic skills and customs of soldiering that the others had to absorb while trying to make it through basic training.

That high-school ROTC detachment made my first days in the army quite different than they might have been otherwise. I would get a chance to thank Captain Hamner a few years later, at the Rex Hotel in Saigon.

So, within hours of joining G Company, 5th Battalion, 2d Training Regiment, I became a trainee platoon sergeant. This was my first responsible job in the army.

We rarely saw our real platoon sergeant because he was assigned to us and to the post football team at the same time. The significance of "additional duties" like his would come to haunt me in the years to come. But while I was in that student company I enjoyed taking up most of the responsibilities normally shouldered by the platoon sergeant, as they were known in the days before they were called drill sergeants.

Within days of becoming a trainee platoon sergeant, I was spotted by the aging field first sergeant as being capable of moving the entire trainee company from point A to point B at double time and without causing traffic accidents. So, within the first week of basic training, I took on the added responsibility of being the trainee field first sergeant. This meant that the housekeeping, the scheduling, and the internal details of the operations of my trainee platoon fell to me. When the company assembled for training I would take the report (to determine if we had all the faces), move the company to the training areas, supervise the breaks and the police calls, and generally catch hell if the trainees were not where they were supposed to be.

It was a good deal for the company cadre. They were able to dump some of the easier and more boring tasks of running a basic-training company on me and get away with it.

For me, it was just the beginning of growing up. I had never before been responsible for the behavior and work of other men. It was also the beginning of overcoming a deep-seated shyness that I only realized I had when I had to step out in front of forty—or two hundred—trainees and give them instructions, information, or explanations. The classic fear of public speaking was damn near crippling for me. I got a knot in my gut each morning knowing that I would have to roll the company out, form them up, take the report, and then report to one of the cadremen or to the company commander.

For this I got: less sleep, lots of ass chewings, the chance to be last through the chow line, a little blue arm band with a staff sergeant's chevron on it, and no time to myself. At the time the trade-off seemed to be a good deal. But I was so involved in the job that it never occurred to me that I might just be learning something about leadership and supervision.

Rarely was there a time that it was not brought to my attention—with emphasis—when I screwed something up in handling the routine field matters for the company.

The NCOs varied in their own grasp of leadership principles, but it is fair to say that even the worst of them had far more on the ball than I did.

A unique feature of basic training is its ability to isolate you from the world. As trainees, our schedule was filled with classes, work details, appointments, more work details, and just plain waiting in line for things.

We rarely, if ever, saw a newspaper, heard a news report, or even saw a television set. The dayroom was off-limits to us even though it had a TV, a pool table, magazines, newspapers, and places to read and write. Dayrooms were like the razors in our footlocker trays—they had to be there, they had to be spotlessly clean, but we were never allowed to use them.

Our only link with the outside world was the telephone, and that was a privilege that came rarely and for much too short a period of time. And even when we did get to a pay phone, we were under intense pressure from the others waiting in line to make our call and get the hell off the line as quickly as possible. As a result, the phones were only used to speak with girlfriends, wives and close family members—briefly.

In those few free moments we spent out on the small wooden steps of the platoon barracks at the end of the training day or on Sunday afternoons polishing brass, shining boots, and cleaning our M-1 rifles, the conversation was always the same—girls, sports, cars, girls, the army, and girls. I can't ever recall any discussion about the Berlin Wall, Khrushchev, Vietnam, the attempt on Charles de Gaulle's life, Linus Pauling's Nobel Prize, or thalidomide.

We did wander into such worldly events as Sonny Liston knocking out Floyd Patterson for the championship, and Marilyn Monroe.

I remember that her death was appreciated from a point of total naïveté. We only knew her as a sex queen who had attacked so many taboos and had gotten away with it. We were totally unaware of her connection with the White House, and I believe that we all silently mourned the loss of the boyhood fantasies we held.

None of us was aware of the important role such fantasies would play for us in the years to come during the long, lonely nights of separation, when we would have drifted off into frightening speculation without those Marilyn-like images to fill our minds and our time.

Still, no matter what we talked about out there on our steps, it took us the entire eight weeks to get all of the lacquer off our issue belt buckles and collar brass insignia.[5]

While a few members of my trainee platoon volunteered for and were sent off to Airborne school, I was still certain that it was interesting—but not for me. I just couldn't make that connection in my mind —me and jumping from airplanes. But in spite of my frequent discomfort as a trainee platoon sergeant, I was happy to graduate as the top trainee in my training cycle. The competition included all the trainees on post who graduated that week. I had no idea by what criteria they

[5] The lacquer put on the brass at the factory had to be removed before it would take the high polish demanded at inspections.

selected me for this honor, but I was flattered by the fuss that was made of it all.

For the recognition, I was given a trophy and a letter in my 201 file.[6] I was to spend graduation day as the commanding general's trainee aide.

That event was preceded by the NCOs in my company whisking me off to Wrightstown, New Jersey, to a favorite tailor. There, a set of my khakis was cut and tapered and formed to a closer fit on my six-foot, one-hundred-thirty-pound frame.

The next day the same khakis appeared back in my platoon barracks starched to a point I was unaware cotton could take. Suddenly, the NCOs who had spent eight weeks calling me a complete incompetent were now hovering around me like mother hens. They took care to get me to the barbershop, have my boots spit shined, make blousing cans for my trousers,[7] polish my three items of brass insignia,[8] and coach me on all of the questions that the general might ask me.

Finally, the big day came. I was driven to the commanding general's office where I was quickly briefed by his aide, a lieutenant. My job was to ride around with the general in his staff car all day and only respond to the general if he spoke to me.

I had never really seen a general before. Sure, when I was a kid at some parade on a Saturday morning, there was always a general sitting up on the reviewing stand as the troops passed by. But then all the focus was on the spectacle and the pomp.

That morning I climbed into the back of a black Chevy sedan with Major General Charles Beauchamp. Our day was a whirl of visits to firing ranges, classrooms, the reception station, the post hospital, and a basic training battalion graduation ceremony.

There, I mounted the reviewing stand with the general and stood at attention to his left. My uniform was starched, my boots gleamed, and on my left arm I wore a bright red arm band with two large stars embroidered on it. As I looked out into the crowd of a thousand new graduates, I became aware of how many of those eyes were on me— wondering who I was and what the hell I had done to deserve being

---

[6] The soldier's personnel file. It contains qualification records, orders, and other papers documenting the individual's training, assignment, personnel qualifications such as test scores, awards and decorations, special skill qualifications, etc.

[7] Number-ten-size cans inserted into the ends of the trousers, to give them a straight, stiff military blouse.

[8] Collar brass insignia and belt buckle. The collar brass insignia are worn on each lapel. They consist of a flat disk through which a "U.S." and branch insignia device (crossed rifles for infantry, for example) are inserted. The "U.S." device is always worn on the right lapel. Basic trainees, who are not yet branch-qualified, wear two "U.S." devices.

singled out. I wasn't aware of being different from the regimented, cookie-cutter soldiers that stood on that parade field, but the notion sank in somewhere and stayed with me as later I made decisions about being in the army. Nonetheless, at eighteen, it felt pretty good.

Planting the seeds didn't end there. While waiting for further reassignment to Fort Monmouth, I was put on KP one morning in one of the huge, ten-thousand-man mess halls. There I was given a greasy job in a greasy kitchen cleaning grease off of trays that were still greasy when they got stacked back in the racks.

I recall making a trip outside where I found a long line of soldiers waiting for the next serving. They wandered in and out of the line, smoking, talking and killing time. Suddenly someone yelled, "Attention!" and as quickly a voice yelled back firmly, "As you were."

I couldn't see who had spoken but had to assume it was an officer. The strange thing was that the entire line stayed silent—all looking back toward the direction of the voice. I craned my neck to see what was going on.

There, just where the line snaked around the corner of the building, was a tall and very lean second lieutenant. He was talking to the soldiers in line, asking about their homes, their mail, and the food. He seemed to be genuinely interested in their answers, although I didn't understand why. He wasn't wearing the two-toned 2d Army shoulder patch with its distinctive large Arabic number 2 that most of the permanent party at Fort Dix wore. Instead, he wore a set of fatigues unlike any I had ever seen, tailored, starched to a point of visible stiffness, and well faded. This being back before the days of camouflage insignia, it was easy to see the gold bar on one collar and the crossed rifles of an infantry officer on the other. His cap was a Louisville pop-up,[9] placed squarely on top of his white sidewall[10] GI haircut. A shiny bar topped by a set of highly polished jump wings was pinned on the cap.

His shirt had a cloth set of wings over his pocket flap and a blue and white combat infantryman's badge sewn above the wings. On his left shoulder was Fort Benning's "Follow Me" patch with its upturned bayonet, topped with a blue arc reading AIRBORNE that was topped with a black and gold arc reading RANGER.

He seemed to be at home with the troops as he talked to them,

---

[9] Also called a "flattop" cap, it had a stiff brim and visor with a wire-reinforced crown, to keep the top perfectly flat.
[10] Where the hair on the sides and back of the head is cut so short it appears shaved down to the skin.

casually but with a presence that I was unable to identify at the time. As he got closer to me, I noticed that there was a very faint outline of a circular patch on each upper sleeve. Later, I would discover that the patches had been the insignia worn by candidates at the officer candidate school.

That officer's presence and ease with the troops went right into my mental file that held the images of those two NCOs at the Airborne school briefing.

The few weeks I was allowed between basic training and advanced individual training (AIT)[11] at Fort Monmouth gave me a chance to assess my summer's experiences and think about the months ahead. It was on leave in Massachusetts that I discovered that the army wasn't nearly as traumatic as I had expected it to be. For me, basic training had some strange quality about it that made it vaguely familiar, even homelike. Though I was moving again, and would continue to do so as long as I was in the army, it wasn't that upsetting to me. I didn't realize that the constant reassignments that faced me in the army were only a reflection of the turbulence that I had grown up with.

It had seemed difficult as a boy, being bounced around from place to place and having to make disguised moves to find acceptance and quickly integrate into my new surroundings. My entire childhood was a series of new faces, new schools, new teachers, and new circles and cliques to break into. To a kid the ground was rarely solid and always promised change. But after those first few months in the army I was more at home than anyone else in my basic-training company.

By the time I entered the army I had lived in almost a dozen states, occupied Germany, and Japan. I don't know of any other way to have had the experiences I had without being the son of a millionaire.

After ten weeks in uniform I didn't know much about the army. But I did know about moving from post to post, assignment to assignment. While others were adjusting, with varying degrees of success, I was able to focus on the other parts of soldiering. I hardly regret being an army brat.

---

[11] The schooling immediately after basic combat training where the soldier is trained for duty in a specific branch of the army.

CHAPTER 2

.

For me Fort Monmouth was a strange transition from the screaming and hazing associated with basic training. First, Monmouth was a signal-corps post and not nearly as rough around the edges as Fort Dix. Added to the sudden release from round-the-clock restrictions, I was unprepared to venture into the world of electrons and cathode-ray tubes. I had no background in electronics and had no idea why the army had selected me to attend such a school. All I wanted to do was get a chance to retake the exam for West Point Prep School and get on with letting Uncle Sam pay for the college education that I couldn't afford and no one else would offer me.

The retesting and selection for the prep school were still a long way off and I had to go through the motions. So I hit the books and learned a bit about electrons, troubleshooting, and army signal corps radar sets—mostly tactical radars, used in combat and combat-support units.

The classes were much more like those at a trade school. We moved about in small groups—still marching everywhere, but we weren't double timing, and we were allowed long and frequent breaks. We could smoke in class and drink coffee while on the practical exercises. And, unlike basic training, we carried large notebooks filled with complicated schematics of the circuitry for everything from the first super-heterodyne radios we built to the large tactical radar sets we repaired. It was almost college coursework with fatigue uniforms—almost.

The academic days were not long. We attended class from mid-morning to mid-afternoon with the rest of the day open for details, other administrative needs of the student company, physical training, and homework. Lots of free time for a trainee in advanced individual training is a delight to those who will quickly reach out and find ways to fill their time.

It didn't take very long for the basic combat skills I had learned at Fort Dix to fade into a less than pleasant memory. At Fort Monmouth there was no need to get wet, dirty, greasy, or cold. It was *nothing* like Fort Dix.

* * *

Fort Monmouth had a totally unauthorized drill team/honor guard and marching band made up of students from the several courses taught there.

Not long after I was assigned to a student company and we began the yearlong course, I was called out to a recruiting pitch for the post band and honor guard.

I had no musical training or talent, so the band was of no interest to me. I was involved once in a small drill team in Junior ROTC and remembered just how much hard work and how many long hours were involved. Still, I listened to the pitch: Weekends free of duty when not performing somewhere . . . no details . . . no guard duty . . . a special mess hall and barracks . . . special uniforms . . . and privately owned cars permitted.

All this occurred in the days when unmarried soldiers were required to live in the barracks. In our case, it was a barracks full of more than 250 other students in a battalion of several other companies where privacy and exclusivity were at a real premium. The honor guard pitch started sounding a lot better.

After an interview by three experienced members of the honor guard, I was accepted on a probationary basis. I was expecting the probation to be based on my ability to learn the rifle drills and the marching. I was wrong.

I was assigned to a squad in the honor guard and spent ten times as many hours as I would have as a regular student polishing floors, starching and ironing my uniforms, spit shining boots, and endlessly practicing the intricate rifle routines.

My average day started at four A.M. and ended well after midnight. In addition to the course work and the homework, I had the honor guard work, which also included a moderately high level of hazing.

As probationary members of the honor guard we were at the beck and call of the more senior members of the detachment. We were required to run errands for them, like picking up their laundry, taking their footgear to the shoe repair, purchasing things for them at the post exchanges, and going on what they called "runs."

A *run* was a late-night trip out the front gate to Eatontown, New Jersey, to pick up one (or a hundred) submarine sandwiches—the best I've ever eaten.

When called upon to make a run, the trick was to memorize the order and to get it right. This we had to do while all of the hungry upperclassmen were yelling out and changing their orders—pressing us to hurry up and get gone. The chore included keeping exact change separated for the money provided by those who placed their orders.

The whole process of taking the order, collecting the money, dressing, running out and getting the order, and returning with the right stuff was all done under intense pressure from the others to be fast. They wanted us to be out the door and back as fast as possible—or faster.

Additionally, attitude was a large component of the testing. If at any time we showed even the slightest resistance or resentment performing those menial tasks, we could count on soon being eliminated from the honor guard and being sent back to a student company.

The elimination process was easy. No one mentioned that your attitude was not up to par. Instead, you would be tested on the precison of your rifle drill and your marching. Most often it was done with another more experienced member of the honor guard. If he wanted to make it difficult or nearly impossible, it was an easy matter for him to be a little late throwing the ceremonial rifle to you or catching your throw. And that was enough to find you uncoordinated enough to be eliminated.

Back in ROTC I had taken a bit of hazing from a cadet officer named Doug "Skunk Boots" Terrel. Doug was a mover and a shaker in the ROTC detachment, starting a Ranger-type training course and never allowing anyone to whine, quit or complain.

Doug's training helped me get through the hazing in basic training and in the honor guard. I became fairly proficient with the precision drills and began to enjoy the status that went along with being a member of the honor guard, performing for post activities and for regional parades and civic events. We were still students in the signal school from Monday to Friday and expected to keep up academically, but we were different, and that was beginning to be a pattern for me.

The other unusual feature of the honor guard detachment was the preoccupation with appearance. Every member of the unit was expected to wash, starch, and iron his own fatigue uniforms, polish his own brass, and shine his own boots and black helmet.

There were other students on post who had figured out a way to send out everything to places off post that would take care of all those little details of soldiering, but their standards would not make it in the honor guard.

A member of the unit inspected every soldier every morning. The inspections sometimes took as long as five minutes. You were gigged if you had a fingerprint on your black helmet liner, so you put it on with your fingers touching only the inside of the sweatband.

You were gigged if you had even the smallest piece of thread sticking out of any part of your uniform, so you learned to go over every seam, buttonhole, and hem with cigarette lighters to burn away any thread rather than pull it out and create more.

You were gigged if you had any unintentional creases in your shirt or trousers, so you learned *never* to bend your knees, squat down, or cross your legs.

You were gigged if your boots were not glass-like, so you would spend as much as an hour each night on each boot.

You were also gigged if your hair was too long or you missed a few whiskers.

All of this seemed to be important at the time. I would come to recognize how really superficial it was, and how little the ironed-in creases in the shirt backs had to do with real soldiering. But much like fraternities, we were largely unsupervised and set standards for ourselves.

Soon I was advanced to squad leader. I had done well enough at passing a large number of inspections without being gigged so I was given the task of inspecting the others. The goal was never to allow a member of the honor guard out of the building without making sure that he met our most exacting standards.

Along with the job came a semiprivate cadre room out of the platoon bay. The significance of the room was no small matter in a platoon bay with only chin-high dividers separating each pair of soldiers.

In the cadre rooms we were allowed such luxuries as throw rugs, small hi-fi systems (before stereo was available), and even a second wall locker to hold our personal things and civilian clothes.

So while others tried to take care of all the housekeeping chores sitting on their bunks or footlockers, my roommate and I were able to spread out in our ten-by-twelve room and take care of our chores in leisure—listening to Peter, Paul, and Mary.

My status as an acting squad leader was a bit heady for an eighteen-year-old with only a few months in the army behind him. I liked the responsibility of answering for myself and a squad of eight others. It was a little like the extra load that had been put on me in basic training. I liked the pressure and I liked the distinction of being a leader. And I sure was enjoying the recognition and the privileges that went along with the job. It all seemed so important to me at the time.

* * *

The academic year was taxing. The size of my class dwindled dramatically at each major exam. I don't know if they were failing because of the difficulty of the tasks, or boredom. The sequence of training after getting us familiar with the basics of electronics was to keep introducing newer and larger radar sets for us to master and then repair.

Rumor had it that dropouts were simply put on miscellaneous details for several weeks, until the army could reclassify them into some other job. The threat that was always held over our heads was that dropouts would be sent to "pole climbers" school. The thought of spending the rest of our time in the army scrambling up and down splinter-filled telephone poles was a motivator.

Somewhere in mid-course I began to lose motivation, thinking that I didn't need the electronics education to make it through West Point —so why kill myself? My grades dropped a little too much and I was informed that I was invited to a mandatory study hall that was held each Saturday. That turned my grades around—I was not going to lose my weekends off. On working weekends we performed as a precision drill team all over New Jersey and New York. But I was counting the days until I could reapply for the exam for West Point Prep School.

I think that a benchmark might help in understanding the mindset at this point—1962. We were feeling the early influences and optimism of Camelot. John F. Kennedy was still alive and criticisms of his administration and his lifestyle were neither focused nor coordinated. The army was undergoing the final changes from a World War II force to a new and uncertain force preparing to enter a nuclear world facing a single enemy, the USSR.

Vietnam was a word in the news now and then. But down at squad level—even in a signal-corps school—it was not yet a threat. We were all aware that there were Special Forces teams in Vietnam, but we were equally aware that since John Kennedy had personally blessed the "Green Berets," there were military missions and advisory teams in virtually every country with which we had a mutual defense pact. From PFC level, it just wasn't a big deal.

A more frequent topic of conversation was the Cuban Missile Crisis —passed, but not forgotten. The Bay of Pigs seemed so far away, and as we understood it, only peripherally connected to the U.S. anyway. That translated to us as not much chance of signal-corps PFCs being involved.

* * *

After pestering the clerks in the personnel section about resubmitting my request to take the West Point Prep exam, I was finally allowed to submit the paperwork. I was required to take another physical and submit it with the request.

It never occurred to me at age nineteen that I could be found unacceptable for physical reasons, but that's what happened. I got a call from personnel telling me that I had failed to meet the vision standards for admission into the prep school.

I was crushed. It was not in the list of possibilities that I had considered when I volunteered to join the army—unassigned—to get in so I could take the exam. I had a foolish notion that I could just waltz into the prep school and then on to the military academy a year later. How wrong I was.

So there I was, looking more than two years ahead of me—fixing radar sets somewhere.

It was the first time I had really faced failure in anything important. It was the first time I ever had to face the letdown of a major disappointment.

From somewhere inside I spooled up the determination not to let the rejection get me down. Instead, I would look for other opportunities. I wasn't sure what it was that I wanted, but I knew it wasn't being a radar repairman for the rest of my enlistment.

I did know that I liked responsibility. Being a sergeant was appealing, but hardly likely any time soon. The army has a minimum time in grade requirement for every rank, and the thought of waiting years to make sergeant was not something I could tolerate.

So I did some more research on what I could qualify for, considering my lack of perfect vision. It didn't take long to find out that there were many opportunities in the army that didn't have such high vision standards.

Becoming an officer seemed the thing for me. I could avoid the lengthy enlisted time-in-grade requirements to move up[12] and in a matter of months become a leader, a supervisor, an officer. I wasn't aware of how sweeping an oversimplification of the process that view was.

So I set out to burn the midnight oil, filling out applications for

[12] Quite lengthy, depending on the army's requirements for various grades in different specialties. Time-in-service requirements were also a major factor in enlisted promotions. For example, a soldier required eight years active service to qualify for promotion to platoon sergeant, E-7, but a second lieutenant could be promoted to first lieutenant in half that time.

officer candidate school, flight school, and an application for a direct commission as a warrant officer in the signal corps.

Looking back, I was clearly unqualified for any and all of the things I was applying for. I had nothing to bring to the army that would make them want to accept me for training or make me a warrant officer. But I was nineteen, and very full of myself.

Personnel was not impressed with my enthusiasm. I received a note from a senior NCO in the student-records section to call him. For my trouble I got an ass chewing "for not knowing that you can't apply for more than one school at a time." He told me that he was sending my applications back and that I had better make up my mind before I wasted any more of his time.

I recall sitting on my bunk in my cadre room with all of the applications and completed physical forms and results of recent physical fitness tests, trying to decide what to go for.

I didn't have much confidence in the army simply making me a warrant officer because I was about to graduate from the radar course, and I had never been in an airplane. So I pitched the warrant officer and the flight-school applications and looked more closely at the OCS application.

Back in the pre-Vietnam days there were only two officer candidate schools: infantry, at Fort Benning, and artillery, at Fort Sill, Oklahoma.

Neither one actually reached out for me, so I opted for what I thought would be the most likely to accept me—Fort Benning—infantry. I have no idea what made me draw that conclusion.

Over the course of the months that had crawled by, the lieutenant colonel who commanded the student troop command became aware of my existence and my performance on the honor guard. Not long after I resubmitted my application for OCS, he stopped me in the headquarters building to tell me that he had recommended that I be allowed to appear before an OCS board—an interview—and that he felt that I would probably fare well.

It was his way of telling me that as far as he was concerned I could be fairly confident that the board he would appoint would probably find me acceptable and send a positive recommendation forward to headquarters. Then it would be up to them to determine if I would be matched up with allocations for OCS at Benning.

To me it was a sign that for the first time things were going my way. I had the troop command commander on my side and I appeared to be qualified—on paper. All I had to do was look sharp, bone up on the usual questions, and not screw it up before the OCS board.

The next several weeks found me studying for the board. I memorized the entire chain of command from my platoon sergeant to the commander-in-chief. I looked up and committed to memory the basic stats on the new infantry rifle—the M-14. I made notes on hand grenades and map symbols and read all of the leadership manuals I could find around the barracks. Still, I knew that I didn't know a thing about the infantry beyond my limited exposure to it at Fort Dix.

The weeks clicked by, and I not only got closer to graduation from the radar repair course, I got a written notification to appear before an OCS board to determine my qualifications for consideration as an officer candidate.

The day came. The board met, but it didn't really meet. I was invited into the room. I was looking as good as my entire squad could get me—fresh uniform without a thing out of place or a loose thread, spit shined boots, and a haircut that was way beyond what the regs demanded. I walked into the boardroom and took my spot front and center, facing the president of the board, and reported to him with a sharp salute.

As he hesitated I took in the board members: a major, two captains, and a sergeant major. The president returned my salute and in a very unenthusiastic tone told me to stand at ease.

I was expecting to be told to take the single chair that had been precisely placed in front of the panel. Something was wrong.

The major started his windup to soften the blow for me. It seems that there was some obscure regulation that said the board could not convene if I was on orders for overseas shipment, and I *had* been put on orders to go to Germany a few days earlier by some computer that matched my punched card to a vacancy in 7th Army.

He told me that I could not be interviewed. I felt as if I had been hit in the gut, and I guess it showed.

The major tried to make me feel better by explaining that my paperwork looked good and that the commander had planned to add a letter of recommendation to my file. He said that I was facing a slight delay that would take me to Germany where I could reapply and certainly be accepted for OCS, and returned to Georgia in just a matter of a few months.

I was crushed again. I had been in the army just short of a year, and I had failed to get into West Point Prep and failed to get by an OCS board. There seemed to be little chance of my getting to go anywhere, except Germany.

Later I sat on my bunk in the dark, listening to the "Duke of Earl" on the radio. I felt very much alone that night.

CHAPTER 3

•

Leaving the States for Germany ended my comfortable status as an acting squad leader. Suddenly I found myself in a troop compartment as far forward and as far down as they could put us on the USS *Geiger* —crossing the Atlantic in the summer.

We were meat. No one had any rank or authority or responsibilities except the compartment NCO, who was an engineer master sergeant with little concern for our comfort or our needs. He herded all 110 of us into the compartment and made us change into fatigues and low-quarter shoes[13] (for safety if we went over the side), and made us close our duffel bags and stack them in the center of the compartment. He then told us that that was the last time we would be allowed to get into our duffel bags until we had Bremerhaven in sight.

We complained and he explained that he wasn't going to put up with a hundred duffel bags scattered all over the compartment. We were furious. He told us we could complain to the chaplain when we got to Germany.

So much for taking care of the troops.

The trip was uncomfortable and pleasant at the same time. It was a wonderful adventure, one that I'm sure everyone who's had it will never forget. A troop ship is a special world of confinement that combines the spectacle of being at sea and the brotherhood of vomiting.

We spent days in a compartment that was only ventilated by air shafts that connected us with the decks, but that's all they did; they didn't force any fresh air down into the compartment, as far as we could tell, or vent any hot air back up and out. As a result, in a matter of days the temperature and the smell of a hundred soldiers in the same clothes got pretty foul.

By the time we hit rough water we were all a bit queasy from our own body odor and the greasy food in the galley. We held our own until the first among us got seasick and threw up. That started a chain

[13] Another term for black, Oxford-style shoes.

reaction of vomiting that went on for the better part of three days. By the fourth day we were coming out of the epidemic of mal de mer, although it took two more days to clean up the mess in the compartment.

My first impression of Germany was that it was the real army. No more schools, no more training post, and no more temporary assignments. I was on my way to a signal battalion in Mannheim and it *was* the real thing—fighting the cold war just a few miles from the iron curtain.

Language was a problem, not just German, but the army's special language in Germany. Even before I had boarded the troop train from Bremerhaven to Mannheim, I was confused by the endless briefings we got from the time we left the deck of the ship. We were given lists of things we couldn't do because we were in transit. Then we were told that we were guests in Germany and that we had a special status under the Status of a Forces Agreement, one that allowed us to be found guilty of crimes against Germans *and* crimes against the army.

Then we were warned about Soviet agents who were said to have bugged every *schnitzel* and hid behind every fräulein. We were given briefings on the menace of venereal disease and the black death that was sure to follow the most innocent experimentation with drugs. And we were warned not to use greenbacks for local purchases, and not to purchase PX or commissary items for German nationals.

We were soon separated by unit and destination, and the distinction between combat soldiers and the rest of us became apparent: The combat units sent NCOs to welcome their new arrivals.

I looked and I waited. Soon the crowd of travel-weary soldiers began to thin out and I could see down the huge train-station platform. There was no one there from the 504th Signal Battalion to meet anyone.

Finally, an announcement was made that those of us who were not going to major units would report to the NCOs representing the appropriate geographical destination. I felt a little conspicuous searching out the NCO in charge of soldiers reporting to Mannheim Post. Second class didn't feel all that good after being fussed over in basic training and the Fort Monmouth honor guard.

I had never seen the trappings of real armored or mechanized infantry division until I arrived at Coleman Barracks in Mannheim. Somehow I managed to show up at my new company on a Saturday— a cardinal sin. It would be the last time.

But since it was Saturday all of the vehicles belonging to the nearby infantry brigade were neatly lined up in the motor park. I rode through the *kaserne*[14] amazed at the collection of steel carriages, all designed to carry men into battle. I had heard about, but never really appreciated, that sheer force of arms before I saw those hundreds of tanks, armored personnel carriers, and command tracks waiting for an alert to be called.

Even empty and silent, they represented the strength of the NATO armies manning the borders with the Soviet bloc, standing ready for a nuclear confrontation so terrible that we never even joked about it.

There was no way for me to know then that in just six years I would be commanding a Long Range Patrol company whose mission it was to leap that iron curtain and provide the intelligence that NATO would need to commit itself to the battle.

No, I was just a PFC trying to find a way to sign in, get a bunk, and avoid any details before first call on Monday morning. I was unsuccessful. The burden of reporting to a new unit on a weekend is that everyone else is gone and when any work detail comes up, you are it.

So I spent that first Sunday in Germany as the runner for a specialist 5[15] battalion staff duty NCO who was old enough to be my father.

I fully expected to find something that would be my home for the few months I planned to spend in Germany. Again, there were many surprises and disappointments ahead for me. I explained to the spec 5 that I really had no intention of staying in the unit, that I planned to apply for OCS and be gone in short order. He suggested that I keep that notion to myself. I didn't fully understand why, and considering the great gap between our ranks, I decided to stop while I was ahead.

It was in Mannheim that I really learned that the army worked by the numbers. For me the number of my MOS[16], 282.1, was matched up with the need for a 282.1 E-3 at still another number—the 557th Signal Company. I was quickly shuffled off to another building, dragging my bursting-at-the-seams duffel bag through the heat of the old German Army barracks. I might add that this was back in the days when you were only allowed to travel in uniform, and your luggage

[14] German for "barracks."
[15] Specialist 5, E-5, equivalent in pay grade to a three-stripe sergeant. Also called spec 5.
[16] Military occupational speciality, or a soldier's "job code." MOSs are grouped by specialty, where there is a degree of interchangeability of skills—for enlisted personnel, 100-series, combat arms; 200-series, electronic repair technicians, etc. The MOS code for a small-unit infantry officer is 1542.

had to consist of no more than one duffel bag and an AWOL bag.[17] In no case could your entire luggage ensemble exceed sixty-six pounds.

As I approached the new signal-company orderly room I anticipated being assigned to a cozy bunk in the small building and finally finding a home—a real TO & E unit,[18] like the big guys. But again I was wrong. I no sooner reported in to the first sergeant[19] than I was informed not to unpack since I was being assigned to a forward-support maintenance team in Kaiserslautern, Germany, or "K-Town," as it was called.

The trip to K-town was in the back of a hot, uncomfortable, tarp-covered two-and-a-half-ton (deuce-and-a-half) truck. I tried very hard to stay neat and clean to make a good impression when I arrived. But the truck was dirty and I was sandwiched in between boxes of GI toilet paper, two skid-mounted generators, and three greasy immersion heaters. By the time I got out of the truck, where my starched khakis weren't dirty and greasy, they were sweaty.

I have to admit that I felt pretty much alone. The army often forgets that the guy on the bottom sees himself as he is treated. For me, that day, I felt like a piece of cargo, just a replacement part. I had processed through my new company so fast that I had only exchanged about fifty words with my first sergeant and had not met my commander or anyone else in the company. I had been expecting more of a reception than I had gotten.

As I walked into the huge barracks building in Daenner Kaserne in K-town, the possibility of convincing the faces along my new chain of command that I should be sent back to the States to go to OCS seemed very remote.

Then I met Bobby R. Foxworth.

After being passed from one office to the next, I found myself standing at a fourth-floor barracks door marked FSM—forward support maintenance.

Entering, I found a small corner of the building had been set aside to house the small signal team. Two connecting rooms held six bunks, six wall lockers, six footlockers, and a single field table with a reel-to-

[17] A small zippered bag with two handles and just big enough for a soldier to pack away his essential personal items, such as shaving gear, toothpaste, etc. So called because a soldier going absent without leave (AWOL) would not need any other baggage.
[18] Table of organization and equipment (TO & E) is the organizational document showing the number of soldiers, their grades and assignments, as well as how many vehicles, weapons, and equipment are authorized in a unit.
[19] The senior NCO in a company-level unit. The grade calls for a master sergeant, E-8, and is identified by a lozenge centered between the stripes and rockers on his chevrons.

reel tape recorder on it. I was told to wait there for the team to come back from work.

Not knowing if I was staying which of the bunks would be mine, I found a neutral place to sit—a large window overlooking the parade ground.

While I waited, I watched the activities out in the *kaserne*. I didn't know it at the time, but the *kaserne* housed a variety of combat, combat support, and combat-service support units, as well as outfits like the Red Cross and a European Exchange Service snack bar/cafeteria. So from the window I could see a cross section of tankers, infantrymen, civilians, and German employees crisscrossing the compound. The soldiers wore a wide variety of uniforms and headgear, which confused me as to just who was whom. I was unfamiliar with most of the insignia, but there was a difference in a mechanic from a mechanized-infantry battalion and a sergeant from an Airborne battalion. It wasn't just the way they walked, or the small silver wings on their headgear and over their shirt pockets—it was an attitude of pride and self-confidence that I could see from even my window ledge on the fourth floor.

Suddenly the door was kicked open. My new boss, Bobby R. Foxworth, Staff Sergeant, Signal Corps, with his large face, short body, and loud voice, had arrived.

He asked me who I was, and before I could answer, he grabbed the orders out of my hand and read them as he yelled instructions about chow and the next day's schedule to the men who followed him into the room and split off to their bunks—a spec 5, two spec 4s, and one PFC.

"Get yer civvies on," he ordered me.

Civvies? I had stuffed a set of cotton pants, a Kingston Trio button-down-collar shirt and a skinny tie into my duffel bag, but they were in no condition to be worn. Foxworth wouldn't hear that. I was to put them on and be ready to leave in ten minutes.

I looked like something out of a laundry bag in my unpressed civilian clothes and my black army low-quarter shoes, but no one seemed to care and no one let me speak.

Within the hour we were out of the barracks, out of the *kaserne* and on the "strass."[20] The team's "mission" for the evening was serious and continuous drinking and scouting for girls. It sounded like a great idea to me. But I hadn't accounted for the potency of German beer

[20] A shortening of the German *strasse*, or "street."

and the inadvisability of drinking the house beer at every German bar we visited.

I spent the better part of my first night in K-town hugging the commode, trying to rid my system of the poison that I had put into it.

My first official duty day was a mixture of confusion and nausea. It may have not been the sickest I have ever been, but it ranked up there with the top five.

We were attached to an armored maintenance battalion, and had a little workshop in the corner of a track maintenance building that was as large as four basketball courts. Our repair benches were separated from the rest of the shop by a homemade wall of salvaged plywood.

Every time they brought in an M-88 tank retriever to tune its engine, they would crank it up and then back it off. The sound of a tank retriever's engine being screwed up to a few thousand RPM and then dumped back to idle is similar to, but more painful than, sitting next to the starting lights at a drag strip. And with a hangover—it is a special experience unmatched in real life. But in the army in Germany there were plenty of opportunities for hangovers, and plenty of M-88s that needed lots of tuneups.

It was the job of the maintenance battalion to keep the thousands of tanks, jeeps, trucks, armored personnel carriers, wreckers, water trailers, command tracks, trailers, and tank retrievers prepositioned in Kaiserslautern in good working order.

Those vehicles were all there to be ready for the 2d Armored Division, from Fort Hood, Texas, to jump into airplanes, fly to Germany, get into the prepositioned vehicles, and roll out to meet the Soviets should the balloon go up.

It was our job in the Forward Support Maintenance Detachment of the 557th Signal Company to keep every radio and radar set in that division's stock in working order. That meant thousands of pieces of equipment went across the top of our workbenches each year for scheduled maintenance, MWOs (modification work orders), and repairs.

Some of the radar sets came to me and some were too big to move, so I had to go to them. Because we had to travel over a large part of Germany to work on the equipment, we were often required to stay overnight at remote sites. This was justification for us to have class-A passes.

The army of the '60s was quite different than today's volunteer army. The sixties army worked on the principle that if there weren't special arrangements and permission for you to be away from your work or your barracks, you just didn't go off the *kaserne* and into town after work. You needed a pass.

And on top of the requirement to have a pass that specified the time and distance you could be away from your unit, there was a curfew. Every soldier, single or married, had to be in the barracks or in his quarters by midnight, unless he was on leave or had a class-A pass.

Class-A passes were hard to come by, but because of our mission our tiny maintenance team had them, and our comings and goings were monitored only by Staff Sergeant Bobby R. Foxworth and his able assistant, Sergeant Rayfield Vann.

Now, the doings of a small signal detachment in the hills of Germany may seem a bit far afield from the memoir of a soldier in Airborne, Ranger, and Long Range Patrol units, but not really. It was these experiences with those soldiers who patched up radios, did the support work, and had little lives staked out for themselves in this small, "best-kept-secret" unit that made me sure there was somewhere else in the army I wanted to be. And it gave me the proper perspective, knowing that on any given day a radio or a radar set or a helicopter just might have been repaired or inspected by a soldier who was suffering from a hangover, or was still distracted by a long night in Paris or Saigon or Nha Trang.

The tooth-to-tail ratio[21] is a large one, and the number of opportunities for equipment to fail in combat is a frightening reality of war. I worked with many fellow junior officers who were compromised the first day they joined the army. They never saw or really experienced the small and jerky world of the PFC and the spec 4. For those enlisted men and junior NCOs,[22] each day that didn't turn out to be a nightmare of changed orders, confusing instructions, and conflicting demands on their time was an unusual day. Much of their day was spent protecting their turf, and their evening was spent in pursuit of women and music and beer.

That's where Bobby Foxworth shined. We would return to the barracks after work and get cleaned up to go to the mess hall for dinner. Foxworth, a very capable NCOIC for our detachment, would immedi-

---

[21] The number of men in logistical and administrative duties needed to support each soldier in a combat unit. In Vietnam this ratio was estimated at from eight-to-one to ten-to-one.

[22] NCOs in the ranks of corporal through staff sergeant. "Senior NCOs" are sergeants first class through sergeant major.

ately go to bed. By 1730 hours each day he would be asleep, and we would be standing in long lines at the mess hall or the cafeteria.

And every night at eleven, Bobby R. would get up, shower, shave, put on his best civilian clothes, and head out to the strass. It was his theory that the highest likelihood of having a good time in the bars was during that golden hour after all the regular soldiers with regular passes had jumped in cabs and headed back to their barracks to make bed check.

Foxworth would have a great time, enjoy the early morning hours, and return to the barracks well before reveille.

But when he returned we knew it. Bobby R. loved country music and on his return to the team room he would turn on his tape player. Every morning we would wake up to Buck Owens singing "I've Got a Tiger by the Tail."

Living in a barracks with soldiers who were from different parts of the country with different tastes in music is a special experience that most civilians don't get to enjoy, outside of prison. Most of us hated country music but kept it to ourselves because to a PFC a staff sergeant was a special god whom you just didn't casually criticize.

Bobby R. was a good team leader, and aside from his musical tastes he was always our best supporter and a fierce defender of our time and energy. He was always there to protect us from the clutches of the battalion sergeant major, who had an endless shit list that he wanted to put us on.

It was in K-town where I discovered the first rule of details. If a crappy detail can be given to some unit that you control but is not made up of your troops—dump it on them first.

Foxworth protected us from this tendency to give the dirty jobs to the tenant units.[23] He also encouraged each of us to do whatever it was we wanted to do careerwise. Bobby rearranged the work schedule to allow a couple of the guys on the team to go to night school, and for another to be able to see his German girlfriend, who had a strange work schedule herself.

As for me, Bobby didn't laugh when I told him that I wanted to go to OCS. He basically rolled up his sleeves and asked me, "How do I help?" I will not soon forget Bobby R. Foxworth. He was a good man who cared for his troops and got the mission done. He was neither chickenshit nor lax in his responsibilities as an NCO. He liked cold

[23] Units assigned to a garrison for administrative and other support but not part of the garrison's complement.

beer, country music, and German women. But he was an unselfish man who could have made our lives hell.

There is a temptation when someone is given plenty of authority and posted far from the flagpole to bend and twist that authority for selfish motives. Bobby R. didn't give into it.

I waited a few weeks to get settled before starting up the entire OCS application process again. Bobby R. helped. He did what he could to cut through the red tape and get me forms, get me on rosters for scheduled PT tests and special appointments at the hospital for physicals. He and Sergeant Vann wrote letters of recommendation and helped me fill out the endless forms.

Once it was all done, the packet went by truck to our parent headquarters in Mannheim. I was sure that I would be recognized as OCS material and quickly dispatched back to the States. After all, what else could go wrong?

I was summoned to Mannheim to report to my company commander. I had never met Captain Fitzpatrick, but I was determined to make a good impression on him when I did. Foxworth and the other team members helped me shine shoes, polish brass, and put together both a traveling uniform and one to see the CO in.

After slipping into the latrine in the Mannheim barracks and changing into a highly starched and perfectly assembled uniform, I reported to the orderly room to make my appointment with the captain.

Fitzpatrick put me at ease and remarked that he would feel a little put out if any other soldier had applied to go back to the States after being in his command less than sixty days. But he had seen in my file that I had applied before, that it was not personal, and didn't reflect on him. I was too nervous to decide if he was kidding or not and didn't want to make a mistake. So I said nothing and just nodded respectfully.

He thumbed through my application, making some grunting noises now and then. Finally, he dropped the packet on his desk and announced that he couldn't see how it would be a problem for me to get accepted to OCS, "but not now."

Not now? I wasn't sure what "not now" meant. I told him so. He looked at me in disbelief and told me that he was sure that everyone in Germany knew that there was a policy that no one—he repeated, no one—was allowed to return to the States for schooling unless or until he had completed half of his tour in Germany.

I had been had again. I was only two months into a twenty-four month tour in Germany and would have to wait until the following summer at the earliest to go to OCS.

As I left Fitzpatrick's office he tried to make me feel better by telling me that I didn't have to wait for a year to submit my application again. I could submit it a few months early, to get everything out of the way in time to go home to the States, just as soon as I crossed that half-way mark.

My trip back to Kaiserslautern was a very long one. I was just about convinced that there was no way that I was going to be able to break out of any normal enlisted track and get to officer training or anything else if the army didn't want me to. And it was beginning to look to me like the army didn't want me to.

Bobby R. Foxworth was as sympathetic as I have ever seen an NCO. He understood my disappointment and immediately encouraged me to not give up and to just keep my nose clean for the next several months until I could resubmit my application.

CHAPTER 4

I think I wallowed around in self-pity for the better part of another day. And during my moment of disappointment I completely missed the event and the significance of Martin Luther King's "I have a dream" speech at the Lincoln Memorial. Little did I know that there was a train picking up speed on a track that would converge with my travels. The civil rights movement seemed so far removed from where I was—in the army and in Germany. We weren't having any demonstrations or sit-ins. We didn't have any problems with segregation, not that we could see. Negro (a term that would stay in use in the army until well after it was replaced by "black" in the streets) soldiers were never asked to sit in the back of a bus. Nor were they denied access to anything that the army offered. Still, there was discrimination, but not to the degree that we saw in the towns outside army posts in the South. The issue would come to consume a large part of my professional life in the years ahead of me.

Still, I pouted and felt sorry for myself until Bobby R. had had enough and insisted that I get dressed in civvies again for another night on the town with him. I resisted. But when Bobby R. said you were going out on the strass, that's where you were going.

As we got closer to leaving he kept turning up the volume on his tape recorder. I was still not a fan of country music and he knew it. I made the mistake of asking him if he had any Beatles music. That night he took me to the NCO club on the *kaserne*. I protested lightly and he insisted that I go with him to the club, listen to some good country music and shut up.

We arrived early and found a good booth near the dance floor. The place was fairly empty and I took the opportunity to tell him that the lack of patrons was because of the country band that was booked there that night. Bobby R. just smiled and ordered us another round.

By midnight I had watched the club fill up to capacity. The NCOs and their dates and wives stomped, laughed, sang, and danced to the fairly adequate band.

We walked out of the club at closing and Bobby R. stopped me. He turned to the club and pulled the toothpick from his mouth and pointed it toward the door. He told me that the club was filled every night a country band played there. And if I was going to become an officer, I had better learn to like country music or I'd have no idea who my people were.

I'm sure that I didn't think that his comment was very important then, but I can say that I never heard country music coming from a troop barracks or a bunker or a poncho hootch again without thinking of what Bobby R. told me that night. It *was* important.

He also made me a fan.

During the day I spent my time on the cold hulls of tracks helping the radio repairmen on our team install new radios and antennae that had just come into the inventory. I also logged quite a bit of cross-training time learning how to repair radios, since there was not enough radar work to keep me busy fulltime.

Occasionally we were called out on alerts and on scheduled exercises to support major NATO field training. There I really came to appreciate the job of the combat soldiers. They were wet, cold, tired, and exhausted most of the time. And when they weren't running across the German countryside in tanks and APCs, they were up late at night fixing their vehicles and pulling scheduled maintenance. Their hours were awful and they always looked like hell.

Somehow, I never made the connection between applying for officer candidate school in infantry and the lives of those troops in the mechanized infantry battalions of the 2d Armored Division.

I was also becoming aware of the routine schedules of small units in a peacetime setting, which can be deceivingly calm and cover up undercurrents of discontent.

Late one afternoon in November a few of us were having a beer at the EM Club when the word spread that John Kennedy had been shot —and killed. We quickly broke up and went back to our barracks.

Later that evening I was sitting in the window in the barracks. Somewhere below my window an argument broke out. A couple of soldiers were hollering at one another, each taunting the other.

Suddenly the argument escalated into a fist fight that drew supporters, and as the soldiers from all four barracks emptied out on the parade field, it became a riot. Soldiers swinging entrenching tools and bunk adapters were splitting each other's heads open for no apparent reason. As we stood there in the window watching the security police trying to break up the fighting, we knew that it had something to do with the sense of loss we all felt at the death of John Kennedy.

A week later I was promoted to Specialist 4. I had been in the army only seventeen months. I was only nineteen and found it just a little awkward since most of the E-4s in the company were in their mid to late twenties. But I figured I was doing something right.

As the days clicked by I realized that I needed to convince myself I really still wanted to go to OCS. So I enrolled in the infantry school's pre-commission correspondence course and studied leadership and small unit tactics. Over the course of the next eight months I alternated nights of studying to get me ready for OCS and nights out with Bobby R. and the others, and an occasional night with Ian Fleming and a James Bond adventure.

Just after Christmas I pulled out the growing applications file and began filling out the paperwork—one more time. I knew that it meant more problems with more clerks and more physicals and more PT tests. I was getting pretty good at it, and even figured out how to get around the added problem of my being in Kaiserslautern when my headquarters was in Mannheim.

So off went the application packet and I waited. And I waited. We had alerts. We went to the field. We came back and repaired broken signal equipment. And still nothing.

When I wasn't reading Ian Fleming I tried to commit to memory all of those niggling little details that every OCS board asks—the nomenclature of the M-14 rifle, the bursting radius of an M-26 grenade, my general orders,[24] the name of the Chairman of the Joint Chiefs of Staff, the lifesaving steps—in order. There was no telling when I would get called for the OCS board. I had to be ready.

Finally, one morning while we were cleaning our barracks rooms for one of his rare inspections, Foxworth announced that I would report to Mannheim the first of the week to appear before an OCS board. The day was set. It was finally time for me to show them what I had.

I scrambled to get ready. My greens[25] were still in the wall locker—fresh from the dry cleaners. Being attached to an armored mainte-

---

[24] The orders governing the duties of soldiers placed on interior guard details. The general orders cover every situation that can occur and must be committed to memory and recited by rote on demand. At that time there were eleven of them.

[25] The AG44 (Army Green, shade 44) dress uniform required to be worn on formal official occasions.

nance battalion didn't give us many opportunities to wear a class A uniform. With the help of the others on the team I was able to get my uniform ready to go. All the while, Bobby R. Foxworth grilled me on every possible question I could be asked, pummelling me with technical questions that I had not even thought I might be expected to answer.

It was Bobby R. who reminded me that the OCS board would be made up of signal corps officers and NCOs and what they knew, they would ask. His assessment sent a shock through my system. But I hadn't focused on anything related to my own MOS. I had the weekend to bone up.

Each member of the team took a piece of the action. The radio guys grilled me on radio nomenclature and troubleshooting procedure. The wire and generator expert grilled me on that and Bobby R. put me through general signal corps questions. He coached me to answer affirmatively if asked would I apply for a signal corps commission when I graduated from OCS. Not all infantry OCS grads went into the infantry. A few were allowed to apply for a transfer to a branch that was a bit understaffed and one in which they had some expertise. It was the first political consideration of my life.

The OCS board was everything I expected. I was nervous and they were picky. I had never seen any of the officers on the board and had only once caught a glimpse of the battalion sergeant major—one of the three NCO board members.

The interview seemed to go on for hours. I sat there trying to look alert and responsive to each of the board members while trying to remind myself to speak clearly and with confidence. Inside I was jelly. I was sure that the next question would be the one that would wipe out all of the correct answers to all of the previous questions.

Finally, the lieutenant colonel—president of the board—shifted from signal corps technical questions to leadership questions. It wasn't so much that the questions were theoretical that threw me; rather, it was the phrasing. He seemed to have already decided what the outcome of the board was when he began asking questions like, "When you become an officer, how will you handle a situation like . . . ?" *He already had me commissioned!* I began to relax. That made answering his questions a lot easier.

Then I was dismissed and told that I would be notified of the board's decision. When I got outside the board room I found Foxworth and another team member waiting for me. All I wanted was a cigarette.

On the trip back to K-town I tried to recall all the questions and my answers so I could tell Foxworth. He agreed with me, that I probably got about all of the factual questions right and did well on the leadership and personal questions about motivation and becoming an officer. Still, we both knew the real obstacle to my becoming an officer: I was only nineteen.

Days and then weeks went by, and I waited for the decision of the board to make it from Mannheim to K-town. Foxworth tried to do a little tapping of the NCO net by calling all of his buddies in Mannheim who might be connected with personnel.

One Friday afternoon when I was feeling pretty sure that the answer was taking so long because it was *no*, Foxworth came in to check out our work. I was leaning over a PRC-10 radio[26] trying to repair a handset cable that had been pulled completely free of the radio body —socket and all. Foxworth told me that he wanted me to go to the PX and pick up a few things. He wasn't specific. I thought he was jotting down a list on the work bench. I put on my field jacket and gloves while he finished.

As I stood by the homemade plywood door to the shop, ready to leave, he looked up at me and told me to go get myself a new AWOL bag. I was puzzled. I asked him why I needed one. He said that in spite of the fact that I was young and stupid, I was going to Fort Benning to become an officer—the board had recommended I go.

That night we did the town. Bobby R. and the rest of the team members moved out en masse to capture and devour all of the German beer we could find. I should have remembered my earlier encounters with domestic brew, but I was so happy to have received the recommendation that all I wanted to do was get a quick letter off to my family and go celebrate with the team.

I paid—that night and the next morning.

I waited for a few weeks for the official paperwork to get to me in Kaiserslautern and when it didn't arrive, I began to worry. So many things had fallen through the cracks in my very short army career that it was starting to become routine.

Several days later Bobby R. was the bearer of news. We didn't know if it was good or bad—I was to get my butt to the company orderly

---

[26] The AN/PRC-10 was the standard field radio of the day. It had a 170-channel capability with a range of 5-8 kilometers and weighed 26 pounds. In 1967, it was replaced by the AN/PRC-25, which had 920 FM channels, weighed only 23 pounds, and had a range of 25 kilometers.

room in Mannheim. No explanation why or instructions on what uniform to be wearing or when I could expect to return.

But I went prepared. Shaving gear and a change of underwear if I had to stay a few nights, class-A and fatigue uniforms—for whatever I was going there for.

The first sergeant made a big deal out of having me there. He didn't like getting called by the battalion sergeant major about people in his company. I was going to see the battalion commander. He threatened me if I brought any problems back.

The battalion commander! That was not a good sign. None of us could think of any good reason why I should be going to the battalion headquarters. It was with considerable trepidation that I walked across the compound to the colonel's office.

The sergeant major made the usual sergeant-major noises. He gave me trouble about my uniform: too much starch. He didn't like my boots: they weren't issue boots but an extra pair I had purchased. He didn't like my initiative and a long list of other minor things.

After he was through, he dispatched me into the colonel's office.

I had never been in an office like his—well appointed and replete with items of heraldry and replicas of United States Army, European, and 7th Army insignia.

He was a small man with a tiny mustache. I saluted, he returned it. He sat down and pointed me to a chair. I took the chair. You were never supposed to take over the chair and really relax in it—just sit up straight with both feet on the floor with your cap on your knees.

The colonel began a slow windup for a pitch that I didn't see coming for a long time. First, he advised me that the OCS board *had* recommended approval of my application, but that didn't sound as final as I had thought *recommending approval* might actually be.

He leaned back in his executive chair, rambling about how everything that the troops do reflects on the commander and how he was responsible for troop performance and failure. He expanded about how very important it was that everything and everyone associated with his battalion be up to his standards and reflect credit on himself and the other members of the battalion.

I could feel something awful coming but had no idea what it could be. I kept nodding and mumbling "Yessir" at the appropriate pauses and the occasional raising of his eyebrow. All I knew for sure was that I was being circled for the kill.

He continued to give me little lectures about how commanders—officers (the first time he had used the O-word) had to take control of their responsibilities to ensure that everything representing their command was trained, inspected, and equipped to reflect proudly on them.

Then he picked up some paperwork on his desk and leaned forward—speaking more confidentially. He simply asked me, "You understand, don't you?"

"Yessir," I answered.

He told me that he had either to endorse the recommendation or disapprove it and forward it through channels to Headquarters, U.S. Army, Europe (USAREUR).

I was suddenly struck with the question, Why would he even consider recommending disapproval?

Some of his exact words still burn in my brain. "What if I sent you back to Benning and you failed? What would that do to my reputation? To the battalion? Would you go back there and embarrass us?"

Of course I stuttered and stammered a few, "No, sir,"s trying to assure him that I would never do that.

He continued, "I don't know you, Foley. I didn't even recall ever seeing you in the battalion." As he spoke I could see the OCS board recommendation and months of trying to get accepted flying away.

Somewhere in his lecture on caution I reconnected with what he was saying long enough to hear him announce, "So, I've decided to send you to the 7th Army NCO Academy in Bad Tolz. If you do well there, I'll feel more comfortable about recommending approval of your OCS application. But if you fail, there is no way I am going to take your application seriously."

I had met my first "careerist," but it would be several years before I could tell the difference between a careerist and a professional.

The 7th Army NCO Academy had a reputation for being the toughest, no-nonsense NCO academy in the army. There wasn't a soldier in Germany who hadn't heard about the 7th Army NCO Academy and how tough it was and how incredibly demanding the instructors were. Horror stories abounded about the inspections and performance critiques there. In reality, its mission was to take new NCOs and specialists and give them an intensive course in the skills required of them. It had a high washout rate and was focused on the combat arms NCO.

The 7th Army NCO Academy was a serious setback. It makes no sense to me now, but back then going there seemed an almost insurmountable test for me. How could I expect to compete with soldiers who were selected from tank and infantry and artillery units? They were far more skilled than I was in the basics of combat arms training. The instructors and the students were light-years ahead of me in experience and would surely blow by me on the most basic combat skills.

The irony was that what was being taught at the 7th Army NCO Academy was a compressed version of the curriculum at Fort Benning's OCS. If I couldn't hack it at Bad Tolz, how the hell did I expect to make it at Benning? But I was nineteen, and such practical thinking was still not a skill I had mastered.

I feared the worst. I was facing obstacles that seemed to pop up everywhere in my pursuit of advancement and recognition. I don't know where I got the idea that my road would or should be easier. But there seemed to be plenty of officers and NCOs around who didn't appear to have had such a rough one as me.

I went back to Kaiserslautern to announce to Bobby R. Foxworth and the team that it looked like I had been stopped in my quest for a commission.

I was just about at the point where I was going to give up on it all. I was past the midway point in my enlistment and could easily have slid to the end of my army life without too much difficulty. I was in a pretty easy unit, the schedule wasn't bad, we had class-A passes, and Foxworth kept the chickenshit off our backs. We stayed pretty warm and dry in our workshop, and when we went to the field we slept in pup tents but worked in five-ton shop vans that were heated. It really wasn't all that bad.

For a brief moment I considered just pulling my application and ghosting the remaining months. I began to make up scenarios in my head about getting my GI Bill, getting out, going to college, and having a real life.

But there was no way in hell that Bobby R. Foxworth was going to allow that. He and the team had gotten me ready for the OCS board, and they'd do the same for the 7th Army NCO Academy. I never got a chance to get serious about quitting, not beyond just feeling sorry for myself. Bobby R. and the team were on me like a surgical team.

Suddenly, field manuals on the skills taught and tested at the NCO academy appeared on my bunk and I read them from the time I got up until I fell asleep. I would get questions about methods of instruction over breakfast, about how to form for shelter tents at the work bench. When we were driving to a repair site, one of the team members would grill me on map reading or leadership.

It was a cram course. And while they were cramming me, the paperwork was wending its way through channels to tell me that I would report to Bad Tolz in two weeks.

Panic really set in when I got the orders. There was no getting out of it. I had to go and make it or come back in disgrace and face that battalion commander and my peers.

I was really scared of failing. It wouldn't be the last time in my career.

CHAPTER 5

•

The NCO academy *kaserne* at Bad Tolz had a reputation: Before the U.S. Army came it had been a Nazi SS barracks during World War Two. As you approached the place its sharp stone lines seemed totally out of place, nestled into the rolling hills of the green Bavarian countryside.

Its facade was cold and impersonal, more like a government office building than a soldier's barracks. No landscaping softened its appearance, all of the windows were open to exactly the same distance from the sill, and nothing personal could be seen.

Bad Tolz also had another unique reputation as home of the 10th Special Forces Group. I had not seen a Special Forces soldier since the day that the iron sergeants mounted the stage at Fort Dix to recruit us for Airborne school. The thought of an entire Special Forces Group conjured up incredible fantasies of men of steel and feats of great courage on America's outposts of freedom.

The two-story academy building surrounded a huge barren concrete courtyard that was devoid of trees, benches, not even any markings of any kind.

We were met by a sergeant first class who looked like he had just stepped out of a band box. Everything from the top of his cap to the tips of his low-quarter shoes was perfectly shined, clipped, polished, or pressed. He stood perfectly still as he waited for us.

We bailed out of the back of the truck, grabbed our duffel bags, and formed up in front of him. He didn't say a word. We lacked a little coordination and to him we must have looked like the Keystone Kops trying to build a military formation. He made a small gesture of impatience.

"Who's in charge here?" he asked forcefully, tapping his swagger stick against his trouser leg.

No one answered.

"I'll ask again. Who-is-in-charge?"

No one answered.

Still standing at a perfect position of attention, he looked each one of us in the eye for a split second and began our first class. "Everywhere and anywhere you are in the army—someone is always in charge."

We weren't sure if that required a response. So we stayed quiet and listened.

"If it isn't apparent just who is in charge—take charge. Organize and lead. I say again . . . organize and lead."

We let that sink in.

"This is the reason you're here. Before you leave here you'll master that or you *will not* graduate."

The instructional philosophy of the 7th Army NCO Academy was not one of screaming or hazing or harassment. Nor was it just a harder version of basic training. Instead, we were put under great pressure to perform like professional NCOs and we were critiqued in detail on our performance. We quickly got into step with the school.

Each day began early and was filled with intensive classes in leadership, physical training, methods of instruction, dismounted drill, school of the soldier, field sanitation, land navigation, and inspections. We were subjected to inspections and taught how to conduct them.

But over all the dominant theme was *attention to detail.* The school at Bad Tolz had gained a reputation for the incredible lengths it went to to drum into the heads of the students that nothing was too small to be unimportant and anything worth doing was worth doing completely and correctly. The importance of that attention to detail was lost on me at the time. But it would not only serve me well; it would make a difference in lives in just a few years hence.

But at the time I thought it was a lot of chickenshit.

And then there was the legendary Autobahn.[27] The Autobahn was not a German highway—it was what they called the hallways in the NCO Academy. The original halls were wide passageways that ran down the centers of each of the two floors. They once were just smooth cement central walkways flanked (against the walls) with single rows of large glossy tiles. But over the years since the NCO Academy had moved in after WWII, the cement had been covered with layers and layers of hand-applied, spit-shined black shoe polish. The end result was an eight-foot-wide spit-shined hallway no one but the instructors and VIP visitors were allowed to walk on.

As students, we were expected to walk along the narrow margin of

[27] The German word for "highway."

waxed (but not shoe polished) tiles that separated the large shoe-polished central part from the walls. And it was on the same tiles we knelt each night and each morning with soft cotton rags spit shining the Autobahn for the coming day.

I quickly fell behind. Sure, I could handle spit shining the floors and polishing the brass fixtures, but it was everything else that threw me.

Each of us was given a job within the student company. I was slapped with being a team leader for the four men in my large room.

And I was designated the maintenance NCO for the company. As such, I was responsible to see that every man in my team was ready for class, ready for training, and ready for inspections. I was also saddled with the responsibility for everything in the barracks that needed to be maintained. That included every window latch, door hinge, bunk spring, footlocker tray, latrine soap dish, light bulb, and every square inch of wall, wood, and tile in the building. I didn't really take the job seriously. At least not at first.

Then came the reckoning. The faculty NCO assigned to my squad came to my room late one night and asked me to explain the form that I had submitted. It was a maintenance form that stated I had inspected all of the items on the lengthy list and found them all serviceable or in need of the repair as specified. On the list were some entries that a blind man could find. A faucet in the latrine needed a replacement handle. The mop sink was cracked and needed replacement, and a few light bulbs were burned out in the hallways.

I had conducted the inspection in less than an hour and was feeling proud of myself for not wasting time. The time I saved I spent on things that I needed to do. I felt that I had done a fairly thorough job of inspecting everything, even though privately I thought it was pretty Mickey Mouse.

He wanted to know about the other items. *Other items?* I wasn't sure what he meant and said so. He invited me to follow him as we inspected the pages of items together. I cringed as he walked out of my room and clumped across the Autobahn leaving heel marks in the shiny black blanket of shoe polish. It would take at least another hour for my roommates and I to repair the damage.

He led me to a wall-mounted ceramic water faucet and asked me if I had inspected it. I looked at the drinking fountain and at my list which indicated it was okay and said that I had.

The sergeant bent down, reached up under and behind the fountain and pulled out a large lag bolt that was loose from the wall. He made me squat down and look at a hole in the wall that was far too large to hold the bolt in place. He explained that a loose bolt was a shortcoming I should have noted. It was important for the function of the water fountain as well as a potential safety problem.

From there he led me to a wall switch that was missing one screw from the faceplate—not on my list. And then to a mop closet that had a large crack in the tile in its floor—not listed on my inspection sheet either. He took me to a few more of my oversights and I was completely embarrassed by my lack of attention to detail. But more than my embarrassment, I remember his attitude. He was neither sarcastic nor condescending. He tried to explain to me in the most professional tone that as a leader I had to make sure things were done and done well. Without resorting to the dramatic, he explained that for lack of a screw or something equally insignificant, an entire vehicle, weapons system, or protective device can be rendered useless. And useless equipment can mean death at the worst or something heavy to lug at best.

He had made his point. He then gave me the opportunity to reinspect everything. That was a very long evening followed by a repair job that I did on the Autobahn since I figured the trip across the glossy surface was my fault.

The killer at the NCO academy was what in the real world would be called public speaking. Though I had been in front of a platoon and an entire trainee company before to give them short announcements, the thought of giving a rehearsed class put ice water in my veins.

They started methods of instruction (MOI) classes the first couple of days at the academy. We were confronted with lesson plans and training aids and lists of things to do and not do. And every single principle they taught they practiced. Each of the NCOs was not only an experienced combat veteran and leader, but an excellent instructor.

They were masters of precise diction, effective gestures, and proper use of pointers and other training aids. Their material was well prepared and well rehearsed. Their uniforms were perfect and their control over the class was unquestionable. And they were exactly on time. If the class was due to start at 0800 and end at 0850, it would. The example they set made our fear of teaching our own classes that much more intense.

It's important to point out here that the army has a different approach to teaching than most civilian institutions. It believes that if the student fails to learn then the instructor failed to teach. Thus, the entire burden of motivating and instructing a student rests on the shoulders of the instructor.

The second unique feature of army instruction is that rank has little to do with it. You are assigned to teach and expected to master the topic and prepare and teach the class, whatever the rank of your students relative to your own. Thus, your authority comes from your ability to teach and not your rank or seniority. Many a colonel has been taught some very important things by a young corporal.

The first monster I had to tame, after butterflies, was a strange training aid from the Dark Ages called the *venetian blind*. The venetian blind was an inspired device that could be used indoors and out, in good weather and bad. It was a wooden frame that held several horizonal pieces of wood that were on pivots and were four-sided. On each of the rotating faces an instructor could tape or tack a single-line entry that supported some key point or principle or step in his class. As the instructor made his point or reached that principle, he would turn the knob on the side of the venetian blind and reveal the key word or statement of importance. By the time the instructor came to the end of the class, he would have revealed all of the essential teaching points in a living, or at least physical, outline.

It was a nightmare to master the apparatus. We would practice well into the early morning hours, until we could make a point precisely at the right time in our lesson plan and then reveal the correct rotating slat to support it. Despite practicing and memorizing the order that our training aid held, we fumbled again and again.

The venetian blind was further complicated by the strict rules on the use of the pointer. The army's theory was that the pointer can be a training aid or a prop for disaster. We were criticized often for having one in our hands when we weren't using it or for using the pointer to emphasize something we were saying rather than something we were pointing to. And we were never able to get away with making wide and sweeping gestures with it like fencing masters. You wouldn't think it was that hard to manage, until you went to the 7th Army NCO Academy and tried to integrate the proper use of the pointer with keeping your class's attention, staying on your lesson plan, and maintaining control. For me, it was a backbreaker.

Each day of the monthlong course added new problems for me and put me further and further behind in studies, maintenance, and sleep. I began missing meals to gain more time to shine something or inspect something or study or rehearse. I had no way of knowing then that it was a pattern I would set for the days when time would be really critical. That was the price of being a leader instead of just one of the troops. I would learn that the hard way, but not nearly so hard as it might have been had I not attended that NCO academy in Bavaria.

Mastering MOI was only part of my problem. Most of the classes we were assigned to give were oriented on combat arms and techniques. While these subjects were familiar to all of my classmates, they weren't for me.

I collected my share of demerits for infractions at personal and barracks inspections, and got much more than my share of critical comments from the instructors on my performance.

I recall one dawn, looking out across the compound just as the sun began to bathe the concrete with a yellow glow. A first lieutenant from the Special Forces group walked through the sally port, the sounds of his paratrooper boots echoing off the walls of the quadrangle. He wore the green beret and not-yet-authorized crossed arrows on his left collar. His self-confidence and presence was unmistakable even from my barracks window a story above. *He had made it.* Once he had been a high-school boy with aspirations of becoming an officer. Just to look at him I knew some of the tests he had been through. He was parachute, Ranger, and Special Forces qualified. He had earned a commission somewhere—OCS, West Point, ROTC. My mind reeled at the thought of all the days, weeks, and miles that he had put into being assigned to the 10th Special Forces Group. I knew that he had also mastered not only U.S. weapons and tactics but those of other nations; that he spoke at least one other language; that he was cross-trained in some other specialty to give redundancy to his team.

He had worked his way through a system that tested and weeded out and then retested soldiers before they could become Airborne–Ranger–Special Forces officers. He was on one end of the process and I was on the other.

As I watched him disappear into a doorway on the far side of the quadrangle, again I began to doubt that I could ever hack OCS. Hell, if I was having so much trouble with the 7th Army NCO Academy, how could I expect to make it through OCS? I had been up all night studying and was in a particularly dark mood. I was almost sure, at that moment, that I could never be an officer.

Someone had on a Beatles song on the radio in a nearby room. I felt homesick for America and for the times that were so much easier and carefree. I missed being a teenager. It is ironic that British music was my connection to the American kids that I remembered. But even if I'd been back in the town where I graduated from high school, that wouldn't have helped my homesickness much, because most of my classmates were gone—to college, the service, or to jobs in bigger towns.

There really was no place for me to go back to. My family had moved again—my father being in the army. The army was my new home and I wasn't feeling very good about how I was fitting into my new family. If someone had given me the chance to chuck it all that morning, I'd have been out of Bad Tolz by sundown.

I have no idea what snapped me out of feeling so sorry for myself, but somehow the tactical NCOs could tell when you needed a boot in the ass and would restart your engine by making you that much busier when it looked to them like were slumping. It must have been obvious to my tac NCO that my butt was dragging because I quickly found myself put in as the acting student company commander for a week. Things weren't demanding enough; I had to be saddled with the responsibilities for the entire student company. It was a bit like feeding a burning man lighter fluid.

The pressure mounted as I tried to keep up. I was sure that I was so far behind in my standing in the class that there was no way I would graduate with my classmates. Still, they were going to have to throw me out; I wasn't going to quit. I was humiliated each day in class, watching the other students pull up their combat-arms experience when needed. They related everything to being a leader of combat soldiers, which came easily to most of them. I was just amazed at how they could do that almost effortlessly.

But somehow I did keep up. I know there were plenty of things that slipped through the cracks, but it wasn't until years later that I realized it was supposed to work that way. The tactical NCOs put far more requirements on me than I could ever accomplish to make me decide what was important. They had all been in combat and they knew you had to think fast on the battlefield.

They made me learn it by myself: setting priorities and standing ready to take the heat for what didn't get done was part of the job. When I realized this they were no longer around to thank, but they forever changed my attitude and my appreciation for NCOs. They became a model for proficiency and professionalism that went into my head along with the memory of those two Airborne recruiters.

Somehow I survived the experience of the 7th Army NCO Academy. But looking back, I consider it one of the best experiences of my career. I learned more about leadership there than any other school in the army that I would later attend. I think what made that school stand out was how those instructors personally demonstrated the leadership techniques that they taught. Every NCO on that school's faculty was a walking example of what they were trying to teach us. Also, we were treated firmly and with dignity. There was a special balance between placing demands on our performance and explaining why it was important to do things the way we had to.

And the atmosphere of professionalism that was ever present among the many members of the 10th Special Forces Group didn't escape me either. Each day I would run into some officer or NCO from the group. They were always polite, businesslike, and distant.

There was hardly even any small talk with them. I don't ever remember hearing any Special Forces soldiers saying something like, "How 'bout those Colts?" Instead, they seemed to have something else to do and were in a hurry to be on their way. I always took the time to study them because they were so different from us. Most of them seemed to have European or Slavic accents. Many of the NCOs seemed young for their rank, while the officers seemed old for theirs.

I didn't know at the time that many of the officers were ex-NCOs, and the NCOs got very rapid advancement once they did get into Special Forces.

The other interesting thing about them was the individuality of their uniforms and equipment. Many of them wore unauthorized leather field boots. Often the belts they wore were made of high-strength nylon webbing rather than the cotton belts the rest of us wore. All of them carried some form of hunting knife or pocketknife in a scabbard on their belts.

They carried a whole spectrum of field gear out to operations or training that looked nothing like the usual load-bearing equipment that regular forces were issued: they carried rucksacks while we were issued butt packs; they carried foreign rifles and submachine guns while the M-14 was our standard weapon.

I wasn't the only one fascinated by Green Berets in our compound. The Special Forces soldiers were often a topic of barracks conversation. We weren't sure what they were up to, but we were sure they were up to something dangerous and very classified. We were impressed.

I graduated at the top of my class. That caught me completely by surprise. I had been on the verge of quitting and was sure that I was only moments away from being dismissed from the course for poor performance. But I had been mistaking corrections by the NCOs for unsatisfactory performance. Their evaluations, along with my test grades and my demerits, were used to calculate class standing and I must have done a whole lot better than I thought I did.

I was suddenly spun completely around. My thoughts of inadequacy were replaced by confidence and pride in having met the NCO academy challenge and completing the course with distinction.

I won't ever forget Bad Tolz. It was a short course and was not filled with any of the danger or risky training that future schools would hold for me. On balance, it was more of a gentleman's course than most other combat-oriented courses. Nonetheless it was important and valuable to me because it taught me plenty about NCOs, the army, and myself.

My return to Mannheim—victorious—was a complete surprise to the battalion commander and the sergeant major. I suspect that both of them had placed bets against me making it through Bad Tolz. But I was proud to walk back into the colonel's office to tell him I was ready for him to recommend approval of my OCS application.

I was treated to another long lecture about loyalty and obligation to my unit and the unit's reputation—in regard to my performance at Fort Benning. I nodded and mumbled agreeably—anything just to get him to sign the papers.

Once my official OCS orders came down, my status changed. The army is a small family and everyone knows everyone else's business. The word of my acceptance and selection went out quickly and there was no place I could go in Mannheim or Kaiserslautern and not provoke some comment about my status as a soon-to-be officer candidate.

At first I was flattered. But as the weeks went on I got tired of the cracks. It felt good knowing that it was common knowledge that I'd been selected for OCS, but the reactions I got soon became old.

If I was working on some equipment and got so much as a little grease on my boots or uniform I was likely to hear a comment from someone who knew me just casually, like, "That'll never get it at Benning, Foley. You'll be out on your ass in no time for looking like that." Or there was always the comment that validated the huge self-identity gap that has always existed between officers and enlisted men, like, "You going to talk to us once you are an officer? Bet you'll forget that we even exist."

What really bothered me was the almost obligatory nature of the comments. So many soldiers felt that once I became an officer I would then be their enemy, and that anything I did would be for myself alone. In some of the comments I sensed a loss of self-esteem and in others a feeling of exclusion. And while most of the comments were laughable on the surface, they were rooted in a feeling of discrimination—like I was joining a club they were not invited to join.

But as much as I took ribbing from others, I never once heard any of that from the members of my team. I attribute that to the fact that they all knew me to the point where I could be accepted. I think they all realized that they too could have gone to OCS, and I was not going because of some connections or privilege that they didn't have.

By the time I was ready to leave Germany I felt that I had a pretty good chance of acquitting myself well at Fort Benning.

CHAPTER 6

•

Fort Benning in the summer of 1964 was a far different place than it is today. That was eight years before the volunteer army came into being and it was almost a year before the first Marines landed on the beaches in South Vietnam.

Benning hummed with officer training courses for basic officers, OCS candidates, and advanced-course students, but the Airborne school was the centerpiece and focal point for everything at Benning. Directions were given there with the three 250-foot jump towers as landmarks.

At Kelly Hill, the 11th Air Assault Division was field testing the Airmobile concept that would change the face of modern warfare before two more years were up. On a daily basis the skies over Fort Benning were filled with helicopters and fixed wing aircraft.

Out at Sand Hill and Harmony Church, soldiers were going through basic and advanced infantry training and Ranger school. Everywhere you went you saw soldiers, student soldiers, and officer candidates in precise formations double timing to some important class or range or appointment. Jody[28] cadence filled the air and the post was clean, crisp, and manicured.

Everything shined. Everything was in neat rows, columns, piles, or stacks. You could hardly go anywhere without seeing NCOs and officers moving smartly along side troop formations or standing atop PT platforms giving precise instructions—the Benning way.

People at Benning stopped for traffic lights, didn't speed—not even a tiny bit, drove clean and perfectly maintained privately owned vehicles (POVs), dressed in the appropriate uniforms or in acceptable civilian clothes. Everyone's grass was cut outside their quarters and their trash-can lids were perfectly seated.

Haircuts were perfect copies of white-sidewall cuts. And every-

---

[28] The name of the cadence songs sung and chanted by soldiers while drilling and marching. Called "Jody" after the mythical civilian who stayed home while all the real men went off to war.

where on post there was evidence of concern for readiness in the form of infantrymen out doing their own physical training. Runners and ball players dotted the training areas and ball fields and filled the gyms.

It was a busy post with a mission—to train infantrymen to lead men in combat.

I reported to Fort Benning thinking I was ready. I was wrong.

The process of turning an enlisted man into an officer had been refined and polished over the course of three wars with input from such distinguished military figures as George C. Marshall, George S. Patton, and Douglas MacArthur. There was not a trick or a move that an officer candidate could make that Benning had not seen before and had not created a policy or reaction to. The tactical officers, the instructors, and the cadre had it all down to a fine-tuned process.

And we were ready to be processed.

The firm but gentlemanly approach to education that had been the hallmark of the 7th Army NCO Academy was gone. I reported to 50th Officer Candidate Company and stepped onto a rollercoaster that would not end for many exciting, frightening, and painful years. But what I faced in those first moments was hazing and hysterical treatment of the highest order.

Within minutes of reporting in we were all quickly reminded that it was the mission of OCS to turn out the finest infantry officers that they could, and any of us who couldn't hack it would find ourselves gone; no exceptions, no compromise. The standards were set and we had to reach them. We would be put in situations on a daily basis that would test our ability to lead and make sound military decisions with dual concern for the welfare of the troops in our charge and the accomplishment of our mission.

If we faltered, if we stumbled, looked indecisive, or demonstrated flaws in character or judgment or moral or physical courage, we would be dropped from the program and returned to our previous enlisted status.

We were tested under the most chaotic and confusing environment our instructors could create. Their intent was to simulate the din and the distractions of combat by whatever means they could. That meant plenty of hazing and lots of Mickey Mouse.[29]

From the moment I stepped onto the grid of sidewalks that to this

---

[29] A term common in the military since at least as early as World War II for anything stupid, inane, silly, chickenshit.

day connect the OCS barracks, I was bombarded with yelling and screaming of contradictory instructions. The tactical officers and senior officer candidates swarmed around us—nearly two hundred of us —as we tried to report in for training. We were screamed at, belittled, insulted, and put through extraordinary antics. I don't believe there was a candidate in my company who did not do at least a hundred push-ups that first day.

If we were going to quit, they wanted us to do it right away and not waste their time and the army's.

I remembered Skunk Boots Terrel, and how he had done the same and expected us to keep our composure. I knew I could do it. I wouldn't let them get to me.

The Negro candidates were called "nigger" to see if it would get a rise out of them, Jewish candidates were taunted about their religion, older NCOs reporting in were teased about being too old. I was identified as a kid. Just twenty, I was queried about how I expected to become an officer when I couldn't even buy a drink.

Once we were finished turning in all the things and filling in all the forms they wanted it was time to get things. Before we could be issued anything we needed to be able to secure the equipment. We were formed up by the senior candidates and double timed to the small branch PX in the battalion area to get a list of essentials which we paid for.

For all of us it was the beginning of understanding a big difference between officers and NCOs. If the army wanted enlisted men to have something, it would be issued to them. Not so with officers. Often, officers were expected to pay out of their pocket for personal equipment and uniform items. We were given a one-time and very modest clothing allowance after we graduated, but that money never came close to covering our expenses.

The second concept we had to accept was that every single thing in the army that was not expendable was signed out to someone to care for and safeguard. That would be a major concern for each one of us from that day forward. If something we were responsible for got lost, broken or damaged, we had to account for it. No exceptions.

So off we went to the PX to purchase marking pens to ink our names on or in our equipment, and padlocks to safeguard the things that we would store away. And that was only the first of these shopping sprees.

Returning from the PX, we were each issued an M-14 rifle[30] which we locked back into the weapons racks as soon as we memorized the serial numbers. Then we drew gas masks and foot lockers, desk blotters, lamps, butt cans, light bulbs, toilet paper, paper towels, and armloads of bedding.

Most of us made several trips up and down the barracks stairs, hauling what we were issued to the rooms we were assigned and stowing things in our new wall and footlockers. Each trip was its own gauntlet of physical demands and mental hazing. The senior candidates and the tactical officers posted themselves at the choke points we all had to pass through. Each stairwell was an echoing chamber of yelling tac officers and equally loud candidate responses. When we were lucky enough to make some progress, we had to carry our loads over the bodies of our classmates doing push-ups or even more ridiculous physical feats.

I got caught. A particularly enthusiastic senior candidate decided that he wanted to see me treat my wooden footlocker like a rifle and maneuver it through commands as he yelled them. Port arms, right and left shoulder arms were particularly awkward to do with a clumsy wooden box. For my trouble I got the chance to do plenty of pushups on the concrete steps of the stairwell—my feet on higher steps than my hands.

By the time I got all of my newly issued gear into my room I thought that there might just be a moment's letup in the harassment. I was wrong. As the issuing process died down, the tac officers and senior candidates searched us out in our rooms and continued their efforts to try to anger and confuse us with more insults and taunts designed to get us to overreact. They were experts at baiting us while counseling that if they could get to us, the average soldier could leave us whimpering in our beer should the day ever come we were given a rifle platoon.

A rifle platoon. Somehow it had not occurred to me that in the hearts of the cadre it was the highest calling—to be a second-lieutenant platoon leader in an infantry company—in combat. I was starting to realize that I hadn't given the entire experience of OCS enough thought. I had been thinking about becoming an officer, and Fort Benning was training me to lead men into combat. There was a wide

---

[30] The standard infantry rifle from 1959 to 1966, it could be fired fully automatic, had a maximum effective range of 460 meters, fired 7.62mm cartridges from a twenty-round magazine, and weighed twelve pounds loaded. Replaced by the M-16.

gap in our relative goals and I would have to adjust mine. Benning was not concerned with how realistic its goals were.

The first day ended well after midnight with a promise of an early call for physical training—OCS style—next morning.

By the time the lights went out I had met my roommates: Butch Entrekin, Ronnie Epstein, and Jon Every-Clayton. We would go through a lot together. Still, we were surprised that we had made it through that first day. We lost some candidates that first day. They were gone before sunrise the next morning. The only easy thing to do in OCS was quit.

The second day was far worse than the first. The pressure was on and we were a captive group. We went everywhere as a company, took all our training as a company, and ate our meals together. So unlike the first day, when we were split into small groups all over the battalion area, we were bunched up, in an infantry sense, and that made us an easy target.

I was never much of an athlete after I seriously broke my leg in high school, horseplaying during wrestling practice. I spent a long time recuperating, and by the time my leg was strong enough for me to go back to high-school sports, I was well behind my peers in the sports that interested me.

So in the army I got off to a slow start in the PT department, which was never my strong suit and an activity that I dreaded every single day. Still, it was unavoidable. As the months and years went by I kept finding myself in units that prided themselves on how much PT they could do, how much beer they could drink, and how many hearts they could break. Pretty stupid of me, as much as I disliked PT. But I wasn't alone in OCS. There were only a few among us who seemed to enjoy the misery of the Army Daily Dozen and the periodic physical fitness tests.

OCS had a special kind of discomfort in mind when PT was on the schedule. We were not just expected to survive each of the long formation runs and the calisthenics; we were expected to execute every move and run every mile like we were teaching it to others. We took PT every day, and when we weren't doing it we were teaching it and being critiqued on our performance.

A humorous feature of our mind-set was that we would complain about the long runs and the breath-taxing exercises, but then as soon as we would stop for a break, we would light up cigarettes. Smoking was the norm. Nonsmokers were rare. But we were brassy young

American men and smoking was a macho thing to do. We did every macho thing we could think of to prove to ourselves, our peers, and our instructors that we had the right stuff.

We've changed a lot since, but smoking, drinking, and hell-raising were expected then. From the moment we arrived at OCS it was expected of us to challenge the system, be out on the edge, demonstrate initiative, and prove ourselves.

Training at Benning was much harder than anything I had known up to then. The hours were longer, the physical demands were more taxing, and the whole notion of being evaluated for an invisible quality —leadership—was very unnerving.

What was leadership? What did it actually look like? How did we know if we had it? All we knew was that we were being tested as leaders while the screws were being put to us physically, mentally, and academically.

For my roommates and me, we were first thrust under the microscope by a large, talented, football-playing lieutenant who was our platoon's part-time tactical officer. He would come around and get in our faces, dropping us for pushups and asking us to explain first one and then another failing during training. But he was rarely around and never at training because he was on loan to the post football team and we were spared the concentrated heat that the other platoons got from their full-time tac officers.

But that too was short-lived. He was soon reassigned to another job on post and we got a new tac officer—a full-time, no-nonsense first lieutenant named Bill Pfeiffer. Pfeiffer hit us like a train wreck. He walked into our platoon area and immediately and effectively got our attention.

It wasn't enough that the system was heaping shock after shock on us—we also found out that we had been given a true man of steel. We knew when we first saw him that he was a serious professional infantry officer—Ranger and Airborne qualified, fresh back from a tour as a platoon leader in the famous and respected 173d Airborne Brigade on Okinawa.

Then we found out that he had actually made a jump in Okinawa where neither of his parachutes opened and he walked away from it. We were stunned when we saw the news clipping that someone's mother or girlfriend had mailed to one of us after she remembered reading his name several months earlier. He had actually leaped from an airplane with two tangled and uninflated parachutes.

* * *

Bill Pfeiffer's first official act was to impress upon us that his primary focus was on our potential as platoon leaders. He promised us that if we didn't convince him that we were the right material with the right attitude, we would *not* graduate or receive commissions as second lieutenants. No one doubted the sincerity of his words.

Our first task was to create our own goals in the form of an immediate objective. He instructed each of us to go out and purchase a gold second lieutenant's bar and put it inside the webbing of our helmet liner. Those bars were to symbolize our goal—graduating and getting commissioned as infantry second lieutenants. He wanted us to keep those bars shined even though they were hidden from sight. We were to take our helmets off when the going got particularly hard and focus on our gold bar. It was our little motivator.

Bill's other techniques were also different from the other tac officers'. He put the burden on us to critique ourselves, to define our own shortcomings and then explain to him how we were going to correct them. We spent hours writing up reports on our own deficiencies and the plans to fix them.

He was a stickler on command presence and appearance. Around Bill Pfeiffer you did *not* slouch, slump, or crap out. It made no difference how tired or hurting or exhausted you were—you would keep it to yourself or have to explain it to Bill Pfeiffer.

We were impressed with his walking away from a bad jump, but even more impressed that he never once mentioned it to us. I believe that he was more professional than the other officers in the company, and more deadly serious about his job than all of them put together. He arrived early and stayed late. He never missed a thing. If we were at training he would be there to check our performance. His counseling technique was formal and, for the most part, private.

Pfeiffer didn't delight in screaming at us in front of our peers. Instead, he would place himself squarely in our path and tell us when we were screwing up. Then he would ask for our concurrence or, if we disagreed with his evaluation, our point of view. He didn't bully us; instead, he led us. He set the example in everything he did. He was meticulous, punctual, competent, and always prepared. Within a couple of days of taking over our platoon he knew every one of us by name. He knew who was married and who was not. He knew where we came from and what our backgrounds were. And within a week he knew each of our weaknesses.

It was virtually impossible to get anything by him. He was smarter by himself than we were as a platoon. Whatever we tried to pull, he was ahead of us and already knew what we were up to.

Still, we were expected to test the minor rules. Everywhere in the army, especially the infantry, there are rules to be followed, but there was also an unwritten challenge for us to show our initiative and skill by figuring out ways to get around them. The object was not to break the law—at least, not any important law, but to be inventive and creative circumventing those that constrained our fun. Mostly we poked fun at the army, the structure, and the system.

One of the strict rules was *no pogey bait in the barracks*. Pogey bait was any food not served by the mess hall *in* the mess hall or at a field kitchen. No food was allowed in the barracks—a totally alien concept in a barracks full of young men, each burning thousands of calories a day.

Not only were we not allowed to bring food into the barracks, we were not allowed to visit anyplace to purchase any. So we went to great lengths to try to slip food in. There was always a chance to get some mailed to us by family, or an occasional visitor would be asked to smuggle some in—like we were prisoners.

The thought of smuggling a large amount of contraband food into the barracks seemed a sophomoric delight that we couldn't possibly pull off. There were always officers around, and anything good would surely be discovered as it came in by the two main entrances to the barracks.

But we still didn't entirely rule it out. We often talked about pizzas and how we would just love to have one. Hell, while we were dreaming, we could dream big.

Although it might have been just a dream for most of us, Les Colegrove, one of our bravest candidates, thought there was a chance of pulling it off without getting caught.

We spent the better part of a weekend planning our great pizza caper, salivating each step of the way. The basic scenario was that late in the evenings we could count on the officers, if they were in the building at all, to be down on the first floor in their offices. The chance of them coming upstairs to our platoon area was unlikely, and we could post sentries to alert us if they left their offices. The hard part was sneaking forty pizzas into the barracks, through the first floor entrances, without the delicious aroma wafting down the hallway to the tac officers' lairs.

Colegrove's solution was to come in through the top. Through some clever maneuvering, he was able to borrow some rappelling ropes, snap links, and gloves. At the appointed time, special teams went into action. Four candidates went to the roof of the three-story building to anchor the ropes to hoist the pizzas up the side of the building away from the offices.

At the same time, a small party slipped out of the barracks and went to a prearranged spot to meet the delivery man, who had been well briefed by phone to be low-key and punctual. In return he could expect a large tip and our eternal gratitude.

The remaining members of the platoon took up security positions looking out for meandering officers, while others stood by to broach made-up problems that would stop them before they got to the second-platoon area.

Colegrove and his team quickly ran the pizza boxes to my team. We helped the others haul them up the side of the building and then slipped back into the barracks.

The team on the roof handed the pizzas down through the rooftop fire door to others who quickly ran them down to the last room on our floor for distribution. On a prearranged signal, a representative from each room would move quietly to the ration breakdown point and pick up his room's pizzas.

Things went like clockwork. We had collected the money, ordered the pizzas, picked them up, moved them into the barracks, and passed them out without arousing suspicion among the officers. Colegrove had even turned on the exhaust fan at the end of our platoon area so that the air would be pulled in the doors on the first floor and out the exhaust vent on our floor, preventing any of the wonderful aroma from drifting down to the first floor.

We probably spent no more than twenty minutes getting the pizzas from the delivery boy's car to our rooms on the second floor. Once we were all back in our rooms with sentries posted to alert us of any approach from the first floor, we were ready to dig in.

I had the first slice of pizza within a fraction of an inch of my mouth when I heard someone yell, "Attention!"

Attention? That could only mean that there was an officer on the floor. How could that be? We had posted lookouts to alert us if any of them made the slightest move toward our platoon.

I leaned back on my footlocker and peeked around the doorjamb. There, standing at the doorway to the stairwell, stood Lieutenant Pfeiffer. He had outsmarted us. He had gone to the other end of the building, climbed the second stairwell to the third floor, crossed to our end of the building, and came *down* the stairway to our floor. We hadn't thought to place a lookout on the landing above our floor.

Pfeiffer called us all out into the hallway. At that point he gave us a long and very straight-faced lecture about the reasons pogey bait was not allowed in the barracks. He listed the ills that could befall us if unauthorized food was left in the barracks. We stood at rigid attention in our silly-looking boxer shorts while he speculated on the perils of insect infestation, rodent and vector problems, and a list of other sanitary reasons for not having pogey bait in our living area.

Once he was through he asked us if we understood. We replied in unison that we did. Satisfied that we understood, Pfeiffer then instructed us to get our pizzas and then to move quickly to the latrine.

He marched us into the showers. There we were instructed to eat all of the pizzas under the streams of water. He explained that it was the only way to make sure that the pizzas didn't go to waste and to keep from creating a health problem.

So, there we stood, crammed into the shower—eating soggy pizzas.

CHAPTER 7

·

After we graduated and received our commissions, I asked Lieutenant Pfeiffer just how he knew we had the pizzas in the barracks. He explained that when we had ordered the pizzas from a young girl at the pizza place we failed to recognize that she was currently dating another tac officer in the OCS company. No sooner had we placed the call, he got a call from the insider, who alerted him to our plan.

While we were trying to be so crafty as to move the pizzas into the barracks by way of the roof, Pfeiffer was downstairs having another cup of coffee—waiting to catch us with the pizzas in hand.

It was funny—*after* we graduated.

The standards of cleanliness and the rigid specs on what our rooms would look like made us adopt some bizarre practices. We also figured out plenty of shortcuts to reduce the amount of time we would have to spend getting ready for the daily inspections.

The major problem for all of us was the amount of dark brown tile in the platoon area and the work required to keep it clean and shined. Our first problem was that there was only one large buffer to share between our platoon and the third platoon. That meant that we had to cut way down on the foot traffic. We made our own rules.

No one told us how to maintain the high standards of cleanliness and polish in the face of eighty boots running in and out of the barracks several times a day. It was just part of OCS to overload us with requirements, to see if we could figure out how to economize on time and energy, a very important skill for any future platoon leader.

We reduced the problem by not wearing our boots in the platoon area whenever we could. We became experts on getting our boots on and off in record time. When we couldn't unlace, do what we had to, and lace back up again to get out of the building, we slipped wool boot socks over our boots to reduce the damage to the floor wax.

If there was not enough time to do that, we took a page out of the 7th Army NCO academy book and walked only on one row of tiles in the hallway. So when we did rewax and buff the hall all we had to worry about was one six-inch strip instead of the whole width.

In our rooms we slipped Kotex pads under the bottoms of our footlockers so they would move smoothly over the floor, polishing as they moved. By placing the four footlockers at strategic spots in our rooms we could move to any point by walking on our chairs, the bunk rails, the footlockers, and the desks, never stepping on the floor. If we were particularly careful, four of us could come back from training, spend the entire night in our room doing a multitude of things, and only have to wipe the dust off the floor in the morning to pass inspection. There were times when we would go for several days without having to wax the floor.

Inspecting the underside of an army cot to see if the edges of the sheets and the blankets were neatly parallel to one another, or if the bunk only looked good from the top, was the kind of inspection that we became accustomed to. We were expected to do things right and thorough the first time. We spent hours doing cleaning and polishing the *inside* of our brass belt buckles, the backsides of our pin-on OCS insignia, the bristles of our toothbrushes, and the bottoms of our soap dishes. Attention to detail was pounded into our heads day in and day out.

We went to incredible lengths keeping up with the demands on our time. We were constantly swamped with classes, homework, maintenance, and housekeeping.

One big problem was laundry. We had to look as sharp as we possibly could consistent with whatever training we were doing. It made little difference that we spent all day slogging through the creek bottoms north of Red Diamond Road; when we got back to the barracks, we were expected to clean up our field gear, clean and turn in our weapons, and *break starch* as soon as possible. Breaking starch is the term applied to putting on a freshly laundered, starched, and ironed uniform.

That also meant clean and shined boots, a fresh shower and shave, and a high polish on our brass and our black lacquered helmet liners.

It was not unusual to change uniforms several times a day. We might start out the morning with PT and trash our uniforms, then go to an indoor class where we would be expected to look clean and sharp. If we double timed back to the company area for lunch we got sweaty—which was hard to avoid in Georgia's weather—so a change of fatigues might be appropriate before afternoon classes that could again be physical and outdoors—nothing like bayonet training to trash still another set of starched fatigues.

The end of the training day didn't mean that we could lounge around in cruddy-looking uniforms either. So there were some "five-change" days.

The army only issued each soldier four sets of fatigues on induction. Four sets was woefully inadequate to get through OCS—eight was the minimum, and somewhere over a dozen sets of fatigues would provide a small margin of insurance. The extra cost for those extra uniform items came out of our pockets. Those of us who were single and didn't own cars could afford it since we hardly had any opportunity to spend the money on anything else.

But the married candidates still had families to support, and the extra expenses were tough on some of them. Nevertheless, there was no way to make it through OCS with only four sets of fatigues so we all found the money to buy more. More changes meant more fatigues and more trips to the dry cleaners. They were always busy and there was always a line there and they cost significantly more than the army quartermaster laundry, which could take a week and a half to send back someone else's uniforms—all with stains, rips, and buttons broken. The QM laundry was a lot cheaper but not reliable.

None of us will forget the cramped fingers entwined in several wire coat hangers while we ran back to the barracks. We ran everywhere we went—for six months.

We figured out ways to use self-polishing liquid floor wax to hold the shine on our boots. It worked pretty well until we got around water, and then the wax would turn white and give away our shortcut.

We also figured out ways to shortcut setting up our precise full field inspection layouts. The standing operating procedures required that we have every item we owned cleaned, serviceable, and displayed in a precise place and manner for inspections.

T-shirts, socks, shorts, belts, razor blades, shaving brushes, sewing kits, Bibles, and an endless list of personal and professional items had to be displayed in their prescribed places. Even our field manuals[31] had to be displayed in numeric order on our desks. The sleeves on our shirts had to be arranged so that they were all exactly parallel to each creased sleeve that flanked them. Boots had to be laced to exact specifications.

---

[31] These are manuals containing instructional, informational, and reference material relative to training and operations. For example, Field Manual (FM) 21-26 is on map reading; 21-30 is on military symbols, etc.

To maintain all that gear in a high state of readiness and cleanliness, we kept duplicate sets we never used.

This meant that one of the most valuable things in our platoon was a candidate with a car—preferably one with a big trunk, because we stowed our extra equipment there since we didn't have space in our rooms.

Field gear was always a problem but we solved it by swapping things with other platoons. If our platoon was having an inspection, we would borrow clean and serviceable gear from our buddies in other platoons who might not need it for inspections at the same time.

As I look back on it, the amount of effort we put into trying to economize our time probably exceeded what it would have taken us to do things the proper way in the first place. At least we felt pretty smug about being so clever.

Now that almost thirty years have passed since those days of inconsequential details, I have to admit that I support the notion but I resent how much time we wasted on things that really never affected the lives of those we were later to lead. I would have far preferred more emphasis be placed on leadership skills.

Not that there wasn't any. Like the NCO academy, there was plenty of emphasis on training us to be trainers and public speakers. We were expected to be tactically and professionally competent to lead and to instruct. But unlike the NCO academy, we were there to become officers and gentlemen.

While we were in Bill Pfeiffer's charge, we were expected to read and submit reports on professional books. Those reports were both written and oral. We were questioned and graded on them. Aside from an occasional TM (technical manual),[32] I had never read a professional book. So amid the homework assignments on the effective range of the Davey Crockett Weapons System and the map symbols for POL points,[33] we had to read hundreds and hundreds of pages of related material.

It was hard to discipline ourselves to read lengthy manuscripts when everything about OCS took place in increments of seconds and minutes. We would try to grab bits of information, not concepts and themes that we found in the reading assignments, and commit them to memory. So from the suggested reading list I found books on men

[32] TMs provide detailed instructions on the operation, handling, maintenance, and repair of material and equipment as well as instructions on technical procedures.
[33] Fuel storage sites. POL stands for petroleum, oil, and lubricants.

under fire by General S. L. A. Marshall[34] and biographies on George Patton, Dwight Eisenhower, Douglas MacArthur, and James Gavin.

When time permitted, we occasionally talked about the observations of biographers and war historians like Marshall. But it all seemed so remote to us. It had been twenty years since the end of World War II and ten since the Korean War. For most of us we were sure that we were studying history—the history of past wars, past military figures—that just didn't seem to apply to our modern, nuclear-threat-dominated, iron-curtain-mysterious world. Trying to place the leadership principles I found in Marshall's *Pork Chop Hill* into a world with the Beatles, satellites, and helicopters was a hard stretch for my imagination.

But Bill Pfeiffer and Fort Benning didn't care about my willingness or capacity to relate the experiences of past decades of modern combat to the years ahead of me. They just expected me to read, absorb, summarize, and report, verbally and in writing.

Our oral book reports were rather unconventional. We would set up a small podium in the hallway of our platoon area. The candidate giving a book report would take the podium, notes in hand, and present his summary and evaluation of the book to the remainder of the platoon, which was seated in the narrow hallway on its footlockers. We spent many Saturday mornings in that hallway trying to stay awake. The exercise was particularly boring for everyone except the candidate who was making the report.

The old fear of making an oral presentation in front of others that had plagued me in Bad Tolz had not completely fled by the time I got to OCS. Pfeiffer was a real stickler for presence, control, and organization of material.

He was equally thorough with his critiques, which were held in his first-floor office. Many nights I would stand, my back pressed against the cinderblock wall, waiting for my turn to enter Pfeiffer's office, only to hear shortcomings in my presentations.

Pfeiffer wasn't much for raising his voice. Instead he fell back on his mastery of the English language to make me, and others, feel like we were really inadequate. His detailed descriptions of my failure to take charge of the situation or the class and get *my* teaching points into their heads made me lose what little confidence I had mustered.

[34] A veteran of World War I, Marshall was chief historian of the European theater during World War II. He wrote many books on men at war that have become classics, among them *Pork Chop Hill* (Korean War), *Night Drop* (WWII airborne operations), and *Bird* (Vietnam).

He would list my shortcomings and I was expected to take notes on them. Then I was invited to recite my own self-assessment. We'd compare points of view, and then I was dismissed to draft a summary of the *counseling* session and my plan to overcome my failings.

Writing never seemed to be important to becoming an officer when I was trying to get into OCS. But for Pfeiffer, writing was as important as proficiency with infantry weaponry, leadership, physical fitness, and integrity. He sent me back to my desk over and over again to rewrite. His usual complaint was the lack of precision in my language.

I hated him for it then, but I appreciated it once I became a lieutenant, especially when I became a staff officer.

If I had a complaint of Bill Pfeiffer, it would be that I'm very sorry I never served with him in a tactical unit. I can only speculate what a fine platoon leader he had been in the 173d.

Our Camelot of idle study of combat as a distant possibility came to an abrupt end in August of 1964. Most of us had been attending OCS with a fairly comfortable sense of security. We knew that our earliest opportunity to get out of the army was only ten months away. And there wasn't any serious situation on the horizon that could possibly force us into real combat, unless the Russians launched a missile or we went well out of our way to volunteer to be one of the few advisors in Vietnam. Even that was a fairly silly notion. How could we advise the South Vietnamese? We had nothing to teach them. Hell, they were already combat veterans—we were just candidates.

We really thought that Vietnam was more distant from the banks of the Chattahootchee than ten thousand miles. So it came as a real shocking wake-up call to all of us when the *Maddox* and the *Turner Joy* reported being fired upon by North Vietnamese gunboats.

I wasn't alone in shifting my preferred reading from the heroes and battles of World War II and Korea to more contemporary books after the Gulf of Tonkin Incident occurred. Suddenly Bernard Fall's *Street Without Joy*[35] became a bestseller in our officer candidate company.

On the heels of the Tonkin Gulf resolution we received word that our previous obligation of six months of active duty after commissioning was changed to *voluntary indefinite*. When some asked what that meant, they were asked why they wanted to know, because if we were

---

[35] Born in France, Bernard Fall served in the French underground during World War II and later became a naturalized U.S. citizen. *Street Without Joy* (Stackpole, 1961), one of the most influential and widely read books on Vietnam during our country's early involvement there, poignantly analyzed the French defeat in Indochina. Fall's long love affair with Vietnam was ended by a Viet Cong land mine in 1967.

serious about being professional infantry officers, then the length of our commitment shouldn't matter. On the other hand, if we were concerned with how long our new obligation was, then maybe we weren't displaying enough dedication to be considered serious candidates for graduation.

That response quickly stopped the questions. For the first time in over two years in the army, I began to see more and more newspapers and weekly news magazines around the barracks.

The Gulf of Tonkin Incident changed our lives like the Japanese attack on Pearl Harbor had changed our parents' lives.

We were suddenly training to lead men in combat, in an actual shooting war. At first that had a chilling effect on us. Then within less than a week I felt the mood change. We had given our word. We had asked to be where we were and there was absolutely no discussion about backing out or quitting. Instead, classmates alternately made light of it or rolled up their sleeves and got more serious about learning for the sake of leading in combat, instead of learning as a means to a gold bar.

I remember wondering if I was going to graduate, if I had what it took to lead men in combat. If I wasn't serious or dedicated before, I sure was after the president announced our new policy and dedication to helping the South Vietnamese repel the advance of communist guerrilla forces in South Vietnam.

We were in it and we would do what was necessary to be ready to go to Vietnam. Privately, we may not have wanted to be called, but none would say so out loud. I think that at the moment we decided to meet our obligation to go to that war, we decided not ever to express what we really felt about the war and about our going. At the very least, we would not talk about things that smacked of uncertainty or of disloyalty or any lack of resolve. It just wasn't done. Not at Benning in the mid-sixties.

For the last two thirds of our OCS training we were no longer being prepared to be generic infantry officers. Instead, we were being prepared to be infantry officers in Vietnam.

The notion was commendable. What was missing was the stuff of which lesson plans and training are made. Benning had virtually no base of information for the faculty at the infantry school to use to create credible and applicable classes.

While low-level insurgent guerrilla forces were overrunning South Vietnamese outposts and ambushing South Vietnamese Army convoys, Fort Benning was still teaching us conventional battle tactics.

Sure, we were told about booby traps, but only those common to the Korean War and World War II. We were aware that the Viet Cong were expert at attacking and then disappearing into the night and the local population, making them invisible to the average American. We were taught nothing about techniques to tell our allies from their enemies.

Now no one was intentionally keeping information from us. It's just that the supply of experience fell short of the demand. And since we were not allowed to leave the battalion area or socialize with anyone but our classmates, there was little opportunity for us to learn anything from the very few veterans of Vietnam advisory duty who had returned to Fort Benning.

Inertia was the order of the day at Fort Benning. Things were done much like they had been done for decades. No one was encouraged to make any radical changes in the curriculum. There was a sense that infantry tactics change very little over the centuries and the basics of attack, defend, withdraw, and counterattack were the staples of our business. No world event was so revolutionary as to cause the infantry school to completely overhaul its Program of Instruction overnight.

It's unfortunate that the tendency to resist change was the order of the day at Fort Benning. Some sort of crash course about how war worked in Vietnam, even if incomplete, might well have saved the lives of many of my classmates. But Benning was like most army schools at the time. Classes were developed in accord with accepted tactical doctrine, then written, rehearsed, reviewed by senior officers, revised, and subjected to a murder board before inclusion in the POI.

Murder boards were the equivalent of a dress rehearsal of a Broadway show for the backers. All of the senior officers in the instructional chain of command came to a dress-rehearsal presentation. At the murder board the designers of the class, usually the instructors themselves, were nitpicked to death. The theory was that the best sharpshooters were the senior faculty members and if you could make a class bulletproof in front of them, then you could survive even the cleverest sharpshooting student's criticism or question.

All of this took time which the army just didn't have. Less than a year after we signed in to OCS, ground forces were committed to combat in South Vietnam. For me it was confusing, trying to reconcile outdated infantry instruction with going to Vietnam, where they seemed to be playing by completely different rules. Still, I didn't have a good enough grasp on the traditional doctrine just to dismiss the instruction I was getting as something I could ignore after commissioning. I had to get a handle on being an infantryman first, and then worry about bending the rules. Every day in OCS reminded me that I came from a signal corps and armored background.

CHAPTER 8

·

From the first minute that we signed in to OCS we were immersed in the psychology of becoming the meanest, toughest, and in the vernacular, baddest Airborne-Ranger-infantry officers possible.

We chanted Jody cadence to and from every single class. The lyrics were filled with the mythical blood and gore of the Airborne combat infantryman, a calling and a job just not everyone could do. Sacrifice and hard work and toughing it out were the common themes of the Jody cadence and our barracks talk. We became conditioned to reply instantly that it was our highest aspiration to become Airborne-Ranger-infantry officers.

Every day I sang the songs and repeated the expected answers to inevitable questions about what I wanted to do after graduation. On top of those reflex responses, we spent considerable discussion time among ourselves about what we thought was possible.

There was an assignment progression that was generally accepted as the plum: to graduate; go to airborne school to become parachute qualified; to attend Ranger school; and then be assigned as an infantry platoon leader to the 82d Airborne Division, the 101st Airborne Division, or the 173d Airborne Brigade. They were the brass rings of assignments.

I really hadn't thought things out that far when I arrived at Fort Benning. But I had to fill out an assignment-preference statement and I would either have to apply to Airborne and Ranger schools or have a damn good reason why not.

I remember looking out the window at the nearest 250-foot jump tower looming over Eubanks Field. I couldn't even bring myself to admit that I had never been in an airplane, much less leap out to the front of the pack, submitting applications for jump and Ranger schools.

But the constant daily wash surge of testosterone and the overwhelming tendency for bravado can be infectious. All the while I was pondering joining the pack, I was remembering those two sergeants at Fort Dix. That image became a composite with that second lieutenant outside the mess hall and Green Berets at Bad Tolz. I tried to visualize myself as a platoon leader in the 82d Airborne Division. It was a real stretch for me, but I had to get some picture of myself if and after I graduated.

I recall sitting up in the orderly room one night while pulling charge of quarters duty[36], polishing my boots, brass, and helmet liner. The little gold bar that Lieutenant Pfeiffer insisted we carry held my attention for quite some time. It had taken on such symbolic importance over the months that it was something like a talisman-icon and good-luck charm. He was right to make us focus on it, and he was right in making us keep it shined and within our reach at all times.

The transformation was so insidious in me that I can't identify the day when I started believing what I was obligated to yell, sing, and say. It just seemed that one morning I woke up at first call and was ready to fill out my wish list for jump and Ranger schools and eventual assignment to one of the Airborne units. That notion seemed so natural and appropriate to me at the time.

But despite my wishes to go to those schools and get one of those plum assignments, that didn't mean I believed that I could hack it. I was terribly unsure of myself and my ability to compete in Airborne school, Ranger school, and on the job as a leader of an infantry platoon in one of the nation's fire brigades.

I think it was a one-step-at-a-time thing for me. I knew that by submitting my application I satisfied an immediate need—to be one of the guys. That application wasn't necessarily going to be approved, and even if it was, I wouldn't be reporting for training or assignment until after graduation, and even that was far from being locked in.

So while all these life decisions were being made, we were still swamped with the business of trying to make it through the remaining weeks of OCS. We were also being bombarded with the reports from Vietnam. All of a sudden there were filmed reports on the evening news and in the newspapers of coups and grenade lobbing and rocket attacks. We were the first OCS class given the chance to look at game films before the game.

Between the time we started OCS and the time we graduated, the world had changed. The contract between us and an ally was being called due and the postwar attitude virtually disappeared from our army.

So we kept on taking classes that we didn't dare declare out of date,

---

[36] The enlisted person, usually a noncommissioned officer, who watches over the company affairs during off-duty hours.

and we kept on making all the gung-ho noises expected of us. And we kept on digging for snippets of feedback from Vietnam. We were on a roller coaster that was slowing and loudly ticking as it cranked up to the top of the first big drop. All of us heard the ticking, and all of us got a grip for that moment when we went over the top.

For me, suddenly there appeared to be a reason beyond being macho and gung-ho for going to Airborne school and Ranger school— preparation! If I was going to war, I had damn well better take advantage of any edge I might be able to get. I was amazed at how fast my attitude was changing, and how often I was being asked to make declarations and decide what path I would take. I found myself rapidly mastering techniques of infantry combat and specifications and peculiarities of infantry weapons beyond just getting me through a test.

I soon found myself permanently committing to memory ranges, rates of fire, weights, and capabilities. I began to get very serious about the consequences of *not* mastering land navigation, adjusting artillery, calling for tac air, or treating a sucking chest wound. I found myself reading S. L. A. Marshall and Bernard Fall for lessons rather than for material to put into a book report.

And while I was doing those reading assignments I was very conscious of the Viet Cong's successful attack on the Bien Hoa air base just north of Saigon.

I'm ashamed to admit that somewhere in the confusion of OCS I completely missed the importance and the warning implied by the discovery of the bodies of civil rights workers Schwerner, Goodman, and Chaney in Philadelphia, Mississippi. I have to think that I was swayed into believing that there wasn't much of a civil-rights problem that wasn't already being solved by the signing of the Civil Rights Act of 1964 and the selection of Martin Luther King, Jr., as the Nobel Peace Prize recipient. How terribly wrong I was to think that civil rights was a small issue in comparison to the war that I was certainly headed for in the months ahead.

Somewhere into the first third of OCS it became obvious to me that the tactical officers and the infantry school instructors were not only charged with making us officers, but with making us gentlemen. It certainly seemed like a goal far afield from all of the training I had received to date in the army.

My roommates and I found ourselves worrying about mastering skills that we didn't even know existed. Who ever knew that there were requirements on our off-duty and personal lives beyond staying out of jail and not acting like fraternity brothers? I had no idea that I would be expected to call on the post commander on New Year's Day and leave an embossed calling card in the silver tray that I could expect to find near his front door.

Receiving lines were a complete mystery to me. The historical conventions that made them customary were lost on me as I tried to master the intricacies of when to arrive and how late was too late; who to introduce to whom, depending on rank and sex; and why was it considered inappropriate for me to carry or use an umbrella in uniform? Or to avoid carrying bulky packages or pushing a baby carriage?

The mysteries of becoming a gentleman were just as baffling to my roommates. We spent hours wading through the instructions on related topics and committing to memory the essentials of the social graces that could be found in condensed texts of the *Officer's Guide*.

We were expected to join the officers club, the Association of the United States Army, and the Army Mutual Aid Association;[37] to have a checking account; and to have our car (if we owned one) properly inspected, insured, and registered in a state and on post. No exceptions!

We were also introduced to a level of peripheral behavior and standards that we had never considered in our previous lives as enlisted men. Suddenly there was a flood of information about what car we should buy and two schools of thought on that—one was the *appropriate* car for an officer to drive and the other was the *popular* car among a group of candidates whose mean age was probably twenty-three.

We all concluded that the army would be just as happy to see us driving Chevy Bel Airs, but we were leaning more toward the new, hot car on the market—the Mustang.

Clothing was still another issue. We had to budget into our immediate expenses the cost of suits and conservative ties and dress shirts and top coats. Most of us owned only a few civilian clothes, purchased since joining the army. They consisted of the low-priced things that we just couldn't do without for a weekend away from an army post; usually items that would fit into a small AWOL bag.

All of our other civilian clothing was at home somewhere and consisted mostly of a wardrobe for high school boys. Hardly appropriate.

Somehow all of this paled in importance when held up against the

---

[37] The Association of the United States Army (AUSA) is a civilian association composed of active-duty and retired army personnel and civilians that promotes a strong national defense and supports army programs and policies. Since 1879 the Army Mutual Aid Association has provided low-cost life insurance and other forms of personal assistance to army officers and warrant officers.

escalating war in Vietnam. For most of us the distance between us and a Mustang was growing, and the distance to Ah Khe, Pleiku, or Cam Ranh Bay was closing.

For me the thought of getting a car was ever more distant because I wasn't yet old enough to sign a contract on one and my family was in Europe. That was a large concern of mine. Who ever heard of a lieutenant without his own transportation?

But first things first. I still had to graduate and that meant mastering leadership, weapons, tactics, and the fine art of becoming a gentleman.

There were several stages of OCS where cuts were made based on academic and leadership evaluations. Toward the end of the course our ranks had thinned considerably for that and a wide variety of other reasons. Health problems and injuries took a fairly high toll. The army's training base was always a breeding ground for upper respiratory infections that often turned into pneumonia. We had our share. With the exception of permanent injuries, if their standing was good otherwise, most who were dropped from our class were recycled into another course later.

A number of candidates were lost due to honor violations. The army set high standards on honesty and integrity. Those qualities were extended to include an officer's word being his bond.

I will long and fondly remember the days when I could go into a store anywhere in Columbus, Georgia, and write a check and not be asked for any backup identification or guarantee that it was good. Most merchants knew that if they got a check from a candidate or an officer, it was the same as money. We took pride in that and had little sympathy for those among us who dribbled a rubber check.

Benning had less sympathy. A rubber check as small as two dollars was considered a major gaffe in officer conduct and was grounds for dismissal from OCS.

Lies, deceitful double-talking, or crafty dodging of the truth were not accepted. The principle that an officer's word was his bond was practiced in everyday business. If a candidate was found to be deficient in any aspect of training or conduct during the course of a day, all a tac officer had to do was point it out, and the candidate was expected to render the exchange to writing and turn it in to the tac officer later. We were on the honor system to *write ourselves up* for these shortcomings. Failure to do so could result in dismissal.

We were particularly lucky in my small group. My three roommates and I—Entrekin, Every-Clayton, and Epstein—made cut after cut although we sweated each one out.

The last few weeks of the course we were elevated to a new and lofty status. We became senior candidates. A senior candidate in OCS was like an upper classman at the military academy. He was a fairly large fish in a very small pond. The respect and the relative avalanche of special privileges we got was quite different compared to the life of a bottom feeder that we had been living.

The night we *turned blue*—the term applied to being vested as a senior candidate and issued the coveted infantry blue helmets—was one of hysteria and hazing. The outgoing senior candidates from the senior company (there were usually three OCS companies in session at a time) bestowed the honor of turning blue upon us by putting us through a series of demeaning drills to mark the end of our junior candidate status.

Each of us was issued a powder-blue helmet liner with a fresh paint job, OCS decals on both sides, and a brand new sweat band. Inside we put a strip of tape with our last names stenciled on it and polished the helmet. Then the helmets were collected from us and we could claim them once we turned blue.

When the senior candidates descended on our barracks to begin the ritual we were instructed to fall out in the company street in shower shoes, boxer shorts, and ponchos.

We knew we were in for a night of fraternity-boy crap, but went along with it knowing that we could stand on our heads for a few hours until we gained our new and privileged status. So we all went along when we were double timed (a hard trick in shower shoes) to Sightseeing Field for more fun and games.

Sightseeing Field at Fort Benning is a huge manicured patch of level grass that has been used for everything from mass physical training exercises to full division review parades to impressive displays of infantry vehicles and army aircraft. Its dimensions were huge, easily a quarter mile wide and over a half mile long.

On that night we were taken to one end of the field and told that we would become senior candidates just as soon as we made it to the other end and found our helmets, which were waiting for us. The only hitch was that we had to low crawl to the other end of the field in our shower shoes and ponchos.

We were a sight, crawling on our bellies the length of that field in those ridiculous outfits. So much for the dignity of commissioned officers.

* * *

As the course progressed and the size of the class got smaller, the tac officers were able to spend more time evaluating fewer of us.

As the intensity of the scrutiny picked up, the detailed analysis of our capacity to serve as officers became more revealing, and things that might have been missed in earlier weeks took on larger significance as minor mannerisms or personal quirks were identified and targeted for elimination. I had thought that Bill Pfeiffer was omnipresent and all-seeing before, but that was a grave underestimation on my part.

I seemed to live in his office after training. I could count on seeing him twice as often as before, after our class size had halved.

While Bill Pfeiffer thought that he was just polishing the rough edges on me, I thought I had been identified as the next man to be washed out. I tried not to look rattled, but I was.

I remembered Skunk Boots Terrel and knew that if they smelled blood, then they would find me unacceptable for commissioning. I took on a stoic and unruffled outer appearance even though inside I was more like Jell-O than the Rock of Gibraltar. I think now that was Bill Pfeiffer's objective—to get me to wear less of my emotions on my sleeve and become a better poker player. His wisdom far exceeded his years.

I found it difficult to take on that tight-lipped, say-little-and-look-like-you-know-a-lot attitude. But that's what Pfeiffer beat, pushed and cajoled me into. And once I got the hang of it, he let up on me a bit.

We were all very eager to get on to graduation and put OCS behind us. By the end of six months of the kind of fishbowl training we had been experiencing, we were getting very tired. At the same time we got more excited about what lay ahead of us. The last few weeks of the course flew by. Suddenly, we had time off in the evenings—no more mandatory study halls. We were allowed to drive and go off post and start acting like we actually expected to graduate.

Right after we turned blue we got our alert notifications. They weren't the final orders, but were notification of what the army had planned for us if we didn't screw up between then and graduation. For me it was Airborne school, Ranger school, and the 82d Airborne Division at Fort Bragg, North Carolina—and in that order.

If there ever was a truer statement than *be careful what you wish for*, I don't know what it is. I was roundly congratulated for getting such great news. A large number of us had similar orders and there was plenty of celebrating—on the outside. Inside, I was sure that I had gone all that way to become a lieutenant only surely to wash out of

Airborne or Ranger school, or at the very least, get relieved of duty at the 82d. I just couldn't imagine myself being successful at the next three stages of my training and ultimate assignment to the most respected Airborne unit in the world. How could I possibly measure up?

I was thrilled and panicked all at the same time. Still, I just knew those assignments would be my complete undoing.

Looking back, I'm amazed at how well I handled the combined pressures of the course, the anticipated schooling, the assignment, and the force of history conspiring to get me into a shooting war half-way around the world. There was one thing for sure. If America were really going to get into Vietnam big time, it would mean that the 82d Airborne and/or the 101st Airborne would be part of it. Those pressures seem mild when held up to those placed on the shoulders of Americans since December 1964, but I was a boy living in the last few days of peace, and things had been very easy for us all up to that point.

On the weekend we got our alert notifications. I recall being on another part of the post and watching large aviation elements of the 11th Air Assault Division flying to some major phase of a large training exercise. The sky seemed to be filled with helicopters, large and small. I'd never even been close to one of them. It never occurred to me that they were soon to be flying those same helicopters over the Mang Yang Pass in the Vietnam Central Highlands, the new colors of the 1st Cavalry Division painted on their hulls.

There was plenty of good-natured kidding around at the OCS company as we all compared assignments. One of the comical and then ironic assignments was given to my roommate, Ronnie Epstein. He delighted in kidding us about going to assignments that were sure to find us in Vietnam. He, on the other hand, was assigned to the 11th Air Assault Division at Fort Benning. He teased us about being able to stay at Benning in a division that went everywhere by chopper while we were going to ground pounding jobs.

We had no idea then that Ronnie would not only go to Vietnam with the 11th-Air-Assault-turned-1st Cavalry Division before we would, but that he would be one of the few heroic survivors of the first big battle of Vietnam—Ia Drang. Ronnie was wounded while serving as a platoon leader in combat—a job we had all been training for all those months. Still, at the time, the teasing was good natured and no one took offense.

During the last week of OCS I took a quiet moment to walk over to Eubanks Field. I found the empty bleachers that faced the jump towers and the other training apparatus on the field. Just looking at the towers was intimidating enough. But the long and snaking track that Airborne school students ran each morning again gave me doubts about my ability to hack it.

It was such a confusing time for me. I had started the whole ball rolling with the goal of just getting to be an officer for the distinction of it and the opportunity to make a few extra dollars. After all, going from $145.00 a month to $222.30 a month seemed like a windfall to me.

But it had all gotten away from me. Suddenly I found myself on the eve of graduating and being commissioned as an infantry second lieutenant with more advanced combat training immediately following graduation. I wasn't really sure how I'd gotten on that track. But I was sure there was no getting off without considerable embarrassment and harassment from my peers and the tac officers. Going back and saying, "I'm not sure anymore that this is what I want to do," was not even a consideration.

I remember sitting in those bleachers and saying a little prayer. The prayer was mostly for some help to get me through what was ahead without embarrassing myself or my family. The thought of failing or being found lacking in the months ahead was every bit as frightening as the dangers I could expect to face on the way.

I decided that night to swallow my anxieties about what lay ahead and just do the best I could. I didn't really feel that I had much choice. I had put myself in that box. Little did I know that it would not be the last time I would do that.

Just a few days before graduation I received a change in my orders. I would be going to Airborne school immediately upon graduation, but I would not be going to Ranger school or to the 82d Airborne Division. Instead, I would report to Fort Leonard Wood, Missouri, for further assignment. There was no explanation.

What I didn't know at the time was that I was being pulled out for an experiment in training. I must admit that I had mixed feelings about the changes. It relieved a bit of my anxiety about Ranger school and the 82d, but made me feel like I was no longer on the infantryman's yellow brick road.

The morning we graduated was one of the most memorable days in my life. It was a thrill finally to feel like I had measured up to something difficult and important. We were all completely convinced that our immediate future would be complicated and totally guided by the needs of Vietnam and the growing idea that we needed more troops to solve the problem.

The day was filled with families, gold-bar-pinning ceremonies, snapshots, packing, moving, clearing post, and saying goodbye to newly made, close friends. If it is true that lifelong friendships are often forged on the field of battle, then it is true also that friendships of similar intensity are formed in infantry OCS. During that six months I met and became friends with some of the finest men I would ever know. It has long been a favorite pastime of mine to take joy in the successes of my closest classmates. Many of them have gone on to be accomplished battle captains and leaders of industry. I'm very proud to call them friends.

By the end of graduation day I had cleared out of the 50th Company and signed in to the 4th Student Battalion at the Airborne school.

Signing in to bachelor officers quarters was a milestone for me. It meant the end of one career and the beginning of another. I was actually acting like and being treated like an officer, and I was really excited about it.

For our first official act of the day, Every-Clayton and I went trolling for someone to give us our first salute. It is a tradition that a newly commissioned officer give a dollar to the first enlisted man who salutes him. For me it was a young specialist 5 medic who was coming out of the PX. He was surprised by the tradition, but glad to take the silver dollar I had held tightly in my left hand for several minutes before giving it to the soldier who had given me my first salute.

Our second priority was to go to the Infantry Bar for our first beer as officers. The IB was the focal point for all things infantry and manly in the sixties. The end of a duty day was marked by a short trip to the IB to quaff some beer, play some liar's dice, and recycle war stories of training and duty at Benning. Also, it was the place to catch up on the latest scuttlebutt on Vietnam.

Every-Clayton and I bellied up to the short end of the L-shaped bar and ordered beer. We had not even finished our first sip when we noticed a captain approaching. He pulled out the stool nearest ours and threw his leg over it.

We both were struck by who had just parked it next to us. Jon and I looked at each other for some confirmation. We were both sure that we knew him, but didn't want to embarrass ourselves if we were wrong.

There, sitting inches away from us was our country's most recent war hero. He quickly realized that we were stunned by his presence and not even sure what to say, so he took the initiative. He smiled and said, "Donlon. Name's Roger Donlon. Can I buy you two a beer?"

Roger Donlon had gained America's respect as a detachment and camp commander of a Special Forces camp overrun in the Central Highlands.

We stuttered and mumbled some reply accepting the beer and said how nice it was meeting him, but didn't mention that we knew who he really was or that we knew he had just been awarded the Medal of Honor for the valiant defense of his camp. Neither of us had ever really met a real live hero. Donlon made the day even better by being down to earth and friendly.

I am sure that both Every-Clayton and I secretly promised ourselves that if we ever became Medal of Honor winners that we would be sure to be as approachable as Roger Donlon.

We stayed for a while after Donlon left and mentally pinched ourselves over the things that were happening to us on that day in January. Eventually we remembered that we not only had things to do, but we needed to be careful how much we drank. We had been in OCS so long that drinking beer was something we needed to work back up to. So we headed back to our BOQ—roommates again—to get ready for our first day at Airborne school.

CHAPTER 9

•

I sat in just about the same seat in the bleachers on the first morning in Airborne school that I had occupied only days before as an officer candidate. But this time was much more daunting. Sitting there in OCS my mind was filled with the possibilities of going to Airborne school. That morning I was now facing it—no turning back. And for some unexplainable reason, the jump towers and the training apparatus and the asphalt track and the Black Hats—the instructors—were much more unnerving now that I was actually signed in for training.

We sat there while Colonel Lamar Welch gave us a stern welcome and a challenge to make it through Airborne school. Welch had been there for several years as the director of the Airborne Department. He started every new class and jumped with all of them. He was older than most of the colonels I had seen, and that was reassuring. That he could make all those jumps and still be around to give the welcoming remarks made me feel a little better. He made it clear to us that not everyone would make it, that not all of us had what it takes to become Airborne qualified.

As he spoke, I looked around at the Black Hats who stood nearby, waiting to begin the formal instruction. I felt a little bit of that awe I had felt in that theater at Fort Dix. All of them looked alike. All wore black baseball caps with their shiny jump wings pinned on them. Instead of fatigue shirts, they wore gray sweatshirts with large master parachutist's wings emblazoned across the chests. And, to a man, they all wore highly shined Corcoran jump boots.

Colonel Welch concluded his welcoming remarks and turned the class over to a master sergeant, who started the orientation-demonstration. For the next two hours we were alternately impressed and warned by the capability of army parachutes and the importance of training. We were promised that if we paid attention and worked hard and did what we were told, that we too could step out of an aircraft twelve hundred and fifty feet above the ground and safely land on a drop zone. Few among us were convinced. Red flags were waving in our heads at every caution the instructor mentioned about points of performance and parachute landing falls.

He continued to dazzle us with dummies falling from the 250-foot tower, reserve parachutes attached—they opened. An assistant instructor leaped from the door of a thirty-four-foot-tower mockup and still others unpacked parachutes in front of the bleachers.

The sight of a main and a reserve parachute being unpacked in front of us was supposed to give us confidence. But most of us thought the complexity of the packing and the maze of spaghetti-like suspension lines were an invitation to disaster. For me, I just kept trying to reassure myself with the recent safety figures I had heard that suggested I had a better chance of dying in my bathroom than in a parachute jump.

But those statistics were for sport parachuting, not parachuting into enemy territory with someone shooting at you.

Once the theory of parachuting and the course outline was covered we were on to the real thing. Airborne school was everything that its reputation said it was. It started early and ended late. The technique of instruction was repetition, repetition, repetition. All of the effort was focused on getting jumpers safely to the ground.

It was simple and smart. The Airborne Department knew well that soldiers get a little scattered and are easily distracted in the heat of combat. The chaos of combat drastically reduces the ability to communicate. So everything that happens in an aircraft and between the aircraft and a successful parachute landing must be done with a minimum of instruction or direction. Essentially, the two basic variables are when to get out of the aircraft, and where to assemble on the drop zone. Everything else is standardized and memorized and practiced over and over again. And that is how the training went.

We ran everywhere. We had no rank. And we did large numbers of pushups for our mistakes. For three weeks we hung in training devices that taught us how to manage the direction of our non-steerable parachutes, and practiced exiting mockups on the ground and on the thirty-four-foot mockup towers. And when we weren't doing that we were practicing parachute landing falls (PLFs), and doing physical training to build up our stamina and strength.

The training was intense, but not impossible. What was most unpleasant was the incredibly high number of repetitions of everything we did. We were soon going through all the steps from *stand up* in the aircraft to *go!* that got us out. The steps in between that insured that we were hooked up and that we were finally inspected all fell into the same place—practice jump after practice jump out of the mockups.

I'm sure that the training was designed to give confidence as the course progressed, but there was something missing in my training because I couldn't easily relate the techniques we were taught to actual flight. Not having flown before made it hard to visualize some of the teaching points. So for me the training was taken just on faith. I had convinced myself that what they were teaching must work and must be the right way to do it.

Our days were filled with jump training but our evenings were free. Free evenings were a wonderful luxury that I really had not appreciated when I had the class-A pass in Germany. But after six months in OCS, I realized how good I'd had it back then.

We would gather at the Infantry Bar or the bar at the Lawson Field Officers Club for drinks and then dinner, and usually ended the evenings early since there was a full day of Airborne training ahead. We would gather around a television in our quarters later, to catch up on the news while we cleaned up our gear and polished boots and brass.

U.S. troop strength was increasing in Vietnam while we were making laps around Eubanks Field and hurling ourselves out of the mockup doors on the jump towers. Rumors were flying everywhere. We were sure that the 11th Air Assault was soon going to send an advance party to Vietnam, and we had heard also that army Special Forces had been tasked to fill up the 5th Special Forces Group that had gone to Vietnam three months earlier. But we knew nothing about the Marines that were already outloading for amphibious landings in Vietnam within a month.

We read everything we could get our hands on and tried to cross-check every rumor for verification. Then we applied it to our own important question: What does that mean to me? We knew the answers before we asked the questions.

All indications were that we too were going. I didn't know how Fort Leonard Wood fit into the scheme of things, but I was sure there was a puzzle piece up at the Pentagon that had my picture on it.

The bravado factor at jump school went up in direct proportion to our manpower commitment in Vietnam. Chants about killing Viet Cong crept into our Jody cadence, and the evening news became a place for us to gather for a little "advanced training" on jungle warfare.

After a week of heavy PT, lots of running, and introductory training on getting in and out of an airplane in flight, the techniques got more intricate and the repetitions became more intense. This was physically taxing but not too mentally challenging. The Black Hats yelled and we performed.

We kept it up and tried not to become casualties. We lost plenty of classmates to injuries, pneumonia, and an occasional quitter.

Quitter was a word that put ice water in all our veins. I had forgotten the term until I was in OCS and considering going to Airborne school. I remembered the film that we saw in basic training. It made a point of how beneath contempt quitters were. I recalled that they just weren't allowed to quit. Instead they would announce they were quitting and they would have to stand in yellow circles at the base of the jump tower and watch all their classmates make exit after exit from the bone-jarring thirty-four-foot towers. During that time insults were heaped on them, and the Black Hats made them do pushups just for being alive.

The custom had not changed by the time we got into jump school. The one thing that was not mentioned in the recruiting film were the consequences to the student leaders when someone did quit.

The interesting feature about quitting in Airborne school was that if it was going to happen, it happened at the thirty-four-foot tower and not later in the course. The thirty-four-foot tower was referred to as the *separator*. Rarely did students who got beyond the thirty-four-foot towers quit at the 250-foot towers or on the day of their first real jump. There was something about the thirty-four-foot tower that did the trick.

As officers, most of us were given jobs in the student company as platoon leaders or stick leaders. A stick was the Airborne equivalent of a squad. When a member of our stick was screwing up, failing to perform or making noises like he wanted to quit, the Black Hats were in *our* faces.

During the ground-training week an instructor decided that it would be good for me and good for everyone in my twelve-man stick if I made an extra jump out of the thirty-four-foot tower each time a member of my stick did—and that I should keep doing it until every member of my stick had made the necessary number of acceptable exits. That little decision caused me considerable discomfort. It was one of many occasions when I had second thoughts about having sought a commission.

* * *

Toward the end of the second week of training we were all given our first real chance to jump from the 250-foot jump towers. There were three, each with four arms extending out to the four compass points. A cable stretched from each tower arm to a detachable parachute on the ground.

Each student would strap into the parachute harness and be hauled up to the 250-foot level, an open parachute above him. When the student was ready to be cut loose, a clever release mechanism would detach the parachute canopy from a retaining ring and cable, and the jumper would float to the soft sandy ground at the base of the towers.

Each of us waited in line to take our first trip to the top. While we waited we were actively involved in rigging the parachutes for other students and yelling encouragement.

Each of us waited anxiously as our classmates got strapped into a well-worn main lift harness, were hoisted aloft, and cut loose after a few seconds at the top.

When my turn came I could hear my heart pounding in my ears. The ride to the top was slow, easy, and exciting. As I left the ground I watched things get smaller as I got higher and higher. Soon I could see the tops of the nearby barracks, the Infantry school, and the other mockups on the field.

The instructor on the ground yelled at me through a bullhorn. At the top, he told me to look around. I had never been that high off the ground in anything. And the visibility was breathtaking. I could see all the way to the front gate in one direction and the firing ranges in another. It was beautiful—and scary.

He had me release the safety strap that held me to the tower, and wait. I then looked up and saw the edge of the chute flutter as the cross wind tried to furl the skirt under the parachute. The thought of a malfunction entered my mind and concerned me plenty.

The instructor cut me loose. The initial sensation was—no sensation. I guess I had expected to feel the wind in my face, but all I felt was a gentle swaying of the suspension lines as I drifted to the right. The instructor yelled at me over the megaphone to slip left. He wanted to control my descent so that I would land in the large sandy circle around the tower. I don't recall even having to think about it—I just did it. That was the whole point—not thinking, just doing.

The landing was soft and easy. It was a wonderful ride and a great confidence builder.

I remember Lieutenant Ronnie Epstein was given several dozen pushups for a wisecrack about the towers. He approached one of the Black Hats and told him that he didn't believe that the towers belonged in the Airborne school because they didn't hurt and they were fun.

The morning we went to Lawson Field to outload for our first training jump, we got the news that the Viet Cong had launched widespread attacks on a number of American and South Vietnamese installations.

The other major announcement was that Lyndon Johnson had ordered bombing raids on North Vietnam to begin. The heat was getting turned up and the roller coaster was getting closer to the top for us. We might have been even more attuned to other world events and the domestic warning signs had we not been getting close to an event of major proportion for each of us.

Every-Clayton and I had coffee at the Lawson Field Officers Club before reporting for training on our first day of Jump Week. Jump Week was the time of reckoning. All the practice PLFs, all the exits from the thirty-four-foot towers, all the running and PT and push-ups were to get us ready to make our five qualifying jumps.

To say we were nervous would be a massive understatement. The instructors were more animated than ever. I don't think any of them ever forgot their first jump, and though they had made the previous weeks tough on us, that Monday they were on our side.

We moved quickly into the briefing hangar down on the apron of Lawson Army Airfield. Outside we saw the huge C-130, four-engine prop aircraft waiting for us to load up. Our first jumpmaster briefing was one of the few formations any of us had stood in the army that didn't require someone to remind us to pay attention.

The jumpmaster explained the type of aircraft we would jump from and descend, and the drop zone and its dimensions. We noted the jump altitudes, the details of the jump lights, the wind speed and directions, the location of the ambulances, the assembly points, and the parachute turn-in points.

The section of the briefing on injuries made us as uncomfortable as the reminder of how to clear parachute malfunctions. But the really uncomfortable part was on what to do if our static lines got fouled and we found ourselves outside the aircraft, slamming into the fuselage. We had heard it all many times in training, but now we were hearing it in a pre-jump briefing. The thought of having to signal the jumpmaster to cut us loose or use the option of foaming the runway to land, dragging us outside the aircraft, was really frightening.

After the briefing we were hustled into the rigger shed to draw equipment. We snaked through the rows and rows of parachutes, reserve parachutes, and kit bags, picking up one of each as we went. Outside we struggled to put on our parachutes. We had done it dozens if not hundreds of times in training. But trying to do it with the real equipment for the first real jump made us a bit fumble-fingered.

The jumpmasters swarmed over us as we tried to stand up under the weight of the parachutes and fought with the straps that pulled our shoulders to our crotches.

Each of us was inspected in great detail by a qualified jumpmaster who performed the identical equipment check that every other jumpmaster did. Nothing was left uninspected or untouched. Once we were okayed, we were given a bight on our static line and moved back in the briefing hangar to wait to be called to the aircraft.

We sat on strange benches built to accommodate us and our parachutes. The walls were decorated with photographs of jumpers and the colorful insignia of all of the Airborne units in the army. The sense of camaraderie was thick in the room, not just with one another —all facing our first jump—but with those who had gone before us.

I remember looking at the huge photos of the first Airborne test platoon and wondering what kind of men could have had so much courage to test a concept like parachute jumping. By the time we got to that morning we had heard all of the horror stories about how the first Airborne test platoon had jumped with parachutes that were smaller, clumsier, harder to control, and impossible to get off on the ground. They had no quick release assemblies on the harnesses so if a jumper got dragged in the wind or landed in a tree there were serious safety consequences.

Periodically a jumpmaster would step up on the stage and change some of the data on the large chalk board. We watched as the DZ time changed. That was the time we were scheduled to land on the drop zone. Everything in Airborne operations is measured backward from that time. So when the DZ time changed, so did the time we would take off, load, and leave the hangar. We were especially worried each time the wind speed changed.

Finally we waddled out to the open tail ramp of the C-130. They squeezed us in to the aircraft, shut the ramp, and we taxied out to take off. I was truly surprised by the amount of noise inside the cargo compartment of the airplane, and immediately understood what all the fuss was about in training, forcing us to recognize commands by hand signals. It was virtually impossible to hear even yelling while the tail ramp or the jump doors were open.

While the others were contemplating the jump to come, I was paying attention to the strange noises and creaking and clanking of the aging C-130 as it strained to get in the air at the end of the runway.

I will never forget looking out of the open jump door at Fort Benning and the Chattahootchee River snaking by below. The distinctive red clay-marked holes in all the pine trees and scrub oaks, and the river tied it all together with a meandering coffee colored ribbon. Had it not been my first time, I might have enjoyed the experience more. But since the drop zone was coming up quickly I stopped watching the scenery and directed my attention to the jumpmaster, who was down on his knees with his head way outside the door, looking at the approach.

We were given the five-minute warning within seconds of leaving the ground, and clearly half of that time had elapsed while we made a large lazy turn to get lined up on the DZ.

For me it was hard to believe the moment of truth was at hand. There was no backing out and there was no time to ask any last-minute questions. I had to be ready to get out of that airplane over Friar DZ. We had been briefed that if we were going to refuse to jump, do it before we were given the command to stand up. That way, we would be pulled out of our stick and taken to the front of the aircraft and strapped into a seat for the ride back to Lawson Field.

The pace picked up considerably when the jumpmaster yelled "Get ready!" We acknowledged the command and replied by stomping one foot on the corrugated metal decking and slipping free of our seat belts.

The next five commands in the routine went by in a blur and we finished checking our equipment and stood ready to go. I was a stick leader and was the first man in the door on my side of the aircraft. The jumpmaster didn't wait for me to step up. Instead he grabbed me by the lift harness at my hip and steered me into the open doorway as he yelled, "Stand in the door!"

Peering out and down, I could see us coming up over the leading edge of the hard, sandy drop zone. I watched the jumpmaster again out of the corner of my eye. He glanced up past my face to the lights and as he did, the red light went out and the green came on. I felt him let go of my harness and slap me on the butt as he yelled, "Go."

I had been rehearsing that moment over and over again in my head and had done it hundreds of times in mock ups. *Push up and out. Feet and knees together. Elbows in tight to your sides. Hands cupped over the ends of the reserve parachute. And count.*

Suddenly, I was out the door and into the prop wash of the huge engines. I could feel the wind blowing up and over the top of my close-cropped hair under my helmet. I felt like I was falling out of control. *Count!* I had forgotten to count. I was supposed to count, one thousand, two thousand, three thousand, and if I got to four thousand, I was supposed to take immediate steps to deploy my reserve! But I forgot.

I was so involved in correct body position that I completely forgot to count. I tried to make up for it by rushing the count. But before I got to two thousand I felt the parachute come out of my pack tray and I realized that I was spinning on a vertical axis.

As soon as the chute inflated and I swung under it, I realized that the sounds of the engines were gone. It was so serene a silence compared to the cacophony inside the aircraft and the yelling of jumpmasters and jumpers. I felt my trousers being pulled out of my boots as the main lift web yanked me and everything on me upward, holding me safely in its grip.

My risers and suspension lines were wound up from where they connected to my shoulders to the skirt of my canopy. Knowing that I had twisted the suspension lines by exiting in a bad body position, I began to pedal as if on a bicycle to create the motion to unwind me. And in a couple of fast rotations I was free and could raise my head to look up at the canopy.

I was very happy to see that my canopy was okay. I made a quick look at the expanse of nylon and found no holes or tears. I realized that I was automatically remembering the next point of performance: steer clear of other jumpers. The sky was filled with dozens of other jumpers. But none was close enough for me to worry about colliding with him.

I remembered all of the cautions we were given about avoiding other jumpers and what to do if one landed on your canopy, or to be ready to run off of another jumper's canopy if you landed on it. We had been warned that to stay on top of another man's canopy was certain disaster, as his would steal air from yours and yours would collapse.

The ride was exhilarating and while I didn't realize it, I was hooked. Unlike so many jump school graduates who get the wings and then never jump again, I was sure I wanted to do it again. But that was during the best part of the jump, after the parachute had opened and before landing. Anyone can love parachuting then. I still hadn't landed.

As I looked down, the distance to the ground was hard to judge. Hell, I'd never been that high. How was I supposed to tell how fast I was falling or how close I was to the ground? Again, the training came back to me. *Watch the other jumpers. If you are falling faster than they are, consider deploying your reserve parachute.* And, *when you get to treetop level take up a good parachute landing fall position.* I remembered to look out for jumpers or obstacles below me and prepared to land.

The jump had gone so well so far that I was a little apprehensive about the landing being as easy as the exit and the descent. I remembered to put my feet and knees together, bring my hands up on my risers and pull my chin into my neck. Training had taught me not to look at the ground for fear of stiffening my legs and causing injury. Instead, I looked out at the treetops that were about level with my eyes and prepared to do a parachute landing fall, hitting the ground on my toes, calves, hips and push-up muscles—hopefully in that order.

I felt and heard myself crash into the ground with anything but a graceful PLF. Instead, I landed in a very small dry wash with half my foot on one side and my heel on the other side. The twisting sent a small sharp pain up my leg, but I was pumping so much adrenaline that I hardly noticed it.

I remained still for a fraction of a second, looking up. I was so excited as I watched the jumpers above me making their own last-minute adjustments as they approached the drop zone. I had made it! I had made my first jump from my first airplane and I was in one piece. What a terrific feeling! Then I remembered that I had to get up and collect my parachute before one of the drop zone safety NCOs found me screwing off and had me doing pushups until he got tired of it.

After stuffing my parachute into my parachute kit bag and clipping my reserve to the handles, I threw the bundle over my shoulder and began the long jog to the turn-in point. Since I had been the first man in the door in my stick, I was the farthest man from the turn-in point at the other end of the drop zone.

As I got closer to the turn-in point I realized that I had done some damage to my foot on the landing, and became angry with myself for failing to do a perfect parachute landing fall. It certainly was an object lesson for me.

For most of the men that morning, that first jump was a real milestone in their lives. For me it was a triple accomplishment. My first flight, my first jump, and my twenty-first birthday.

CHAPTER 10

•

Several of us decided to celebrate our first jump at the Infantry Bar. We consumed plenty of beer and did plenty of talking about our individual experiences. The tales got taller as the beer flowed and none of us cared if the stories were all that accurate. All we knew was that we had *done* it. We had actually stepped out of an airplane in flight and lived to talk about it. It was about as good a reason to drink beer as I have ever had.

But by the time we got back to the BOQ my foot was bothering me enough to overcome the numbing effect of the beer. Every-Clayton had had some medical training as an enlisted man, so he took a look at me. His best guess was that I might have fractured one or more of the small bones in my foot, just behind my two smaller toes. The news was frightening! I couldn't go on sick call because injured students in Airborne school were recycled back to a later class. I remembered the students who had been recycled into our class, and the ones who were recycled in OCS and in basic training. I couldn't remember one of them who eventually graduated. They all washed out. I couldn't imagine turning myself in for an injury that wasn't bleeding or serious.

Jon told me that a fracture that wasn't poking through the skin could become serious if I jumped on it again. I could tear up important tissues and ligaments in my foot and do some permanent damage. All that notwithstanding, I was *not* going on sick call. After considerable begging and pleading, I got Jon to help me tape up my foot.

The litmus test was the morning check run. During Jump Week the company was formed up and double timed around the end of the access road that circled the runway. While we ran, the instructors looked for students who were limping or otherwise unable to make the run. They obviously had experienced trouble with students like me who were more concerned about being recycled than about jumping injured. I was plenty concerned about jumping injured, but not enough to speak up. I did *not* want to get recycled.

As I approached the first formation of the day I made every effort to not show that I was walking on a very sore foot in a sock filled with adhesive tape. Walking was hard to do and running was even worse. I wasn't sure if I could conceal my limp, so I devised still another plan. As we began the run I noticed that there was another soldier in my platoon who was favoring his leg with some kind of a hip injury. A few steps after he started, I fell out of the formation and bent down, as if retying my boot laces and then fell back into the running formation just behind the guy who was limping.

As we ran down the straightaway toward the end of the runway the instructors were all bunched up on the other side of the long formation of runners, so I was okay there and able to work some of the tape loose so the restriction of the tape itself didn't add to my tendency to limp a bit.

As we made the gentle rounded turn to cross beyond the active runway, a pair of airplanes came in and landed. Everyone watched, most of us having never been underneath an airplane just a few feet before it touched down. That too distracted the Black Hats.

Attention was finally focused on us at the far side of the runway. First one, then a second instructor came up alongside my outside file and looked at the runner in front of me. He knew he was being watched and straightened out his stride. The instructors left again.

This process happened once more as we returned to the rigger shed and the injured runner in front of me was again able to straighten up.

Then they called the formation to a halt and the instructors walked through the ranks pulling out the lame and sending them to a truck posted nearby, to be taken to the dispensary for sick call. I held my breath while the instructors prowled the formation and pulled the man in front of me. I didn't exhale until I saw the truck leaving.

I had made it through the eyeballing, but still had two jumps ahead of me that day—one with an M-14 strapped to my side. I wondered just who had gotten over on whom.

The second jump was wonderful. The day was a crisp, beautiful February day and the winds were calm. We loaded up like veterans and soon found ourselves back at the turn-in point on the drop zone.

I remembered my foot as I floated toward the drop zone for my second time. By then, feeling really cocky about my ability to control my parachute, I devised a plan to reduce the impact on my left foot. I waited until I had a full and safe canopy over head, and then tried to gauge how much room I had to maneuver and not drift off the drop zone into the trees. Looking down, I could see that the chances of missing the huge drop zone were remote, so I tried to set myself up to do a right PLF. That would put the first point of impact on my right boot and I would roll up the right side of my body. I figured that would be the least traumatic on my sore foot.

To do this maneuver I needed to figure out which way the wind was blowing and get my left shoulder into it. At first I couldn't tell. I looked down and saw a purple smoke grenade at the far end of the DZ, the cloud drifting upward with a very slight deviation from the vertical. The wind was almost dead calm, but had a direction, and then I reached up and pulled down on my right risers to turn. I overdid it and found myself with my back to the wind. I began to panic a bit and tried to turn back without overcorrecting. By letting up on my risers early, the huge canopy coasted me into a ninety-degree difference between the wind direction and the way I was facing. With no time to spare, I saw the treetops coming up and prepared to land. While I was trying to guess if I could raise the injured foot just a bit to protect it, I hit the ground like a bag of rocks. No neat PLF, no clever protection for my foot. Just a perpendicular collision with the earth.

My lack of performance was noted by one of the drop zone safety NCOs. He began yelling at me for trying to make a standing landing— a cardinal sin in Airborne school—and instructed me to give him twenty push-ups when I was out of my parachute.

The impact was only slightly uncomfortable on my foot and I was almost happy to give him the twenty. I had made it to the ground without being recycled or breaking my foot into little pieces.

Riding back to the airfield I realized that I had two parachute jumps and two airplane rides under my belt, but had never landed in an airplane. That notion was quickly replaced by my concern about the second run of the day, and the prospects of making a safe jump with a rifle in tow.

The second run was easier to fake than the first. The pain in my foot was not as sharp, and the tape had loosened up to give me support without adding to my limp. I made it through that one without generating any interest in me as a potential medical problem.

The weapons jump was not nearly as difficult as we had all expected it to be. We all worried about landing awkwardly and having the rifle injure us. For most of us, we hardly even knew we had it attached when we landed. The most difficult part of the jump was sitting in the aircraft with the rifle up the left side of our bodies.

Once we were out of the aircraft we had to lean over and find the small tie-down to release it. Failure to do so kept our leg tied to the weapons pouch that held our rifles. Like the others, I had a bit of difficulty reaching the tie-down and once I did, I focused my attention on making a satisfactory landing.

A third successful landing and I was really starting to get the hang of it. At least I thought so then. There were hundreds of jumps ahead of me that would teach me some really important things about jumping in conditions not nearly so perfect as over Friar DZ at Fort Benning. Days would come when the conditions would be marginal, the aircraft would be flown by allies who had different standards of safety and limited flying experience, the weather would be threatening, and the ground would hide hostile forces instead of safety NCOs.

As I jogged to the turn-in point, I never gave a thought to the possibility that some day I would be a jumpmaster myself, inspecting and supervising other jumpers.

The final day was our true test. We not only had to jump with our rifles, but with our combat gear hooked to our main lift web, up under our reserve parachutes. We spent several hours rigging and rerigging what we thought were large and heavy combat packs and other gear into kit bags to hook to ourselves for the jump. We couldn't quite understand why the instructors didn't think it was much of a feat.

We were sure that carrying all that extra gear was an added safety risk and would certainly make our exits difficult and our landings more painful. Of course we had never actually seen a real combat jump. Our training jump was child's play in comparison to the really heavy loads that were rigged for actual combat jumps.

Once I got into Airborne units and jumped with the really large combat loads, I realized how simple the *equipment* jump was in Airborne school. And for all the worries over the difficulties of larger personal loads, the last two jumps were as thrilling and accident free as the first three.

We were formed up near the turn-in point after our last jump. Colonel Welch came out to congratulate us and help pin our blood wings. The origin of the term *blood wings* is not hard to imagine. That was not their official definition, but whatever they were called, we stood proudly at the end of the drop zone as the faculty of the Airborne school swarmed into our formation and pinned them on.

As a stocky young staff sergeant Black Hat stepped in front of me to pin on my wings he smiled and said, "Don't you think it's about time to have that foot looked at, Lieutenant?"

It clearly reminded me that just because I had become a lieutenant, my commission didn't make the NCOs stupid. I had learned plenty about myself and about training at the Airborne school.

I had suffered through the endless repetitive training demands of the school. At the time, I only gained a moderate respect for the technique of drumming procedure into everyone's head by constant repetition, so that when it was needed it would be almost automatic. My appreciation grew dramatically in combat.

To pin on gold second lieutenant's bars and silver parachute wings in the same month was certainly a mark of personal pride. I finally felt I was getting somewhere after two and a half years of delays and disappointments.

Clearing post at Fort Benning that February of 1965, I was filled with mixed emotions. I had come to love lots of things about Benning. It was a place of professional validation. No one came to Benning and got through its tougher schools on anything but their own effort. There were no shortcuts.

There was no way of telling, the day I drove out the front gate, that I would be back many more times before writing this book.

I am forever sorry that I didn't properly thank Bill Pfeiffer for the hard work and faith he put into training me and encouraging me to become as good an infantry officer as I could be. Bill died of cancer just a very short time after we were made lieutenants. I won't forget him.

While I was on leave, en route to Missouri, Malcolm X was assassinated in the Audubon Ballroom in Harlem. I didn't appreciate the significance of the event at the time. But it was still another incident that would come to influence greatly the course of the army in the near future.

I still had very little to go on concerning the army's reasons for sending me to Fort Leonard Wood. I wasn't alone. Jon Every-Clayton, my OCS and jump-school roommate, got the same orders and he didn't know why either.

Right after graduation from Airborne school and before we reported for duty, a series of important events occurred. President Johnson began the bombing of North Vietnam, the first American combat troops landed in Da Nang, the civil-rights march from Selma to Montgomery took place under National Guard protection, and the first teach-in was held at the University of Michigan.

But Leonard Wood was a confusing wild card.

We were assigned to different basic-training battalions in the same training regiment. But it wasn't the kind of training that we had taken when we joined the army.

We discovered, right after being assigned to our battalions, that Leonard Wood had been singled out for an experiment. The pool of available draftees was limited and the Selective Service planners, in collaboration with Defense Secretary McNamara, decided that they would fill the need for more troops by dropping the induction standards.

Before Vietnam, the army was the only service that filled its manpower needs from a draft pool. Those draftees were not only physically qualified, but mentally qualified. There were minimum educational standards, and mental qualifications were determined by testing. Those ranked in the lower mental categories were routinely rejected.[38]

Fort Leonard Wood was tasked with putting the lower category draftees through modified basic-combat training. While we had no idea why, we were told that one of the modifications was to pick a larger number of junior officers who had been enlisted men to serve as cadre. That was why so many of us found our orders changed at the last minute to divert us to Fort Leonard Wood.

Leonard Wood was an engineer post. The sudden presence of a crop of unruly infantry officers was not well accepted by the engineers that had homesteaded there. Within a few days of our arrival, all of us who were infantry were called to a meeting and read the riot act about being low profile while we were there and not drawing attention to ourselves, our units, or our differences from the engineers.

It was easily the least desirable place I had yet been in the army. There we were, plunked down in the middle of Missouri outside a wide spot in the road called Waynesville. The post was plain, calm, and dull. The job was something less than taxing, except for the incredibly long hours.

An officer had to be with each basic-training company when it left its company area for physical training in the morning. That meant being in at four-fifteen each morning. And as company training officers we were little more than baby-sitters. We would double time a company of 260 trainees to a classroom, training area, or firing range, and wait. At each of the sites there were qualified instructors there to give them their training.

[38] Known as "McNamara's 100,000," or "Project 100,000," between 1967 and 1971, the program actually inducted about 350,000 men who scored in mental category IV on the Armed Forces Qualification Test (AFQT). "Cat IVs" are those who scored between the 10th and 30th percentile on the test; category Is, the highest, scored in the 93d to 100th percentile.

As the junior officer in my company, I spent almost all day, every day, waiting at a range or in the back of a classroom while the instruction took place. There was very little for me to do but dispense a little bit of lightweight discipline for trainees who got into trouble in class.

When I wasn't with the company at training, I was swamped with paperwork. Hundreds of forms needed signing on a weekly basis. And the routine additional duties that traditionally cluttered up the lives of all junior officers were given to me: I was the supply officer, the voting officer, the vector control officer, the mess officer, the pay officer, the fire marshal, and the safety officer. In addition, I was responsible for classified documents, inventories, sanitation, the Army Emergency Relief, Red Cross blood drives, and a long list of even less important projects and events.

It was nothing like Germany or Fort Benning. The soldiers at Fort Leonard Wood were of a different kind than I had become accustomed to. They were completely unmoved by the spirit that I had experienced in combat units in Europe and the schools I had just attended. There was no visible demonstration of pride in their units, their accomplishments, or even themselves. They were just guys in uniform who seemed satisfied to punch a clock and head home at the end of the day.

Esprit de corps was just not there. And I was not happy there. Within a month after reporting in I was investigating the possibility of getting out of there and back into an environment that, while more taxing, would certainly be more rewarding.

Volunteering to go to Vietnam was as easy as a phone call. But I quickly found out from Infantry Branch in Washington that I would have to wait until I had fulfilled all of the requirements before I could go overseas.

Requirements? I was surprised to find out that there was a waiting list to go to Vietnam. There were very few units there and the total force strength had just reached fifty thousand. A gung-ho major who handled the assignments of infantry lieutenants told me that he would put me on the list to go and I would get my orders the minute I had qualified to go. He went down the list of requirements for me. I had to be either an OCS or West Point graduate; I had to be jump or Ranger qualified; and I had to spend one year with troops as an officer before going to Vietnam.

So I had all the qualifications except the last one—a year with the troops.

* * *

In the late summer of 1965 I had suffered through the boredom of two and a half eight-week cycles of trainees when I got my alert notification to go to Vietnam, just before Christmas.

During those months I got a chance to get a sense of myself as a junior officer. I was loaded down with work. While none of it was very important or crucial to the accomplishment of the mission, I liked finding out that I could do things and do them fairly well. It was the first place that I had been in the army where I was somewhere instead of on the way to somewhere else. And though I knew I was going to Vietnam soon, I still had work to do there that didn't have anything to do with me preparing to go to Vietnam. It was a short delay in the sequence of events that put me into the war and into special operations units. I wish now that I had appreciated the breather a bit more. But the hours were long, and there was always something that needed to be done around the company.

During that same year forces were in action that would affect me in the years to come—General Westmoreland asked for 125,000 more troops for Vietnam; Selected Service doubled the draft; the national anti-Vietnam movement began to gain momentum; Nguyen Cao Ky was appointed South Vietnamese premier; Students for a Democratic Society held an antiwar rally in Washington, DC; and President Johnson permitted U.S. ground troops to conduct offensive operations in South Vietnam. Riots broke out in Watts, the 1st Cavalry Division fought the battle of the Ia Drang Valley, and by December our troop level reached 185,000 in Vietnam and we had our first thousand-casualty year.

Over beers at the officers club and on smoke breaks in training we discussed the world events at great length. The number of headlines that affected me personally was growing.

CHAPTER 11

•

It was a mistake to think that we were trained for our jobs in the States and then sent to Vietnam. The stateside training base was controlled by a central headquarters that decided every detail of every formal class that was presented at every service school. And unit training was set up to meet the annual training requirements of the unit to which you were assigned. Those requirements were tied to the unit's mission. Since most units had no Vietnam in their mission until they were alerted to go there, the training was for cold war commie fighting.

So if we were going to learn anything about Vietnam it would be only weeks, if not days, before leaving the States. In 1965, that meant most of our training took place in Vietnam where there was precious little time for it, and most of that was on the job.

My personal inventory of Vietnam-oriented training was a short one. The scraps of things that we had picked up in OCS had become obsolete in the several months since then. Real American units were on the ground and finding out that their assessment of the guerrilla enemy was only marginally accurate at best.

The loop stayed closed in Vietnam. When infantry units there found out an important lesson it rarely got from Southeast Asia to Benning, Bragg, Campbell, or other posts where it was needed.

The same was not true of aviation. Their style of instruction was one-on-one, and the instructor pilots at Forts Rucker and Wolters were coming back from Vietnam with their helmet bags full of good information to feed back to the students. They prided themselves on breaking with the formal instruction that was laid out for them in the lesson plans. Instead, they would pound Vietnam into the heads of their students as they flew together over the Texas and Alabama terrain.

But the maneuver or combat units didn't get the benefit of the instant feedback from those few returning Vietnam veterans because all infantry training was subject to inspections, and when inspectors dropped in on instructors, the first thing they checked for was adherence to the standard lesson plans that came out of master training schedules written in training headquarters ten thousand miles and two wars away from Vietnam.

So trained or not, I was off to Vietnam. The trip over was as unconventional as the war itself. I had to hitchhike to the war.

My port call instructed me to go to Oakland Army Base for movement to Vietnam. At Oakland the army had no seat to put my tail in, so I was put up at Fort Mason in San Francisco and was told to call Oakland every day to see if they could find me a ride to Vietnam. Those days on North Beach in the topless bars and amid the emerging hippie culture was an experience worth a book of its own. But that's where the army wanted me to wait, so I did what I was told and tried not to enjoy it too much.

Once I finally did get a ride to Vietnam, it was by commercial jet—one leg at a time. The first leg only went to Honolulu. I then had to hop a ride to the Philippines, then one to Wake Island, then to Japan, and finally to Saigon.

The near-vacation atmosphere of the trip was brought up short when I arrived in Japan and got a day to visit a friend. Lieutenant Ronnie Epstein, my old OCS roommate who was going to sit the war out at Fort Benning with the 11th Air Assault Division, was hospitalized at Camp Zama.

Ronnie's division was one of the first American combat units tested in battle. He found himself one of the few surviving lieutenants in his battalion in spite of the fact that he was wounded several times during the course of the battle.

Finding my first classmate-casualty was a very sobering moment for me. But Ronnie wasn't going to let it get me down. He escaped from the hospital and took me to the local officers club for plenty of Scotch and lots of quick lessons on what I needed to know before I arrived in Vietnam.

Regardless of what I had picked up in training, or figured out on my own, all of it lost credibility in the face of Ronnie's experiences as a platoon leader in Vietnam.

I clearly remember the sinking feeling in my stomach as I boarded still another airplane to make that last leg to Vietnam. I had never felt so close to the test of battle, or so unprepared. Ronnie's words kept banging around in my head. I had to get tough fast and be ready for anything. Training was over. Peacetime assignments were behind me and the real thing was only a few hours away.

* * *

South Vietnam in the Christmas of 1965 was a war zone in a heightened state of flux. Confusion was the normal state of affairs, and chaos would flare up here and there to make things appear even more disorganized.

The troop strength was nowhere near its peak yet, but there was construction going on all over the country. New airfields were being built, and old ones were being upgraded to support outposts and base areas that were rising out of the paddies and the rain forest. Vietnam's economy was on the way up, and its people were being drawn into a new decade of unparalleled turmoil and loss.

For the Americans there it was equally turbulent, but our mindset was that it was just a temporary situation. We were only committed to a yearlong tour. That we might have more than one tour in Vietnam was the last thing that we thought of as we touched down in Tan Son Nhut Airport. Rather, at that moment we just wondered if we were going to finish our tour and make it home unharmed. Looking back, none of us left unmarked. Some paid the ultimate price, but even the luckiest Vietnam veterans paid dearly.

For the Vietnamese it was something altogether different. They had never known peace—but the arrival of large numbers of Americans took the burden of the war off their back and flooded their economy with money. American soldiers, sailors, airmen, Marines; civilian politicians, U.S. government workers, diplomatic corps members, contractors, and others were there in huge numbers—all with greenbacks and piasters.[39]

All of us on my flight had either missed or cut short our Christmas celebrations at home with our families to make our port calls. As we got off the chartered 707 we were herded into buses with chicken wire over the open windows. The windows were open to give us some relief from the oppressive heat. And the chicken wire was to keep hand grenades from being pitched into the windows by passing enemy terrorists on bicycles.

Camp Alpha was a tent city equally unprepared for the influx of troops on their way to their final in-country assignments. It was poorly equipped to handle the bedding, feeding, and sanitary demands put on it by an ever-increasing flow of new arrivals. But what it did have

---

[39] The basic unit of currency in Vietnam during the French occupation. Although the Vietnamese, both North and South, called their currency the *dong*, "piaster"—abbreviated "P"—was still commonly used throughout the years of America's involvement in Vietnam. At this time, the Vietnam piaster was worth 73 to one American dollar.

were plenty of rumors and long lines. There were lines for food, lines for the showers, lines for shots, lines for bedding, and lines for pay. While in those lines the topics of conversations, in priority of importance, were: the recent major battles fought by the 1st Cavalry Division, where each of us thought we would end up; and the growing popularity of the miniskirt back in *the World*.[40] And in every line there was someone with a radio. It seemed so symbolic to hear the McCoys singing "Hang on Sloopy" over and over again. We had 365 days to go. All of us were promising ourselves that we would hang on.

Things never go the way you expect them to in the U.S. Army. Our first disappointing news was that it would be a few days before any of us would find out what our final assignments would be. Like so many others, I thought that the orders I had in hand were the ironclad documentation that would determine my final and ultimate unit of assignment. I had had orders to the 101st Airborne Brigade for months and had come to grips with the job and what I would be doing —I thought. The only other possible place that I would want to go would be the 173rd Airborne Brigade. What could be the problem?

I was told that the assignments were based on *projected* needs and not the *actual* needs of the gaining units in Vietnam. Basically, we were told that Department of the Army was full of crap and that United States Army Vietnam (USARV),[41] would decide just where we would go. To top that off, they would take their time about doing it, too. We stood formations every few hours where names were called out for those lucky few who finally had a home to go to.

I was a bit disappointed at still another chance that I might end up in some job other than the one I had set my mind on—infantry platoon leader.

I recall sitting on the edge of my bunk smoking a last cigarette for the day, wondering just what awful alternative USARV could come up with. In the chow lines we heard nightmare stories about officers ripped off of their orders to choice units. As the rumors went, they were assigned to mortuary duty, the Saigon Post Exchange system, Vietnamese service schools, advisory duty, and press-relations assignments. Each a kind of slow death of its own. Each formation was a moment of anxiety as names were matched to new assignments.

The next day my assignment was confirmed. It turned out to be the 101st Airborne Brigade after all. What a relief—I thought.

[40] The United States.
[41] USARV was the headquarters that exercised direct operational control over U.S. Army forces in Vietnam.

* * *

Riding through the streets of Saigon, making my way up-country by truck, jeep, and air, I began to discover that there were many more Vietnams than I had anticipated. And most of them were not at all what I expected, and before a year was up, I would see all of them. It wasn't until years later that I realized the differences.

First, there was part of the Vietnam I expected to see. That was a country in the middle of a war. Then there was the Vietnam at war that the press wanted me to see. And then there was the Vietnam that the U.S. and South Vietnamese governments wanted me to see. And the strange thing was that not one of them looked like any of the others. The only thing they had in common was a national border. And sometimes that too was in question.

I suppose that any soldier who spent a year in one job in Vietnam went home thinking that he had seen it, and that he could pretty much believe that his experiences were typical for his type of unit and his type of job. I would come to find that I had no such typical experiences. None of my jobs was routine. I never stayed in one place. I would serve in the coastal lowlands, the Central Highlands, the Mekong Delta, the rolling terrain north and west of Saigon, and the reed plains along the Cambodian border. And my experiences covered both sides of Vietnam's blurred borders with Laos and Cambodia. Before the last time I was evacuated from Vietnam I would travel to all those locales on foot, by boat and chopper with leg,[42] Airborne, Ranger, Long Range Patrol, and Special Forces units.

I guess what I missed were the jobs in air-conditioned buildings with waxed floors, scheduled sit-down meals, regular floor shows at the officers clubs, going to work in taxis, wearing civilian clothes off duty, and being *off* duty. My experience was with fighters and not with administrators. And I am sure that if I were to compare war stories with those administrators and headquarters personnel that our points of view would never resemble each other's recollections.

I didn't have the time to assess or even to recognize how deliberately factions in Vietnam were trying to sell a point or justify an expenditure while I was part of the sales pitch. I'm just as glad that I didn't. I would have hated to go to sleep at night out in the field knowing I was there for reasons other than to help.

* * *

[42] A derogatory term for a non-Airborne soldier. It may have originated from the idea that ordinary infantrymen walk into battle on their legs instead of getting there via a parachute.

I was lucky to start in the brigade of the 101st Airborne Division, a unit with a reputation for professionalism and readiness. If I had to break in somewhere, I'm glad it was there.

Before Vietnam, the 101st Airborne Division was at Fort Campbell, Kentucky. All its resources were poured into creating a separate brigade to deploy to Vietnam in the summer of 1965. To create this brigade out of the Airborne division's assets meant stripping the other two brigades of a considerable amount of manpower and equipment. Everyone who went to Vietnam had to have at least enough time remaining in the army to get them through the summer of 1966. And all of the equipment needed to be in top condition. Everything and everyone had to be operational before loading onto the USNS *Le Roy Eltinge* to sail for Vietnam.

Once the *Eltinge* landed in Cam Ranh Bay, they unloaded the troops and equipment and sent the maneuver battalions directly to the field to begin combat operations in the immediate vicinity. As with most units, their first efforts were a little shaky, and there were the usual overreactions on the part of the command structure to over-supervise the troops and the use of ammo. In time, they settled down and became more comfortable living in an environment where everybody was carrying loaded weapons.

During the four and a half months of combat operations that took place before I was assigned to the brigade, there had been plenty of time for them to discover what would work in the field. Many were disappointed to find their organization and equipment poorly suited for the type of combat and the terrain that they were now working in.

The division had been modified over the years since World War II for deployment to a European battlefield, or for immediate use in domestic civil disturbance situations. The 1st Brigade had been specially trained in desert operations. As such, there was little in the training schedule and the inventory that was well suited for Vietnam. And when the division got alerted to send a fully independent brigade to Vietnam, there was no time to upgrade its training.

Since the brigade would be expected to operate independently of a division headquarters, its staff and support components had to be augmented by more artillery, aviation, civil operations, transportation, maintenance, personnel, communications, and medical units. But the basic structure of the infantry maneuver battalions remained unchanged and their organization for combat was traditional and conventional.

So while I was trying to get out of Fort Leonard Wood to join the 101st, they were trying to keep up with the combat demands of Vietnam and adapt. For the first months they received a whirlwind of missions in diverse geographical areas that took them from Saigon to An Khe. Those missions required them to operate as a brigade, and sometimes as separate battalions. And during that time the inadequacies of the modified brigade organization became much more apparent.

The term *fire brigade* was attached to the 173d and the 101st. As enemy concentrations were discovered by or reported to the intelligence network in Vietnam, one of the two brigades would be dropped into an area to develop the situation into contacts.

The continuous change of missions, terrain, and targets caused the 101st to refine many of its operational techniques, but still it was difficult for them to work out tactics they could use as SOP. Additionally, the constant turnover of personnel—reassignments of officers from staff to field jobs and vice versa—worked against standardization and made continuity in command a big problem.

By the time I arrived on the brigade's Phan Rang rear area, they had been committed to combat for almost six months. Their operations had taken them to the central highlands terrain along Highway 19, the coastal lowlands of Qui Nhon, and the manicured rubber plantations near Lai Khe.

Each area presented a new enemy. The idea that the brigade was going to face small guerrilla and occasional main force[43] units was far from the reality of what it found in its travels. The troops were exposed then to a wide variety of enemy combat techniques.

I had very high expectations of the 101st and an even greater estimate of what I thought would be required of me. What I discovered was a combat unit that was trying hard, but was as confused about their role and their mission as I was. Nothing seemed to fit and no one seemed to have answers to the obvious questions: Who are the bad guys? When can I shoot? What can I shoot at? What am I supposed to do with all the civilians in my area of operations? How can I tell who is friendly? Can anyone speak this language?

When I arrived at the brigade command post to meet my brigade

---

[43] Viet Cong units. Main force units were better trained and equipped than the guerrilla forces.

commander I was brought face-to-face with the realities of our mission in Vietnam. The headquarters was well-equipped, clean, and sparkled with whitewashed rocks marking all of the pathways to the major tents and buildings. The soldiers looked sharp and moved with a purpose. No one was lounging around, killing time, looking useless. There was plenty of business going on. I just wasn't sure yet what it was.

What came clear to us from the briefings we got was our unspecified mission as junior officers in the unit. We were to be careful not to step on toes. Sure, we were encouraged to be aggressive, bold, self-assured, and visible. But the subtext was to assess the impact of our moves on everyone else we had to work with in Vietnam.

There was an overriding caution against offending the South Vietnamese or the intrusive American government agencies that were everywhere in Vietnam. The dedication to this mission was crystallized in our new brigade title—*Diplomats and Warriors*. It had been a while since I had seen a unit so concerned with its relations with the civilian population.

When I was a PFC in Kaiserslautern, Germany, the tank battalion I was attached to had a policy about drunk driving. If you were caught by the German police and ticketed for driving drunk, your car was impounded by the army provost marshal. Then, to make it worse, your car was placed on a flatbed truck and displayed in the center of the parade field outside the headquarters building. Alongside your car was a large sign that read: "This car belongs to Sergeant John Doe. He has lost the use of it for 90 days for breaking German law by driving drunk."

The motivating factor behind the display was relations with the locals. When the same preoccupation was adopted by American forces commanders in Vietnam the policies translated themselves into confusion, death, and injury for soldiers in the field.

I'm sure that I would have had a much more difficult time fitting in had it not been for the quality and the dedication of the troops assigned to the 101st. They were all volunteers and, in 1965, they all believed that what we were in Vietnam for made sense and needed to be done.

I don't mean to diminish our grasp or belittle our understanding of the world and how it worked back then. But we were children of the forties who grew up during and after World War II believing that it was our obligation to help any country with which we had a mutual defense pact. Vietnam was one of those countries and they reached out for our help.

We were also living through the fading days of the Kennedy era. It was unusual to find among us any who did not believe JFK's words when he said, "we shall pay any price, bear any burden, meet any hardship, support any friend, oppose any foe, in order to assure the survival and the success of liberty."

Why we were there was not in question. *What* was how to take a piece of a division configured for conventional desert warfare and close with and destroy a guerrilla army. We were not trained to fight the enemy we found in Vietnam.

To compound our problems, we were not the only bears in the woods. We had to contend with the sensitivities and the jealousy of partnering with the South Vietnamese, a dozen other allies, the CIA, and the White House. Everyone was in charge and no one was in charge when I arrived in Vietnam that winter.

Somehow, we were expected to make the problems go away for the South Vietnamese without taking too much credit for it, lest we embarrass the Vietnamese or the other U.S. government agencies. It was an extremely confusing situation for a boy of twenty-one being asked to lead men in battle.

From brigade I was assigned to the 1st Battalion, 327th Infantry. On arrival there I was sent to the operations tent to report in.

Inside that tent I met a man who would have a great impact on me in the short and the long haul. David Hackworth didn't look much like a highly decorated, combat-hardened, field-grade officer, but I would come to find out plenty about him in the days to come, and we would serve together more than once in combat. We would drink, play poker, get wounded, and mourn losses together. And the quick decision he made about me would completely change the course of my future assignments and my life. But I had no way of knowing that on that dry, hot morning.

Everyone called him "Hack." In official business or in front of subordinates he was referred to by his telephone call sign of "Steel Five." When you were told that Steel Five wanted to see you, you knew that something was about to happen. He was tough, demanding, and boyish all at the same time.

That morning, three of us were assigned to the 1/327 and we had to report in to Steel Five. We didn't know he was the battalion executive officer. We were most concerned with our immediate futures. Were we to become Airborne infantry platoon leaders that morning—or not?

Hack was stocky, with a slightly leathered complexion, in his thirties. His light hair and deep tan made it hard for us to tell how old he was. He wore jungle fatigue trousers, shower shoes, a green T-shirt, and a Rolex watch. In the corner of his mouth was a large and foul-smelling cigar. As we entered the tent he was bent over a field table looking at a map overlay and drinking a bottle of San Miguel beer.

The initial signs were confusing, to say the least. I had been brought up on a steady diet of staying in full uniform and never drinking during duty hours. But I had never been to Vietnam before, either.

One of us announced that we were looking for Major Hackworth, and the intelligence NCO, Master Sergeant Hawk, pointed at Hack.

He immediately lit up and threw us his trademark smile. I was pleased to see that the first response was a friendly one.

We saluted and reported for duty and Hack shook our hands all around and told us to stand at ease. We waited uncomfortably while he looked quickly at our Form 66s[44] that we brought with us. He sized up our backgrounds and decided on the spot where to put us.

Lieutenant Gene New went to a rifle company to be a platoon leader, Leland Roy went to the mortar platoon, and Hack hesitated when he got to me. I wondered what he saw in my records that made him pause. To this day he has never told me. I once asked and he couldn't remember the meeting except to say that he liked me when we first met.

Hackworth dismissed New and Roy and then he looked at my 66 again. I was starting to worry when he finally said, "I've got a special job for you. I'm sending you to the Tigers."

I looked passed Hackworth and saw the reaction on the faces of Master Sergeant Hawk and Leo B. Smith, the headquarters company first sergeant. Though they gave away little with their expression, the announcement seemed to be something between good and hard. I had no idea what he was talking about but didn't want to look stupid, so I replied, "That's great, sir."

He didn't acknowledge how stupid my reply was. Instead, he just gestured for me to follow him out of the tent. Outside, he pointed to a section of the headquarters company area and said, "Head on down to that tent over there and find Phil Belden. Tell him you are with the Tigers. He'll get you squared away. And, we'll talk more later."

I saluted and picked up my duffel bag. On the walk to the area he had pointed out I was filled with mixed emotions, but I had no idea what the hell a Tiger was and I wasn't going to make a fool out of myself by asking any questions. I was sure that when I met Phil Belden

---

[44] Department of the Army Form 66, Officer Qualification Record.

I'd find out. The problem was that I'd never met anyone in the army who had a name without a rank. Was Phil Belden a civilian?

A passing soldier told me that *Sergeant* Belden was out in the *ville* getting his laundry done and that I could wait for him at his tent. I dropped my duffel bag outside and sat on it. I just figured it was good policy to not make myself at home in someone else's tent when I hadn't been invited. My mind conjured up expectations of a hardcore, battle-tested, no-nonsense Airborne NCO. I remembered those two sergeants at Fort Dix again and wondered what the hell I had gotten myself into. If I had just laid low I could still be sitting in the Ranch Room at the Fort Leonard Wood officers club listening to Erik Burdon and the Animals singing "House of the Rising Sun" while I ate a juicy cheeseburger and drank lots of cold beer. I was really starting to wonder about my choices and just who the hell I thought I was when a jeep rolled into the area.

It was a 106mm recoilless-rifle jeep with the gun dismounted. I hadn't seen one since OCS. And as I stood to see who it was, I saw someone who was a cross between those iron sergeants and a kind and gentle parish priest. Platoon Sergeant Philip Belden was a New England boy, complete with a distinctive Boston accent. His eyes twinkled like a jolly Santa Claus and his smile was as genuine as any I have ever seen. All of the nightmare stories about how you were not going to be well received by your new platoon sergeant and how you would have to assert yourself immediately evaporated as he jumped out of the jeep and saluted me.

Belden must have expected me, because he immediately recognized that I was *his* new second lieutenant and his to break in. He was an NCO of the old school and frequently lapsed into speaking about me in the third person—"Would the lieutenant . . . ?"—as all of the old pros did. But he was one of the most personable and friendly NCOs I had met since Bobby R. Foxworth.

After getting me out of the sun and finding me a place to drop my gear, Belden began to give me his angle on what the Tigers were and what their mission was.

First of all, the Tigers were brand-new, a bastard unit that was totally unauthorized, unfunded, and invisible on our TO & E (table of organization and equipment). It is the TO & E that's a unit's reason for being, its license to draw men and equipment and the basic document that creates and describes it to the army and to itself. But we weren't on it.

Tigers? It was our nickname. Our not-much-more-official name was the Tiger Force. But even that didn't tell anyone much about who or what they were. The name came from an old call sign that the antitank or recon platoons had used sometime earlier in Vietnam. No one seems to be clear on exactly how it originated.

The unit was of David Hackworth's design.

Some years later, Hack explained to me what he had in mind when he sold the battalion commander, Lieutenant Colonel Joe Rogers, on the idea. It seems that Hack quickly realized that there existed several fundamental problems using a conventional Airborne battalion in Vietnam. They were fighting guerrillas with conventional force organization, capability, and equipment. Late in 1965 it became painfully apparent that most of the Viet Cong's activities took place at night. Americans were not yet skilled at night-fighting techniques.

Since the battalions were being committed individually, they were routinely given an artillery battery to provide supporting fires. The artillery fire bases were impossible to conceal and needed continuous protection by infantry units in order for them to handle fire missions. Thus, the isolated artillery firebases routinely tied up an entire rifle company to provide for their security.

On a battlefield that demanded offensive operations and plenty of patrolling to find the enemy, it was counterproductive to leave one of the three rifle companies at a firebase to protect the artillery because the likelihood of finding targets for that same artillery was reduced by at least a third.

And, while securing the artillery batteries was a constant problem, so was the question of what to do with the antitank and reconnaissance platoons. Early in the first months in Vietnam it became obvious that the AT and recon platoons were ill suited for Vietnam. There were few targets for the powerful 106mm recoilless rifles, and the jeep-mounted machine gun crews made both platoons roadbound.

The battalion's organization called for the antitank and recon platoons to be part of headquarters company. They were filled with highly trained antitank crews and recon infantrymen, who were totally malassigned to the Vietnam environment. But because of the recon platoon mission and organization, there was a much higher percentage of Ranger school graduates than was normally found in a rifle platoon.

Fifteen years earlier, in Korea, Hackworth was given command of an all-volunteer unit to organize and train as he saw fit. They became known as the Wolfhound Raiders of the 27th Infantry Regiment.

When Hack's boss, Colonel George B. Sloan, gave him the mission, he explained that the regular rifle companies just didn't have the specialized skills to conduct successful night operations. He wanted to have a special unit for the purpose of conducting combat patrols against enemy positions, with the added mission of taking prisoners as a means of gathering information about the enemy.

He allowed Hack to call for volunteers from every outfit in the 27th Regiment. He got four hundred volunteers when he only needed forty. That put him in the enviable position of picking the best from a very large number of qualified combat veterans.

The screening process was difficult and exacting. If someone didn't measure up, Hack sent them back to their units. In his words, "The weak fell out, the strong made it."

His training method was decentralized. He gave the volunteers to their squad leaders and then held the squad leaders to a high standard of training. If the Raiders failed it was because of the small-unit training, a great motivator for squad leaders in any war.

Their training heavily emphasized ambush and counter-ambush techniques, hand-to-hand combat, physical fitness, and the ability to think under pressure. Hack wanted every man in the Raiders to be able to infiltrate enemy positions with a degree of stealth, to compensate for the small size of the patrols they would conduct.

Weapons and equipment presented a problem. The Wolfhounds were not given light and lethal combat equipment that could carry a punch while being carried. Colonel Sloan left it up to Hackworth and the Raiders to *improvise* and *acquire* their own equipment. Their ingenuity on the battlefield was a perfect match to their inventiveness in matters of supply.

Hackworth's history with the Raiders became the blueprint for the creation, manning, training, equipping, and deploying of the Tiger Force. The legacy was a double-edged sword. The successes of the Raiders under the command of newly promoted First Lieutenant David Hackworth in Korea were what gave him the confidence that the Tigers could hit the street running and do the same in Vietnam. Normal cautions that might have been attached to such an experiment were cast aside because both Hack and Joe Rogers knew that it could be done and that time was short.

This attitude was passed to the Tigers, and they might have assumed a level of confidence that exceeded their actual combat capabilities except that the Tiger Force had a believer for a battalion commander and it was clearly David Hackworth's baby. And once you had Hack on your side, there was little you couldn't do.

CHAPTER 12

•

The birth of the Tiger Force was announced a few weeks before my arrival. It was to be a long-range reconnaissance and ambush element that would operate independently and also serve as a fourth maneuver unit for the battalion.

The unit would be created out of the skeleton of the antitank and recon platoons. The Airborne soldiers who filled those slots were given the opportunity to stay or be reassigned somewhere else in the battalion. Every man in the Tiger Force was to be a triple volunteer: Airborne, Vietnam, and the Tiger Force. Hack didn't want anyone in the Tigers who didn't want to be there, and no one would stay who didn't measure up.

The Tiger Force commander was a bright and engaging first lieutenant named Jim Gardner, a West Pointer who washed himself out of the military academy when he discovered he had committed an honor violation. Undeterred by his dismissal from West Point, Gardner got accepted to officer candidate school and graduated several months before his classmates at the academy. His seniority within the battalion helped him gain command of the Tigers when there were many qualified officers clamoring for the job.

I couldn't have had three better mentors than the ones I found in the Tiger Force. Gardner, Phil Belden, and the platoon sergeant of the old recon platoon, Lawrence C. Smith, were the best of the best.

All of my new-lieutenant anxieties about being accepted and integrated into the unit faded that hot day when I met the three drivers behind the newly minted Tiger Force. I had the feeling that they needed another officer and I was it. I felt at home that very day. But as soon as I became comfortable with my new home, I realized that there was plenty of work ahead of us.

Hack was a tough taskmaster. He didn't let up on the training or the operational requirements until the Tigers could get their act together. He knew that they would take whatever time they were given to get ready for the new change of mission, the infusion of new personnel, and the new working relationship with the battalion.

It was a very tall order. But tall orders never bothered David Hackworth. And no one working for him would be intimidated by the job— or they'd be looking for a new one.

My introduction to combat came under the watchful eye of Phil Belden. But in our first hours together he got me ready for what was to come. I was a mess. I had all the wrong equipment, no field gear, no clean clothes, too much underwear, not enough plastic or waterproof anything, and no control over my bowels.

Belden got me organized and got me the equipment I needed and to the places I needed to go. While it was happening, I wasn't quite sure if Belden was trying to kill me with all of the gear he assembled for me, or if he just wanted to avert explaining my death due to a lack of some piece of gear he'd neglected to get.

By nightfall I had a stack of things on my bunk that spilled onto the floor. Much of it I didn't and wouldn't need, but Belden obviously wanted me to have the option of what to take and what not. There was a moment when I thought this was some kind of test of my field skills: what I decided to take and what I would leave behind would determine the degree of field skills I had.

I quickly concluded that no one in the Tiger Force had the time to contrive such a test for me. But I did take close stock of what everyone else was carrying, washing, rerigging, and repairing for future combat. And I tried not to look like I was looking. Bill Pfeiffer would surely kick my butt if he thought I was letting *them* know what I was thinking.

All of the nightmare stories that we had heard in OCS about platoon sergeants making new second lieutenants' lives miserable couldn't have been more exaggerated in my case.

Gardner's time was limited since he was taking out a patrol to set up ambushes in the brigade's tactical area of operational responsibility (TAOR). But he found the time to welcome me, offer half of his small tent to me, and turn me over to Belden. As was the case with most people who knew Jim Gardner, I liked him immediately. He was open, gregarious, positive, optimistic, and capable. He gave off gallons of that undefinable quality that Bill Pfeiffer had tried to pound into us at OCS. You know it when you see it, and you sure saw it with Jim Gardner. He was a leader, no mistake about it. I knew that from the first few hours we spent together, before he led a patrol through the barbed wire.

Belden, on the other hand, was one of the quietest, most capable, and gentlest warriors I have ever met in all my years around LRP, Rangers Special Forces, and Airborne units. His smile was infectious and his laugh was reassuring. He struck me as a man who was incapable of deceit and did not include acting among his job skills. When Phil Belden felt something, you knew it.

It was clear to me that he had spent years developing his own skills and leadership techniques to fit his personality. He was well liked and well respected by the soldiers in the Tigers, and I was equally pleased with him. I am sure that there was a moment in my first hours with the Tiger Force when I said a private prayer of thanks for having found myself in such good company.

I would only find out later that it was Hackworth's personal involvement in the design and execution of the Tiger Force that caused it to have such capable leaders and such a terrific sense of purpose and mission.

During my first two days, Belden tried to explain the history and the lessons learned by the battalion in the months before I arrived. But each of his short stories was interrupted by a constant stream of questions from soldiers and subordinate leaders, demands from the company and battalion headquarters, and the routine demands of any day in Vietnam.

He told me the straight scoop on things like what I needed and what I wouldn't need to worry about in Vietnam. He was most concerned that I get the proper equipment. Regular fatigues and Corcoran[45] jump boots were just going to be worthless to me, so he scrounged a set of Jim Gardner's jungle fatigues for me to wear and a mismatched set of used jungle boots to hold me over until I could find my own stuff in the supply system.

In addition to finding jungle fatigues to wear in the base camp, I would have to draw the tiger-striped fatigues that we wore on operations. They were heavier than jungle fatigues, hot, slow to dry, and poorly cut for Americans, but they were what set the Tigers off—the tigers stripes and floppy tiger-striped hats.

I sat on my folding canvas cot cutting the cloth Combat Infantryman's Badge off of Jim's shirt. I was not authorized to wear one yet, and we took the wearing of unauthorized awards very seriously. I wondered how long it would take for me to earn one and how I would

---

[45] The name of the bootmaking company that manufactured the sturdy paratrooper boots favored by all soldiers, Airborne and non-Airborne alike.

hold up under the reality of close combat. As I sat there I felt a clock ticking and almost heard its pace pick up. The pressure was on and I was in the squeeze. The knots in my stomach were getting tighter than I had ever experienced before.

All I knew was that I wanted very badly to do a good job and not embarrass myself. I was surrounded by combat veterans who had come to Vietnam more experienced as airborne soldiers than I was on that day in Phan Rang.

My first lunch with the officers in the battalion was a real eye-opener for me. We had only one mess tent for all the thirty-six officers assigned and about half of them were in the base camp that day. It was my first introduction to the brotherhood of West Pointers.

Over the course of my three and a half years in the army I had been nowhere where West Pointers congregated. Basic training posts, signal battalions, and maintenance battalions were hardly the plum assignments given to the cream of the officer corps. West Pointers and distinguished graduates of ROTC got the good jobs, and the good jobs were in the Airborne divisions.

I had met West Pointers, had heard about them, and I had even wanted to be one. But I had never served with one. They were a complete surprise to me. Their distinctive brotherhood was evident even when you couldn't spot their class rings.

Every single officer in that battalion outranked me and most of the West Point lieutenants were classmates. The captains all seemed to share the same years at the military academy, even though they might have been members of four different graduating classes. They even spoke their own language that evolved in their years together.

Several of them finished four years at West Point, went to Airborne and Ranger schools together and joined the 101st at Fort Campbell as second lieutenants. The best I could say about our relationship in those first days was that I was clearly an outsider.

To top it off, I was given a job that almost every lieutenant in the battalion wanted—the Tiger Force. What I didn't know when I entered the mess hall was that Jim Gardner had been selected for promotion to captain. And, as a captain, he couldn't stay with a platoon. So Hackworth had decided to move him to a captain's job sometime in the not too distant future.

The news of my arrival and my assignment preceded me into the mess tent. I am sure that I was a great disappointment for those who bothered to be jealous of me. Still, I was welcomed roundly by all and made to feel like they really wanted me there. I was too young, naive, and uneducated to know that there were officers in that group who were thinking about how being assigned to the Tiger Force could make a significant difference in their career. I was focused on much more immediate goals—like adapting to the heat and getting over the case of the runs I had picked up in Camp Alpha. I just wasn't conscious of career planning or what is known as *ticket punching*. One thing was sure—being assigned to the Tiger Force would forever change my future in the army.

I had so much to learn about so many things that my head was filled with the issues that were most immediate to my survival and to doing my job. So I tried to shut up and listen to the war stories that flew across the plywood sheet that served as our mess table.

The food was awful. The heat was unbearable and my diarrhea would not be ignored. A couple of times during the lunch I had to excuse myself and head for the three-hole latrine that had been constructed near the mess tent.

I tried so hard to achieve a Zen-like, stoic control over my feelings and my condition, but Bill Pfeiffer would have been disappointed in my lack of success. I just felt awful and was completely paralyzed at the thought that someone would take my weakness as an indication of my lack of potential to lead men in combat. As I sat on that wooden crapper I couldn't even imagine leading anyone to do anything.

Over the months that followed I would rid myself of the gross generality that *all* West Pointers were somehow motivated by selfishness and personal gain. There were enough examples to convince me that there was some merit to the notion, but a West Point ring didn't automatically mean that I was dealing with a careerist who would step on my face to get a leg up. And during the course of combat I would learn which ones I could count on. There was no such thing as a stereotypical West Pointer any more than there was a stereotype for OCS grads or ROTC grads. We all had tough jobs to do, and each of us had to prove our own mettle when the tests of the battlefield came and found us.

But that first lunch made me aware of the clique that had formed during their years together at a tough academy, and the months of reinforcement that had taken place in battles.

The boys from the Hudson River were not the only officers in the battalion. There was also a smattering of ROTC and a couple of OCS grads. But the leadership was West Point trained—except for David Hackworth. He had earned his commission on a battlefield in Korea, and I always felt a very slight trace of friction between him and the West Pointers around him.

For me, I had no local chapter of a club to check into. Even the other OCS grads were not my classmates so the only thing we had in common was source of commission. I probably would have been well advised to pay a bit more attention to some steps that would have been career enhancing in my relationship with the other officers in the battalion. But I wasn't as worried about where I was going as I was about what I was going to do—right then.

I still had to break in as a platoon leader. As I left that mess tent I didn't know that my baptism of fire was only hours away.

By mid-afternoon I was called to the battalion tactical operations center (TOC) to see Hackworth again. I wasn't sure what it was about and had no idea that I would be getting combat missions directly, instead of through my boss, Jim Gardner. But Gardner was out on an ambush with half the Tigers and I was the next ranking officer. Neither did I expect to get missions from the battalion executive officer.

Hack had a way of doing things that was anything but by the book. There was the army way and there was Hack's way. In the 1/327 you were better off adjusting to the way Steel Five did business and not bothering to remind him that he was a bit out of line with the SOP in other infantry battalions.

I quickly found out that Hack and Lieutenant Colonel Rogers had worked out a good-cop bad-cop routine and Hack was the hammer. He was tough but fair, but he had absolutely no tolerance when it came to leaders who did not do their jobs or know the basics of soldiering.

While field phones rang and tactical radios hissed and crackled, Hack spread out a map on a field table and gave me an order. It was the moment I had spent so many months waiting for: my first combat mission.

Instead of getting it from a captain or a lieutenant, I was getting an order from the most combat-experienced man in the entire brigade. Though he never wore a combat badge or ribbon or medal, he had been anointed with gun oil and baptized by fire long before I had entered the second grade.

I was aware of all that and my ballpoint pen didn't work. Hack just went on describing the mission while Master Sergeant Hawk slipped me a fresh GI pen. I scribbled the details furiously in my notebook as

Hack pointed out the two important coordinates on the map: where we were and where I was going.

There was a report of a Viet Cong unit operating near a coastal village south of Phan Rang. The plan was to send a rifle company down there to cordon off the village and search it for VC.[46] But Hack had a sense for bad guys and never focused on the actual enemy target. Instead, the Tigers were to send a patrol to a likely route into the village, set up an ambush, and wait.

Now, I had hoped that my first mission could have been an easy area recon or a small ambush patrol—to get my feet wet. Getting my feet wet had a completely new meaning to me when Hack explained that the mission was to infiltrate enemy territory by water, at night—a night, amphibious ambush patrol with the South Vietnamese Navy. In the order of complexities on a battlefield, an amphibious operation is the only thing more difficult to pull off than a retrograde movement while in contact with an enemy force. The amphibious operation is so peculiarly difficult that it is the major reason behind a separate Marine Corps to train, organize, and equip itself to conduct them.

And I was to take a fifteen-man patrol to an allied base, link up with a naval detachment that spoke a different language, take a boat out to sea, turn south for several miles, then turn inland to make a clandestine amphibious landing; infiltrate the enemy area, set up an ambush, execute the ambush against enemy forces (attempting to capture prisoners if I could), and finally get out of the enemy area and back to the base camp.

I did all I could to hide the panic that was starting in my unstable intestinal tract and working its way to my vital signs. To me, the scope and complexity of the operation were overwhelming. Still, I swallowed hard, and true to Bill Pfeiffer, said, "Yessir. Will do."

Before I got out of the tent Hack stopped me. I turned to see if I had missed some detail and found him relighting a cigar stub. He blew the smoke up and dropped his lighter onto his patrolling cap, which was on the corner of the field table. "Belden's in charge," he said.

I must have questioned his statement with a puzzled look because he went on. "I've known Phil Belden for a long time. He's as good as they come. He'll lead the patrol and you'll go along and try not to get yourself killed."

The statement flooded me with even more confusing emotions. Was

---

[46] The Viet Cong (VC) was the military arm of the National Front for the Liberation of South Vietnam (NLFSVN or NLF). "Viet Cong" was actually a contraction of *Viet Nam Cong San*, which the Communists considered insulting.

he telling me that he didn't think I could do it? How was I to accept being just a patrol member? Was I relieved of all the responsibilities of leading?

He filled in the blanks. "You get on down there and get that patrol ready to go. But you do it Belden's way. He's in charge until he tells me that he thinks that you can handle it. When Belden tells me you're okay, that's when you take over that platoon. Until then, you listen to Belden."

The walk back to the Tiger Force area still stands out in my memory. I tried not to be angry about being benched and not to be pleased that the weight of the complicated mission had been somewhat lifted off of my shoulders. I would have to develop a relationship with Belden that would make him my superior without making me feel foolish. My ego was bruised and my stomach was revolting over the bacterial and emotional beating it was taking.

But Phil Belden was as gracious in his accepting the unusual command relationship as he had been in everything else he had done. He put me in the middle of every step that happened from that moment forward. *We* selected the patrol members, and *we* prepared the patrol order and *we* inspected equipment.

When it came time for the patrol order to be issued, I did it. But I included my role as understudy as I explained the chain of command in the order. To my surprise there were no negative responses from the troops. Instead, they seemed to be pleased that their new platoon leader wasn't going to wade in and learn his job at their expense.

Breaking in a platoon leader that way is not the army way and would not be the school solution at the Fort Benning infantry school's leadership department, but it worked perfectly for David Hackworth, Dennis Foley, Phil Belden, and thirteen other Tigers.

I didn't find out until later that Hack had used the same technique several times. And I would see him do it many more times before our days on the battlefield together were over.

The mission allowed only an afternoon and an evening of preparation before we were to depart for the Vietnamese Naval base near Phan Rang. While the Tigers were not well oiled as a team yet, they were experienced in preparation for operations. Everyone quickly kicked into high gear and the weapons, equipment, ammunition, and supplies suddenly appeared in the platoon area in near combat-ready condition. The packing, testing, cleaning, and inspecting went off like clockwork. There was no need for anyone to prod the troops to do something or to do something better. They were motivated and they had been trained well. Whatever was missing when they had left Fort Campbell was quickly being improvised and adapted with each new day in Vietnam.

I was impressed with them and intimidated by them all at the same time. They made me that much more aware of how much I had to learn to make myself qualified to lead them and make the important decisions that would make the difference between life and death for all of us.

We finished rehearsing the few things we could and inspecting the last few items that were packed for sea duty, and called it a night.

The tent that Jim and I shared was very empty and very lonely that night. My mind raced over the list of details that I was sure needed to be checked and rechecked. With my notebook in one hand and my map spread out on the wood-pallet floor of the tent, I traced the land and sea route under the yellow light of a Coleman lantern. The light made it hard to distinguish map symbols and colors, and the mosquitos made it nearly impossible to concentrate. And my gut was beginning to feel like raw hamburger.

I made trip after trip to the latrine, hoping that I wouldn't run into any of the troops because I was worried they would think that my gastrointestinal distress had been brought on by stone cold fear. They probably wouldn't have been far off. To say that I was anxious about the upcoming patrol would be a gross understatement.

After still another trip to the latrine, I went over my notes one more time. Things that had been beaten into my head at Bad Tolz and Fort Benning began leaping out from the mental training files in my head into my cluttered consciousness and onto my notebook pages. The value of the army's boring but effective repetitive training was becoming more clear to me. The lists of things to do, the mnemonics that we had memorized and the keywords that sparked vital items volunteered themselves in my moment of need. Suddenly, I had an even longer list of things than I ever thought needed to be checked or rechecked. The thought that any of the things on that list might not be ready or that I might have forgotten something worried me greatly.

As I was trying to decide what to do about it I heard a voice outside my tent. "Sir? You still up?"

It was Belden. He had been up to operations for a last check on some of the details. He was considerate enough to let me know what he had found out. I had forgotten to get the challenge and password for the day. He hadn't. He also made a last-minute weather check, and a double check on the availability of the drivers and the truck to take us to the naval base. And he made sure that battalion operations and the liaison officers had copies of our patrol overlay. He wanted to make sure that no one who should know we were out there was missed.

He was still reeling off the last-minute things he had checked and updated as I invited him into the tent and into the light.

After he finished briefing me on the changes and the status of all that he had checked, I asked him about my list. Just about everything on it he had taken care of. Still, there were a few things that I was worried about that he had not considered important. But rather than telling me I was full of crap, he looked at his watch and reminded me that it was late and we could do what was still on my list in the morning. He thought that it was more important for the troops to get some rest than for me to be satisfied that everything was done that night.

He was right. He was trained. And I was sure glad to have Phil Belden. He passed a few pleasantries and then left my tent. It got very quiet again and very lonely. That was the last night I would spend alone before a mission.

Between trips to the latrine and my brain racing, I got almost no sleep. I was up long before dawn and found my way over to the mess tent to scrounge some coffee. In the back of the tent a young black soldier known as Lucky was preparing for the morning meal.

He had his shirt off and there were several very ugly scars that broke up the strong musculature of his twenty-year old body. He had been a rifleman and had been one of the very first ones wounded in combat when the battalion arrived in-country. On his return from the hospital he was given the job in the mess hall.

In the corner of the kitchen area he had a tiny, battery-operated record player setup playing Ramsey Lewis' "Wade in the Water." It was so incongruous with the sounds of the choppers in the distance and the H & I[47] fires. I made many more trips to his mess hall before my tour was up, and I found out the music was right for Lucky and it became right for us.

He was a quiet and very pleasant soldier who always had a nice word to say and a great smile. But more than that, there was a peace-

---

[47] Harassing and interdicting, random artillery fires delivered to preselected targets to disrupt enemy activity.

fulness about him that was somehow mixed up with his brush with death and his passion for jazz. As I got to know him better I discovered that he loved each day and nothing seemed to rattle him.

But that morning the coffee did absolutely no good for me. My stomach problems were worse than before, and I was very concerned that to say something about it might be taken as a weakness on my part. It was at that moment that I was very sorry to remember what Bill Pfeiffer had pounded into us about command presence. There is no command presence in a man who is about to soil himself with uncontrollable diarrhea. But with Pfeiffer effort counted for a lot. So, I just loaded up on GI toilet paper, kept my mouth shut and tried to walk like I didn't have any problems.

CHAPTER 13

Sergeant Lawrence Smith, formerly the reconnaissance platoon sergeant, had made arrangements for gun jeeps with pedestal-mounted M-60s[48] on them to act as convoy escort. But our convoy would only consist of our two-and-a-half ton truck and the two jeeps.

Belden assembled the fifteen of us for a final inspection in the dusty street outside the Tiger Force area. I was amazed at the size of the loads that the troops had rigged for themselves. They each had either dropped their canvas rucksacks on the ground until we loaded up or stood bent over at the waist to compensate for the weight.

Belden and Smith went through every man's load inspecting equipment, weapons, and ammunition. As they did, they asked question after question about who was carrying extra ammo for which weapons, what the radio frequencies were, the call signs, passwords, rules of engagement, and the whereabouts of dog tags, malaria pills, and cleaning rods.

As I stood in line to wait my turn I was impressed by the number of things that Smith and Belden were checking that I hadn't thought of myself. I tried to burn the items into my head so that *I* would not forget them when it became my turn to ask the questions.

By the time they got to me I was sure that I would be asked something that I could not possibly remember, and that every man in the Tiger Force would be sure that I was the wrong man for the job. There was no way out of it. I had to stand inspection like everyone else and I had to measure up.

* * *

---

[48] The standard general-purpose light machine gun. It can fire 600 rounds of disintegrating-belt-fed 7.62mm ammo per minute with a muzzle velocity of 2,800 feet per second (the M1911A1 .45 caliber pistol fires ammo with a muzzle velocity of around 850 feet per second). The M-60 has an 1,100-meter effective range and a 3,700-meter maximum range and weighs 23 pounds without a tripod.

Smith grabbed my M-16[49] and Belden handed me a copy of the signal operating instructions (SOI).[50] Smith didn't as much ask me questions as he asked me if I knew where and how to find frequencies and call signs in the SOI. Instead of testing me he was coordinating with me. Smith asked me if I had enough ammo and enough magazines and if I had been shown where the water trailer was, and if I had enough Halazone water purification tablets.

When I think back on how tough those two NCOs could have made my life I am sorry that I never had the time to really thank them for the way they handled me and broke me in. I had landed in the best infantry job in Vietnam and I didn't know it yet.

Loading into the truck reminded me that we were actually going out into bad-guy territory. The floorboard and the truckbed were lined with filled sandbags to reduce the blast of mines. I made some remark about it and Belden pointed across the motor park. There was a Tiger Force jeep with almost the entire front end missing. It had been hit by a command-detonated[51] mine on a convoy a few weeks earlier. The driver and crew of the gun jeep were casualties and the jeep was salvaged for the few usable spare parts that were left of it.

We were outside of the battalion area and through the wire, onto the narrow highway and in VC territory in a few minutes. My condition didn't need the extra bowel tightening that this awareness brought on.

As we rolled down the road, loaded weapons pointing out at the scrubby vegetation, I tried to organize my thoughts around the scope of our mission. We were to find a suspected VC battalion headquarters somewhere south of Phan Rang and a few miles in from the coast of the South China Sea. The chances of sneaking up the road were remote since the vegetation was so sparse we would be detected moving from miles off. The amphibious landing at night would give us the concealment of darkness and the reduced chance of being detected. At least that was the theory.

As someone once said, all operations plans are for flat terrain on

---

[49] The M-16A1 automatic rifle that replaced the M-14. The M-16 can fire 650-800 rounds of 5.56mm (.223 caliber) ammo per minute with a muzzle velocity of 3,250 feet per second to an effective range of 460 meters. The M-16 is fed by a 20-30 round detachable box magazine.

[50] The radio codes and frequencies that are used by units in the field and changed frequently to prevent enemy eavesdropping.

[51] A mine that is set off by an observer operating a detonating device, as opposed to mines that are exploded by the victim.

sunny days. Everything else is a field expedient adaptation to the plan. The sun and the flat didn't last very long for us.

The trip was long and tense. We had to assume that everyone we saw along the roadways could be VC, or passing the word to the VC that we were on our way. I looked at each of the Vietnamese civilians walking along the roadsides. It was then that I discovered what every other soldier, sailor, airman, and Marine in Vietnam already knew: you couldn't tell who the good guys were by looking at them.

At least in my father's and my grandfather's wars they could tell who was the enemy by the way they looked and how they dressed. No such luck for us.

We arrived at the naval base and found it to be not much more than a couple of shacks next to a dock that allowed small craft to be tied up out of the damaging surf. The Vietnamese sailors all looked like little boys in two kinds of uniform: one American-size and too large for them, the other the same uniform taken in by a tailor and made skintight. Both looked ridiculous. The fact that they looked silly wasn't nearly as disturbing as their complete lack of concern for our arrival, mission, or our operational needs.

There were a couple of American advisors at the port but they were not much help either. They didn't speak the language well enough to translate and they didn't know much about our operation. And to top it off, they left right after we arrived, and we were on our own.

We were supposed to meet up with a Vietnamese Army interpreter to help us with the language difficulties with the Vietnamese Navy. But he never showed up. So there we were, embarking on the most difficult of patrols; we didn't have a clue who was taking us to sea, if they knew where we were going, if they had the boats ready, or even if they had any competent sailors to get us there.

Belden and I spoke with a little sailor who seemed to be in charge. He kept gesturing and taking stabs at English, trying to tell us not to worry, that everything would be all right.

Aside from the fact that we were unable to communicate with the Vietnamese Navy, there seemed to be a lack of water craft of any type —just a couple of woven bamboo skiffs that looked like wide canoes and a very weathered, motorized sampan. It was no more than thirty feet long with a little house built on its flat deck that held an engine of suspicious origin. It looked like it had once been in a jeep or a generator. Somehow, they had adapted it to the fishing boat and had built a crude box to protect it.

It had seen plenty of sea days and from the looks of the well-worn tiller connected to the rudder, had seen its share of captains too. It was quaint, but not something we could use.

We asked about the captain and about our boat and were told to wait.

The sun beat down and we soon realized that we were not going anywhere for a while. Belden thought we ought to take the time to get something to eat and to see if we could scrounge some drinking water to conserve what was in our canteens before we boarded the boat.

Then we got some more bad news. There was no drinking water to be had. The Vietnamese sailors had a few soft drinks and the local vendors who clustered around the little base had plenty of beer. So we settled for beer, thinking as long as we didn't have too many we could stave off thirst without cutting into our water supply.

Bier LaRue[52] is a particularly unpleasant brew in the first place, but drinking it warm and in the hot sun and on a stomach that had not yet acclimated to living in Vietnam was less than a wonderful experience. I was as thirsty or even thirstier than the rest, and they were not concerned about downing a few Vietnamese beers. So I went along and threw out my instinctive notion that it was somehow a cardinal sin to drink during duty hours.

The afternoon dragged on, the navy boys lounged around and giggled like children, and we kept quenching our thirst with warm Bier LaRue. By late afternoon nothing had changed except our stamina. We were baked in the midday sun and tired of waiting for the navy to do something and had taken on a little buzz from the beer.

Finally, around dusk, a sailor appeared who was in a big hurry to do something. He kept pointing at the motorized fishing boat and back at us. Eventually we were alarmed to find out that he wanted us to board it and head out.

That fishing relic was our amphibious infiltration vehicle. There was no other boat coming. There never had been. We had just assumed that we were waiting for one when what the Vietnamese had in mind all along was the fraternal twin to the *African Queen*.

Just moments before we shoved off, four Vietnamese sailors jumped on board and began to ready the boat to get underway. During the day not one sailor had boarded it, checked on the engine, the crankcase, the bilge, fuel, navigation lights, or safety equipment. It just

---

[52] Brewed in Saigon by the French-owned Brasseries et Glacieres de l'Indochine (BGI), the label showed the silhouette of a tiger.

sat there until the appointed hour and then was somehow magically ready to go.

Unfortunately, the boat was enough unlike the *African Queen* to cause many problems for us. First, we had to get on it and not in it. Fifteen of us and our equipment took up quite a bit of space and the sailors were picky about where we went. We were required to spread ourselves out in small deck areas at the bow and in the stern and along a narrow walkway on either side of what could laughingly be called the engine house.

We thought we could figure this out by ourselves. But the Vietnamese told us with wild hand gestures and plenty of squawking that we'd be in the way or we couldn't sit here or there or damn near anywhere on the deck without being in the way. Eventually we found places that didn't upset the sailors.

As the sailors rushed about, all aflutter over the mission at hand, we tried to figure out how we were going to get from the deck of the thirty-footer to the beach near our patrol's intermediate objective. The draft of the boat surely was too deep for us to slip up to the beach and just offload as we might with rubber assault boats.

But Belden came through. Somehow, he was able to divine from all the excited talk and gestures and hand waving what the Vietnamese were going to do. Their idea was to take us to a point just outside the breakers and offload us over the side—into the bamboo boats. We would then quietly paddle ashore and slip across the beach and into the skimpy tree line.

There were enough Rangers in the patrol to rise to the challenge and we all nodded that we understood. The sailors then tied the smaller boats to a line and got ready to get underway.

One of the crewmen wrapped a rope around the flywheel pulley on the engine and gave it a yank. The engine came to life on the first pull. That was the good news. The bad news was that it had no muffler, and the exhaust port was not much more than a manifold with a hole in it. The exhaust noise and sparks flew from the hole, out of the opening in the engine house, and filled the air with sparks and noise. We were sure that the sparks could be seen for miles in the clear night sky and that the noise would easily travel over a mile.

For some reason known only to the sailors, they had to keep revving the engine to keep it from dying. And each time they cranked up the RPM, the plume of sparks became a comet-like stream of bright red, yellow, and blue flames. And when the RPM dropped, the exhaust report sounded like a five-ton truck with no exhaust manifold.

We asked about the light and noise and only got giggles from the sailors who obviously had never heard a word about being clandestine. Finally we gave up, thinking that if we stayed out to sea far enough, the racket we made wouldn't be discovered. At least we could paddle ashore in the smaller boats and that would take care of giving away our position at sea.

Our trip out to sea was just awful. The boat bobbed and pitched in the surf, and we had little to hold on to. And as we floundered, the Vietnamese sailor on the throttle kept trying to rev the engine at the appropriate moment to overcome the powerful surf.

The helmsman was a man of no more than ninety pounds. As our tiny craft struggled to get to calm, open water, he tried to keep his footing on the deck. The leverage that the long tiller exerted on him was the amplified transfer of the water's fury on the rudder. A large wave would hit the boat, it would pitch up and come down sideways, and the next wave would hit the rudder broadside and almost take the helmsman off the deck.

As the struggle continued for the Vietnamese sailors I started to notice the effects of the surf on myself and the other Tigers. First one and then another Tiger moved to a point where he could vomit over the side. Seasickness is contagious and within half an hour just about everyone was throwing up. I'm sure this was aggravated by our hours in the sun and the bottles of Bier LaRue we drank.

So there we were, on our way to a very complicated operation— fifteen strong—and throwing up.

The trip became a bit more bearable once we got out of the rough water and turned south. I tried to figure out how far out to sea we were by using triangulation with my map and compass, but I couldn't get the deck to quit pitching long enough to get a compass heading on any of the landmarks I could pick out on the shoreline. Suffice it to say, we were at least a couple of miles off the beach and heading south —to our tiny beachhead.

I remember thinking how much more complicated and lethal the Normandy landing must have been twenty-one years earlier. But that fact didn't make me any more confident that we were going to arrive in one piece, or even find our landing point on that sandy beach.

No sooner had my seasickness started to settle down a bit than there was a commotion on the deck. Three of the Vietnamese sailors were all arguing and pointing out to sea. I couldn't see anything out there and began to wonder just what manner of threat there was—VC frogmen?

One of the sailors pulled out a navy light that had a strong beam. Before anyone could stop him, he pointed it out into the dark and turned it on.

There, in the yellow beam of the light, was something floating in the water—about twenty-five yards off the port side. I strained to see what it was. It looked like a tree or a plank or a board. It was the tiller from our trusty craft. One of the sailors had pulled the tiller out of the rudder and rested it on the roof of the engine house and it had fallen overboard.

Now we had no way of steering our boat and the sailors were arguing what to do about it. If there had been any doubt about our location, the light confirmed our exact position to anyone watching from the shore. Though I couldn't make out the shoreline in the dark from where we were, I was absolutely sure that our exact location and our intentions were now known by every local VC for twenty miles inland.

To me two terrible possibilities existed. Either we were desperately lost at sea and doomed to drown in the leaky *Asian Queen*, or we would somehow make it to shore only to be ambushed by the largest, most well-positioned VC force since the loss of the French Mobile 100 in the Mang Yang Pass.

After a considerable amount of silly bravado over who was going to jump into the black and briny ocean to risk his life to retrieve the tiller, one sailor stripped his shirt off, and after dumping his boondockers on the deck, dove in and swam out to the floating tiller while the other sailors cheered him on, whistling and screaming encouragement louder than the rat-tat-tatting exhaust noise.

I looked at Belden and we both knew we were certainly compromised. We knew that there was just no way we were going to teach the sailors anything about light and noise discipline with the time we had left together. The best we could do was lean over the side and help the scrawny little sailor lift the heavy, six-foot-long tiller back onto the deck.

Finally the sailors were able to get the boat back on course and find some magical spot in the ocean that told them to end the southbound leg and turn west—for the beach. It was time to steel ourselves for what might be a disastrous landing. All we could hope for was that the winds had been favorable to us, not allowing the sounds to travel all the way to shore. And that the marine layer was thick enough to hide the trail of engine sparks from anybody on shore.

As the sailors set our course for the beach, we went to the stern and pulled the lines to bring the two small boats alongside. During the last leg we would split the patrol up into two loads and paddle in quietly. At least that was the plan.

I was at the stern and could see both sides of the larger boat as the offloading progressed. A member of the patrol was lowering the base plate for a 60mm mortar over the side when the pitching of the boat caused him to lose his grip. The heavy metal base went through the bottom of the bamboo boat and it began taking on water at an alarming rate.

As I saw this, I looked over at the other boat just as someone stepped into it, an M-60 machine gun in hand. As he struggled for footing, the machine gun bipod ripped a hole in that boat, so that within thirty seconds we lost our landing craft. Both of them sank within another minute.

The loss of the landing craft started up the hysterical jabbering and arm waving among the Vietnamese crew. They were upset at the loss of the boats and arguing about what to do next. During all this the boat we were on was steadily putt-putt-putting toward the shore.

Someone in the navy contingent made a decision and tried to explain to us that they were going to risk crashing the boat on the beach and take us into shore on the *Asian Queen*.

By that time the water was getting rougher and the seasick-prone among us were starting to turn pale again. That included me. Between the dysentery and the seasickness I was sure that it made no difference, I would surely die on the beach from my compound ills. Anything that the VC could do would mercifully put me out of my misery.

The swells got bigger and the thin ribbon of white beach became more visible as we motored toward our landing. I tried to scan the shoreline with my binoculars but found the pitching made it difficult to focus on anything and the eyepieces were getting wet and salty as the spray from the surf blew up and over the bow.

I was somehow satisfied not to see any fires or lights on the beach. Even with the pitching I probably would have been able to see the streaks of light that would be painted in the binocular lenses. Thinking about it later, it wasn't the folks who might have fires or lamps on the beach that we were worried about. Why I didn't think that then had something to do with my vomiting over the side and trying to maintain some kind of decorum. I never appreciated how hard it was to look like an officer when you were expelling body fluids from both ends. It never came up in the *Officers' Guide* and Bill Pfeiffer never went into that much detail in his lectures on presence.

Just when we thought things couldn't get worse for our doomed patrol, the swells turned into waves that would make a surfer salivate. The boat rose and crashed at the passage of each successive wave as we got closer and closer to the beach.

Each of us grabbed for something to hold onto as we readied ourselves to reach the beach. The noise and flame from the engine exhaust was even louder than the crashing waves, and we were all sure that it carried to the tree line beyond the beach.

As we tried to convince the sailors to quit revving the engine one of them suddenly cut it completely. The engine sounds disappeared and the noise of the waves filled the air until suddenly a huge wave hit the flat, square stern of the boat and propelled it up and forward.

The *Asian Queen* traveled the last few yards until its bottom dug into the shallow beach just under the water line and brought it to an abrupt and jarring halt. Some of the Tigers on the bow immediately disappeared over the side and into the shallow surf; others lost their footing and slid forward to join the men overboard.

I slammed up against the engine house and lost contact with my rucksack, which was still a few feet away on the bow. I crawled back toward my gear and hooked my arm through one of the shoulder straps of my ruck. Just then I looked up at the moment the next large wave hit the stern of the boat. It was nearly six feet over the deck, a wall of rushing white water.

The impact of the wave catapulted the back end of the boat up and out of the water and then swept across the deck. The force of the wave hit each of us who were no longer in contact with the boat and swept us off the deck.

I felt myself flying through the air and at the very same moment became aware of the ultimate sin. I had lost my grip on my M-16 and it and I were flying separately toward the armpit-deep surf. My mind went into panic mode. There are few things less excusable than a lieutenant losing his rifle. And when the loss is not accompanied by enemy fire and massive combat confusion there is *no* excuse.

While I was falling toward the water I was conscious that my first patrol hadn't really started and I had already done something worthy of the worst fate. I could be relieved and sent to some paper-pushing job where I couldn't get into too much trouble. That would be followed by the possibility of a second such assignment, I would never make first lieutenant, and I would have several months' pay docked to pay for the lost weapon.

If I didn't feel bad enough, I was being beached like a whale, was as sick as I could ever remember being, and had lost my rifle while being swept off the deck of an amphibious landing craft.

Then the water came up to meet me as I landed not more than thirty feet from the beach. My rucksack was caught by yet another wave and I went where it went. As I felt myself being dragged across the bottom, toward the sand, I felt something fall into my open hand. It was my rifle! I had bumped back into my own rifle in an ocean that should have easily swallowed it up, never to be found. What luck. I could never be that lucky again. Never.

Water flooded my mouth and nose and I started gagging on the burning salt. My glasses disappeared somewhere and I felt myself rolling over from the backwash of an outgoing wave. I struggled to fight against it and continue moving toward the beach but did *not* let go of my grip on my rifle.

The waves finally gave me up to the sand and I found myself facing the stars, my rifle in my hand, coughing and gasping for air.

The others met with variations of the same landing. In seconds the waves had scattered a fifteen-man patrol along that line in the sand where the water becomes foaming bubbles for a moment at its highest point on the beach. I looked toward the boat and saw the crew trying to wrestle it back out to sea. Each time a wave came in it freed the boat's stern from the sand and one of the sailors revved the engine to try to move to deeper water, only to have the wave subside and leave them aground again. They kept trying, moving a few feet at a time, until finally they broke out into deeper water and regained control of the boat.

Belden didn't waste any time assembling the patrol and getting us off the beach. In our dark, wet camouflage uniforms we stood out clearly against the white sand that almost seemed to emanate its own light.

I stood up and water slopped out of my heavy cotton tiger fatigues and rushed past my boot tops. Everything I wore and carried was waterlogged and added plenty of extra weight to my load. I tried to run in a bent over crouch to the tree line where Belden was assembling the patrol. But the added weight and the loose sand made the effort difficult.

The feeling of weakness that I was experiencing from the diarrhea sapped my energy after only a few steps and made the effort almost impossible. How I thought I could ever make it over the miles that were ahead of us I don't know. I just dragged my butt over to Belden and collapsed in the sand. And we hadn't even started the patrol. We had only reached our dropoff point. Just the first leg—the easy leg— was over. Next we had to go find bad guys.

The few minutes of rest while Belden counted noses and inventoried equipment gave me a false sense of confidence that I might just be able to make it. In the end, it made no difference what I thought I could do. I was going with that patrol—no matter what. I would rather die of a coronary than admit to Belden or the other Tigers that I didn't think I could hack it.

Listening to the beach winds swishing through the grasses near the trees was different that night. Never before had I listened with the thought of death hanging over me. I knew that I needed to develop some field skills quickly to help me survive.

The break was over far too soon and we moved out into the night. Just inside the skimpy tree line that marked the limits of the beach, Belden set up a small perimeter while he quickly assessed the situation. We had taken some equipment losses in the crash landing but all the patrol members were accounted for. A major concern beyond wondering if we had been discovered was the condition of our ammunition and our radios.

Belden checked each man to make sure that we were still able to move on. He didn't want to spend anymore time at that rally point on the beach than he absolutely had to. He wanted to move out as soon as we could to get where we had more control over our own security and a better idea what was around us.

We huddled together and tried to cross-check the map and the terrain to see if there was any chance that we had actually landed anywhere near where we were supposed to be. But without landmarks to use or key terrain features, all we could be sure of was that we were somewhere on the coast of Vietnam. We weren't really sure that we were south of Phan Rang, although we were fairly confident that we had traveled south.

As we stepped off in patrol file formation toward our objective, I wondered what more could happen to our well-laid plan.

CHAPTER 14

•

The concealment that we had found near the beach was only a shallow ribbon of vegetation. As soon as we had moved less than a hundred meters inland, we came upon rolling sand dunes and washes carved by the monsoon rains on their way to the sea.

The visibility was good enough to require us to stretch out our file intervals, to get the distance between us that would provide a bit more protection should we get ambushed. The last thing any patrol wanted was to be ambushed. But if it did happen, one of the actions it could take was to spread out to avoid having the entire patrol trapped in the killing zone at one time. So the fifteen of us became such a long file that one end could not see the other end.

I suddenly had my first sensation of nakedness in enemy territory. Out on the boat there had been a false sense of security offered by the darkness and the distance from the shoreline. But as we moved through the uneven terrain it was clear that we could be taken under fire from any of the bumps, bushes, or trees in our field of view, not to mention the possibility of incoming mortar fire or mines or booby traps.

That knowledge immediately ran my vigilance factor up to a point where it put an unusual strain on my senses of hearing and sight. I tried to watch everything and hear as much as I could, but both senses were limited. Vision was only good for several hundred meters due to the darkness and the marine layer that painted a light gray wash over the ground around us. And distinguishing features was made harder by the extreme contrast between the bright white sand and the blackness of the night.

Hearing was made more difficult by the prevailing offshore wind that blew against our backs making it hard for sound to travel toward us. The wind also made noise as it passed us. I even had to carry my rifle at an awkward angle to keep the wind from whistling as it blew across the several holes in the front handguard.

And the sounds of my boots against the sand and the corduroy swishing sounds of the wet trouser legs of my tiger fatigues created their own interference with hearing of the night sounds.

I was getting more and more convinced that there was little use for the wearing of the tiger-striped fatigues as the night wind began to dry them out and the evaporation caused the uniform not only to be wet and uncomfortable but cold and uncomfortable.

We stopped frequently to check our location on the map. It was difficult in the night and using a 1:50,000[53] map to tell where we were. It took over an hour to pass enough terrain features to confirm our locations.

The amazing thing was that we were not that far off our intended landing site, and had to make only slight adjustments to our direction of march to get on our patrol route.

Even though they weren't made for my benefit, I appreciated the frequent halts. I was extremely fatigued and in bad need of a latrine. But there was no latrine and I wasn't going to stop a combat patrol to relieve myself. I gritted my teeth and tried to replace my fluid losses with canteen water.

After the better part of an hour, I got clammier and weaker. My mind was not able to reconcile the heat of that afternoon at the naval base with the cold night air I was experiencing. I just kept walking across the uneven sand until it suddenly became dirt—real ground. We were no longer near the beach. We had traveled a few thousand meters inland to what looked like abandoned rice paddies. That meant flat and low land. In that part of Vietnam there were rarely any terraced rice paddies. Thus, we were walking in the lowest terrain around. Not good and not comfortable. But the nearest high ground wasn't anywhere near the route of march to our objective, so we had to avoid risk by moving quickly in the darkness.

We moved as quietly as we could and hoped to cover as much open ground as we could without being detected by the VC units we had been told were in the area. It would be an understatement to say that for a newly assigned platoon leader the situation was tense.

We kept moving for a few hours until the terrain suddenly changed from wide-open, flat fields to somewhat more hilly terrain. Belden stopped us again and made still another map check. From our terrain

---

[53] That is, one unit of measure on the map equals 50,000 units of the same measure on the ground. This is known as the scale. 1:50,000 is the standard scale for U.S. Army tactical maps.

association and our pace count from the beach it appeared that we were approaching the hill selected as our observation point.

During the mission planning, battalion had decided to place us on a high point overlooking the approaches to a village that was reported to harbor VC at night. Since the operation would include using a rifle company to cordon and sweep through the village for any signs of those VC, we were set in place to be able to interdict any who might escape the cordon.

Belden reorganized us to send an advance party to the base of the hill to make sure that we weren't walking into a trap. It would have been very easy for an enemy force occupying the hill to take us under plunging fire and obliterate us if we failed to discover that they were there. Walking right up to the hill would have been very foolish.

The recon party left two thirds of the patrol behind and moved off toward the hill. In the dark it didn't look as steep as we would find it to be.

As we waited behind in a small perimeter of ten men, we began seeing lights or small fires, a long distance from us but in the direction of the village we were concerned with.

We made radio contact with the rifle company setting up the cordon. They were on the far side of the lights and could see them too. There was no doubt about it. We were not alone out there. And it was sure that not everyone out there with us had our best interests at heart.

Reaching the hill and seeing the lights seemed to give me a faint second wind. Partly that was due to the feeling of getting somewhere, and the rest was the relief of confirmation that there were other Americans out in that dark night. I was able to muster up enough adrenaline to fuel the final few hundred meters of our movement to the hill. I didn't have any idea how much was going to be needed to get me up that hill. But at that point I didn't anticipate it to be much of a climb. So while we waited for the recon party to return, I tried to take stock of myself. I wasn't very happy with my performance, and was even more concerned that the others in the patrol would think that I just wasn't up to the job. As crappy as I felt, I just knew that if I could ever get acclimatized to the weather and over the runs that I could cut it.

Still, in the hours we had been at sea and walking to our observation post (OP), I had been without sleep, dehydrated by diarrhea, half buzzed by the Vietnamese beer, seasick, washed overboard, drained of my remaining energy, chilled to the bone by the cold, and exhausted by the march. I didn't think I had any reserve left, but I wasn't given any option when Belden tapped me on the shoulder and said, "We're moving, Lieutenant."

We approached the black hill with a great deal of anxiety. It loomed up over us—almost straight up. On the map it was something over three hundred feet above sea level. We had been only a few inches above sea level during our entire trek from the coast.

It was fairly heavily covered with a variety of trees and shrubs, with a few rock outcroppings on its steep slopes.

Contour lines are a mapmaker's way of telling you what the terrain looks like from above. The more distance between contour lines, the gentler the slope. The closer together, the steeper the slope. That hill's contour lines were almost touching on the side we had to climb. Touching contour lines and easy climbs are not ever mentioned in the same sentence.

We threaded our way through the scrub brush at the base of the hill and soon found a wall that we had to climb to get to our OP.

The transition from forward to upward movement was not an easy one. Our equipment got fouled in the brush, and the footing was difficult as we tried to climb with our heavy loads. Within a few yards of starting up, the climb became nearly vertical. We were crawling, chest to the earth, straight up. Looking up was impossible because of the falling gravel, dirt, and debris dislodged by the patrol members ahead of us. Roots helped for some but gave way for others. Every few yards someone would slip and fall back onto other Tigers behind him. The recovery of fallen Tigers and the retrieval of equipment that invariably fell free and slid down the hill slowed our progress.

Each time someone would fall or slide back down the hill the noise of the event seemed to be so loud that anyone nearby was certain to hear us.

As I crawled, hand over hand, that reserve energy I had thought I had mustered quickly ran out. It was harder than any obstacle course I had ever run in OCS or the Airborne school. The effort was totally draining, and I was afraid that if I lost my grip or footing and fell backwards that I would be unable to recover and catch back up. So I held on as tightly as I could and took advantage of every little pause in our progress to catch my breath. Somewhere on the side of that hill I promised myself that I had smoked my last cigarette and would give up the habit that night. I broke that promise at first light. So much for self-discipline. The irony was that this was just a week before the surgeon general's warning was put on cigarette packages.

And God, we were a long way from home that night.

The climb took its toll on all of us. A few sustained minor injuries from falls, and some were injured trying to break the falls of others. Equipment was broken and lost and we fell well behind schedule making it to our OP.

Finally, after what seemed like hours of climbing, slipping and climbing, Belden held up the patrol. He didn't want to take the entire patrol into what might be a VC defensive position so he took a small recon element forward first. I had planned on holding on to the side of the hill while he went forward with a radio operator and a couple of riflemen, until I found out that I would be one of those riflemen.

Belden sent the word back down the file for me to *come forward*. Those words always upped the heart rate of any soldier on any combat patrol.

Going forward on a recon is always spooky. You know that you are part of a smaller element than the one you just left. You know that you are entering an area that if you thought it was worth occupying, someone else might have thought so too. And you know that the position was selected for its defensive potential. The process is usually accompanied by lots of breath holding and hypervigilance. So you move slowly and as quietly as you can, all the while getting closer to what may be a meeting engagement that finds you on the move and them ready for you.

We found a small pocket on the side of the hill that might have been a saddle if it had been a bit larger. But whatever it would be called in cartographic terminology, at that moment it was unoccupied and free of mines and booby traps. The only thing we didn't know was whether or not it was under enemy observation. We easily could have been sucked into occupying that spot on the military crest of the hill only to find it registered[54] by enemy mortarmen and likely to be obliterated.

Belden was skilled at patrolling. He checked out the position for how he wanted to organize the patrol, made some mental notes, and then walked to the edge and looked out over the rocks at the valley floor below us.

I stood next to him trying to figure out what he was looking for. The

---

[54] That is, previously ranged by enemy mortarmen to determine accurate firing data for subsequent bombardment of that spot.

flatland below spread out to the sea. I could see from that vantage point the route we had taken and was impressed by our success, but I would have bet it was two or three times farther than it actually was. I was letting my fatigue and not my military training make judgments. It was something I had to work on before I started making decisions, or there would be expensive consequences.

Belden was satisfied with the position and motioned for us to go back and pick up the patrol and guide it forward. He left two members of the recon party in place to hold what we had cleared and make sure it stayed that way.

I watched Belden and the other young NCOs move everyone into his respective position with almost no confusion. Belden was unflappable and had learned how to communicate without talking in his years of Airborne operations. I would find, over the years ahead, that the best communicators were Ranger school grads and master parachutists because they had mastered the technique of getting a man's attention in a tense moment and clearly transmitting to him what they wanted done.

Belden was good—patient, and he gave clear instructions. It took less than ten minutes to feed each man off the side of the hill into his position, where he would stay for the rest of the night.

I realized how important Belden's vision of the layout was. If he hadn't known where he wanted his people before we got to the small position, moving them around afterward would have been dangerous and confusing. That night the reality and the importance of small-unit planning ceased to be a training exercise for me. We were living it and poor planning could result in unnecessary noise and confusion that could get someone dead—fast.

Within an hour after we closed on the position Belden had tied everyone in, assigned sectors of responsibility, identified a rally point if we were run out of our position, checked us for personal injuries and our equipment for losses and damage, and made sure everyone had eaten. I was impressed.

I know now that the Tigers were *not* well trained as a unit. They had only been assembled just before that patrol. And while they had almost six months of field experience in rifle companies, the antitank or recon platoons, they were not yet trained as a team. I wasn't aware of their limited experience in patrolling and independent operations, but from *my* inexperienced perspective, Belden made it look easy.

I could not have appreciated the stop more. I had just about run out of strength from the diarrhea and the seasickness. I might have thought that I was in shape when I had left the United States, and might have been a little cocky about being twenty-one, but I was completely wrong. I was whipped and on the edge of holding up the patrol's progress when we finally closed the observation post.

Belden organized us to sleep in shifts and I drew a number to be one of the first to get some rest. I realize now that he planned it that way.

We were almost straight above a grassy path between us and a stand of trees that was about four hundred meters from the base of the hill. The path ran across our front at almost 120 feet below. Anyone wanting to get through below would be smart to use the trees to conceal his movement for as long as possible. But there was a point where the trees ran out, and then any movement would be exposed to observation.

That night the patch of trees looked like a black splotch of vegetation and there was no way to tell how thick it was. So while we didn't see any activity in the trees—no lights or sounds—that didn't mean there wasn't someone in there.

Belden didn't eat. Instead, he came over to where I was and explained that he had checked in with battalion by radio and made sure that we had commo. They knew that we were in position and were clear to fire any artillery or mortars into the valley below. He had also asked Sergeant Newton, our artillery forward observer, to make commo with his battery to be sure that we could call for fires from them if we needed to.

He continued to explain how and what he had done to establish our own local security and a plan for escape from the position if it came to that.

In his own special way, Phil Belden was telling me that if I disagreed with any of his decisions, it was okay for me to say so. Not many men would be as generous when put in charge of such a complicated patrol.

The night chill touched each of us after we had stopped climbing. The sweat we had generated in the climb up the hill, the remaining moisture from our perpetually wet tiger fatigues, and the damp ground resulted in a bone-chilling loss of body heat for each of us. I had just not anticipated how cold Vietnam could be. That night was cold enough, but it was nothing compared to the months of night operations we had ahead of us in the Central Highlands.

I caught a quick catnap only to awake shivering with cold. I couldn't stop the shivering and had to roll up into a tight ball to conserve my body heat. As I lay there I looked at my watch. It was just after three A.M. but it seemed we had been there for hours. Night patrols and ambushes made the clocks stop.

The others seemed to have come to grips with the problem. Those that were supposed to be awake were—and paying attention to their respective sectors. They made no noise and seemed to be aware of their responsibilities to the others. The others slept soundly. There was nothing different about Vietnam when it came to a soldier's capacity for getting sleep. It always amazed me that no matter how dangerous the situation, men could still sleep when time permitted.

But all were ready if we were probed or mortared.

I tried to get some more sleep, but within a few minutes I was tapped to take over while someone else slept.

My first dawn on my first combat patrol was uneventful, but still unforgettable. The sun came up and painted the blackened valley below with a bright beachlike glow. I was surprised to find how normal the terrain looked, and how easy the climb we had made looked in the daylight.

The trees across the grassy field at the base of our hill were not as threatening as they seemed at night. Our view of the surrounding area was excellent. Belden had picked a perfect observation point. If it was out there, we could probably see it and identify its grid coordinates from our shady perch on the hill.

We expected to have a full day if the assumptions at battalion and brigade were correct. They were betting that the rifle company could catch some of the VC who were reported to be in the village. And should any VC units be moved in to reinforce their comrades in the village at the expense of our rifle company, we were there to spot them and stop them. On the other hand, if the rifle company was unable to tighten the noose around the village and some of the VC were able to escape, we were there to catch them.

We waited for some time to hear of the progress of the rifle company. For one reason and then another their cordon and search operation was delayed. We didn't realize the importance of the delay at the time, but later we would understand that for every minute surprise was postponed, the VC were somehow able to capitalize on the delays and cause our efforts to fail. They knew our every move and were usually able to move sooner. Our only advantage was our high mobility, which was lost when we hurried up only to wait.

* * *

My expectations of what a day in an OP was going to be like were formed at Fort Benning where breaking the rules was important, but not life threatening. By the time the sun was up over the hill mass behind us the temperature began to rise. I quickly remembered the sun from the previous afternoon, when we waited at the Vietnamese naval base. Funny how I completely forgot it during the night while I was shivering against the cold, wet ground.

Local security was the first order of business. Belden picked a few Tigers who weren't otherwise busy with other tasks and sent them out to crawl around our OP to see just what it looked like and what we looked like from the outside.

While they were gone there was an early-morning flurry of radio batteries to replace, weapons to be cleaned, wet ammo to be exchanged, personal hygiene, and adjustments of the perimeter.

I watched as Belden and the other NCOs executed a routine that they had been going through since they had arrived in Vietnam. Born of their experiences, they were quick and organized.

The day dragged on. I sat near Belden looking out and down over the dry paddy fields and the tree lines below. The radio crackled with cross-talk between the rifle company and the battalion headquarters. Sometimes we only got half of the conversations.

By midday nothing had happened over the radio and we had not heard any firing from the direction of the village. And suddenly I realized it was time for lunch. For the first time since arriving in the Tiger Force I was hungry. Something had turned around in my system and I was beginning to think that I would live. What I didn't take into account was that I was just standing or sitting in one place for hours. Anyone can feel better doing almost nothing, not exerting himself, so I thought I was getting well.

The heat turned what might have been a beautiful day into a sweltering, fly-infested endurance contest.

By midafternoon I was getting anxious for something to happen. The plans for finding VC in the village just didn't seem to be panning out. And we were only guessing what the situation was since the battalion headquarters was under no obligation to keep us informed of everything that was going on in one of its rifle companies. So we guessed and we watched and we listened. For us it added up to a dry hole.

I was able to marshal enough energy to get cleaned up a bit and get

some food into me. I was still way behind in hydration but was unaware of it. Sweat kept pouring out of my skin and soaking my still-
damp uniform as if there was no end to the supply of body fluids. I just
passed it off as getting acclimatized and didn't worry about forcing
water.

I have to put the issue of water in perspective here. The mid-sixties
was still the time when we thought that salt tablets were what you took
in a hot environment and *not* drinking water was a sign of military and
personal self-discipline. It was just not in our training or operational
philosophy to consider encouraging one another to drink as much as
we could. There was also the problem of availability. Up on that hillside there was no source of water. So we were conscious of water
conservation and unaware how counterproductive that was.

In faint whispers I was able to talk to Belden and Sergeant Newton
about our fire support plan. Newton had plotted what we used to call
artillery concentrations all around us for our defense and on the valley
floor along likely enemy routes. He spent the entire morning replot-
ting them once he had the opportunity to actually see the terrain.
What had looked good on paper back at Phan Rang wasn't the best
fire support plan for us when we finally got there.

Newton was a skilled forward observer and gave me confidence in
his ease and familiarity around things artillery. I have to admit that I
just never got it in OCS. The lack of importance I placed on the use
and adjustment of mortar and artillery fire as a student came back to
haunt me on that morning. I wasn't as up on it as I needed to be and I
knew that I had to get with it—and fast.

I couldn't ask a lot of questions because of the noise discipline so I
just watched and followed Newton on my map. In just those few hours
I learned more from Newton than I ever picked up in days of training
at Fort Benning. I sure was glad to have him in the Tiger Force. I
didn't know how much—yet.

Night fell without anything of consequence happening. I was sore
from sitting on the damp and rocky ground and I was bored. We
finally got a summary update that the rifle company had turned up
nothing important on their sweep through the village. We were given a
warning order to be prepared to move the next day to link up with
another rifle company working nearby and to expect a change in mission. I didn't know what that meant. Neither did Belden.

The bottom line was that it was a dry hole and we were to get ready
to do something else, as soon as battalion figured out what. We
couldn't just sit out there on that hillside without the mutual support

of a rifle company within reinforcing distance from us. Things just weren't done that way—at least not up until the Tiger Force was formed.

The second night was a much longer version of the first. Unlike the first night, there was more activity in the valley below. Occasionally, we would pick up a light or a flicker of some kind that had to be man-made. Also, there were some new sounds. A dog barking or a clunking sound that just had no reason to be happening unless there was some enemy or civilian activity out in the darkness. We couldn't see enough to determine exactly what was going on, so we just stayed on enough of an alert status to be able to react if we had to.

By dawn the noises and the flickering lights had gone, and we were exhausted from the lack of sleep and the energy the patrol had ex-acted from us so far.

The morning's activities were identical to the previous day's. I pulled a shift on radio watch and could tell from the cross talk that the operation was winding up and arrangements were being made for one of the rifle companies to rendezvous with a truck convoy for transport back to Phan Rang.

By mid-morning it looked like a complete zero for the operation, and the patrol was beginning to repack equipment for an order to move out.

Suddenly, a Tiger alerted us that there was someone on the valley floor.

I pulled out my waterlogged binoculars and eyeballed the area start-ing at the base of the hill and working out. Belden and I saw them at the same time. An entire reinforced platoon or a light company of VC, armed and moving through the open area between us and the far tree line.

A major complaint of many of us in the course of the Vietnam war was the assessment of success or failure by using numerical measure-ments. The issue of body counts became a standard reporting proce-dure early in the war and tended to be exaggerated in even greater proportions as time went on. So I will not try to perpetuate that sys-tem. Instead give you what I knew and you can make up your own mind.

It is important to understand that our terminology about enemy squads came out of what constituted a small unit in the Korean War. And to use the same standard of measurements—numbers—to deter-mine a unit was completely wrong in Vietnam. What might have been called an enemy platoon in Korea would be a Viet Cong company. We were generally one unit size under what the VC called them, and we tended to apply force to the nominal description of the unit rather than its actual size. That would become a very big problem for the Tiger Force in just a few days.

But in this case the unit walking the valley floor numbered between thirty-five and forty-seven, depending on whose report you consult. I am sure there were thirty-two, at least. I counted the ones I could see in the grass. There may have been more, but there were plenty for us to go into action.

It was a completely stupid move on their part. Somehow the nearby cordon and search operation had taken place without their knowledge. Or they were misinformed as to the size of the American units in the area and they were going to mount an attack. Either way, they had made a big mistake.

Before I could even pull my binos away, Belden was on the horn to battalion reporting the sighting and Newton was getting clearance to fire on the enemy column below us.

It was my first real VC sighting and one of the most memorable. It was not like the VC to walk in the open and in broad daylight. They would pay for their boldness.

Clearance came more quickly that morning than on almost any other fire mission I ever called. Newton had confidence in the battery firing the mission for us and put up a volley of artillery all at once. Without warning, six rounds of artillery left the tubes in a distant fire support base and arced toward the enemy column on that valley floor.

They heard the incoming fire about the same time we did. They reacted in panic and began running in all directions—none of them finding cover.

Before the smoke from the first volley had cleared, the second volley landed. The radio was squawking with instructions and requests for information. We were told to saddle up and get down to the valley floor to exploit the contact and see if we could get some prisoners.

My heart began to pound with the stuff combat is made of. It is a special state of mind and body that just can't be duplicated. Sports parachuting or car wrecks are nothing like the level of alertness, the pump of adrenaline, and the urgency to do what is right as fast as you can that you experience when men are dying.

The destruction the artillery did on the valley floor was easier to see on that patrol than in any other fire mission I have ever witnessed. We had an unobstructed view of the enemy and the incoming fire. As the rounds impacted, bodies fell. It was nothing like any movies. Men weren't hurling up into the air like stuntmen off of air rams. Instead, they were collapsing under the fatal impact of red hot shreds of ragged steel flying into and through their flesh at hundreds of feet per second.

Some were down and crawling and others were trying to help fallen comrades. But most seemed to run or cower in an effort to avoid the rain of steel that had turned their morning into a hell and the last day on earth for some of them.

We ran, stumbled, fell, and slid down the hill to get to the valley floor before the remaining enemy could disappear or take up firing positions to defend themselves.

As we left the top of the hill the second volley had just landed and everyone was talking and the radios blared with non-stop traffic. We knew that the longer we took to get to the enemy unit, the less we could capitalize on the shock value of our attack. But the less deliberate our move, the more likely we were to approach them haphazardly and in a disorganized mob rather than as a maneuver unit supported by covering fire.

We had to take the chance or risk losing them all into the nearby tree lines.

CHAPTER 15

•

I thought my heart was going to burst out of my chest as we ran and half fell down that hill. It had taken us so long to get up it two nights before, but the trip down was a roller coaster ride with dirt, clanking equipment, and desperate men gasping for breath.

There hadn't been time to make a plan and get it out to the patrol. We all knew what we were doing. How we were going to do it was a question. But whatever we ended up doing it had to be done fast if we hoped to capture any prisoners.

Hitting the paddy fields, we spread out without being told to. We all knew that somewhere in the grasses around us there was the remains of a unit two to three times our size.

Belden set up the machine guns and the grenadiers to cover our sweep as we stretched out to fill the gap between the hill and the far tree line.

We didn't talk about it, but we never lost momentum from the time we started down the hill. Our speed slowed considerably, but we kept moving from a running file to a loose shoulder-to-shoulder rank moving across the waist-high grasses.

There had not been any shooting that we were aware of. The artillery came in and caught the Viet Cong unit without warning, and they had no targets to shoot back at. By the time the second volley hit them, those who were alive were down and crawling in the grass. Soon we began finding blood trails—everywhere.

Each Tiger moved cautiously with his weapon at the ready. I could hear the others breathing heavily and I tried to control my own breathing enough to be able to listen for any signs of life in the grass.

It was nerve-racking moving through the grass and finding blood trails, but very confusing not finding anyone. We couldn't have taken so long getting down the hill that they all could have dragged themselves off. After seeing my first real artillery fire mission close up, I couldn't conceive of anybody surviving.

They must have been incredibly motivated because we traveled nearly the entire length and width of the enemy position and found only the blood trails, shredded equipment, hair and bone fragments, and footprints in the dirt churned up by the artillery. But the footprints petered out when they moved to the hard-baked paddy fields.

I had still not caught my breath when suddenly something popped up just a few yards in front of me. I was looking away toward Belden when it happened. Out of the corner of my eye I caught some movement and when I spun around and aimed my M-16 at it I found a rifle barrel sticking up out of the grass—at me. I thought I was a dead man. The VC soldier on the other end of the rifle had me full length standing in his sights and I could only guess where his body was.

Before I could react the Tigers on either side of me turned, got the enemy soldier in their sights, and someone yelled, "Don't shoot!"

I had already pulled in the trigger slack on my M-16 when I heard the words and caught myself reflexively dropping to a bent-over squat to make myself a smaller target. Just then, another hand came up out of the grass with something in it. I heard someone yell, "Don't shoot!" again.

It was a bolt! A rifle bolt. I took one more step forward and saw the soldier raising both hands. In one was an aging bolt-action, single-shot rifle, and in the other was the bolt. The rifle was inoperable in two pieces. The VC wasn't trying to shoot us, he was trying to give up, showing us that he was not going to shoot by holding the two parts of his rifle over his head.

We ran up to him and snatched the rifle. Two Tigers tried to stand him up, only to find out that he had been wounded and needed help. He chattered and pleaded in Vietnamese, but I had no idea what he was saying. It was clear that he didn't want to be hurt and was begging for some kind of mercy.

Our medic ran in to where the soldier sat and began to attend to his wounds.

Belden finished reporting what had been found in the target area and received instructions to call off the search. I found out later that one of the rifle companies involved in the cordon was given the mission of picking up the search in and beyond the tree line where most likely the VC had escaped to.

It was still several more minutes before I put my rifle back on safe and stood up full length. My first enemy contact was over and I was in one piece and I had gone through a day's worth of adrenaline in less than thirty minutes.

We would all come to find that most contacts rarely lasted longer than that. Any that did usually were major actions with large units, and the results were plenty of casualties on both sides.

On that day we were plenty lucky. The number of blood trails and the amount of body matter that we found in the field confirmed that we had severely damaged that Viet Cong unit.

I was astounded at how fast and how effectively they were able to drag their dead and wounded away. It wouldn't be the last time I would see that, just the last time I would be so surprised.

Things didn't slow down after a contact in Vietnam. Suddenly, the radio traffic brought incredible demands for comprehensive reports on who and what and when and what were they wearing and on and on. We were also told to find a place to set up a hasty perimeter to be able to land a chopper. Brigade headquarters wanted the prisoner and they wanted to waste no time getting him interrogated.

Since we were on the valley floor the selection of a landing site was not a problem. We were concerned that we were within firing range of the tree line and the hill, and sent out two-man security elements to keep an eye on both. There was little else that we could do. If we moved to a more secure location, then there would be difficulty getting a chopper in, and there would be a delay getting the prisoner evacuated to the rear.

We didn't have to wait long. The chopper arrived and off stepped Major David Hackworth and a couple of others from battalion headquarters. He talked to Belden and then gave the prisoner a quick once-over. I couldn't tell what they were talking about, but it was a short conversation. I remained on one side of the perimeter to help provide the security, and before I had a chance to find out what was going on, the chopper lifted off.

We were close and had to duck and turn away to keep from getting faces full of blown grasses and dry paddy dirt. As I shielded my eyes the radio operator tapped me on the shoulder and yelled, "It's for you."

I picked up the handset and answered. Hack was on the other end. He said, "Hey, look up here."

I looked up just as the chopper was coming across in front of my position.

He continued, "Belden tells me you're okay. You got it. Now take those Tigers and link up with the element to your north and await further instructions. Out."

I wiped the dirt away from my eyes and looked harder. There in the jumpseat of the departing chopper, both with big grins on their faces, sat Hackworth and Belden. Hack threw me a loose salute and Belden gave me a simple thumbs-up. I was in command. I had somehow passed some test, although the standards were not clear to me. But I must have passed because Hack had gotten an okay from Belden and decided to take him back along with the prisoner.

The announcement caught me completely by surprise. I had no idea that I had done anything or enough of whatever I was doing to satisfy Platoon Sergeant Philip Belden that I was worthy of assuming responsibility for the patrol. In later years I asked both Belden and Hackworth what they talked about to make that decision, and both of them claimed faulty memories of the day. I guess I can understand that.

Taking over my first patrol in the field and after a successful contact was a moment I will never forget. I had spent months and months being trained and warned and prepared for that moment. I don't expect that it was that monumental a moment for either Belden or Hack. I'm also very pleased that all these years later both of them are still alive and we can laugh about it.

I wasn't sure what my first move should be, but I was positive that I had to make one—fast. There we were, out in the open. Everyone in Vietnam already knew where we were, and our location was confirmed by the landing and takeoff of a chopper. Someone in the trees or on the hillsides surrounding us had surely counted noses and knew that we were only fourteen strong and lightly armed.

I also had to assume that whoever was watching us knew that if we made the first move in the direction of the rifle company that they could just about guess our route to a linkup—ambushes are made of this.

We moved in a direction away from the rifle company and then turned back toward it when we were inside a tree line that bounded the north side of the clearing we had been in.

Suddenly nineteen months of training to become an infantry platoon leader was over. No more school problems and school solutions. No more easy mistakes and student critiques. No more pretending. That day my life changed. That day I became a combat leader, and that day the lives of others became my full responsibility.

My mind was filled with all of the lists, techniques, and details that I was sure I would need to have at my fingertips. But there was no time for deliberation and complete attention to detail. I had to get us out of the open and into a concealed route to our rendezvous.

They were right back at Benning—thirteen sets of eyes were looking at me to make some decisions and not be stupid. I swallowed hard and said a small prayer. But I wasn't nearly as confident as I'm sure the members of that patrol hoped I was.

Moving any group of combat infantrymen through the bush is a strain comparable to few other things in life. Every single step of the way you are surprised that you haven't taken incoming fire, and you are reminded that there was something you should have done and didn't—yet.

There was no more time to study. No more chances to look something up or ask a question about the business of leading men in combat. It was clearly like having someone strap a heavy weight to your load and then press down on it.

My first experience as a field leader was uneventful. We made no contact and sighted no enemy on our way to link up with a sister company.

Once we did link up I encountered my first very selfish act on the part of another junior officer. I had seen officers make moves that were in their own best interest and even some who did so and used the excuse that it was good for their unit. But I had not run across such a blatant act before.

We were told to stay with the company while it moved to a pickup point. That early in the war the availability of helicopters was very much exaggerated in the press. You got helicopters when there was no other way to move you or when the time was so crucial that other methods of transport would take much too long.

We were headed to a point a day and a half's walk away to meet a truck convoy in a more secure area. From there we'd be trucked back to Phan Rang.

When I reported to the company commander—protocol since I was a second lieutenant and he was a captain—he treated me like his own personal find. He immediately gave me details that he wanted my patrol to accomplish before we moved out of *his* company perimeter. Somehow, he was able to feel comfortable telling me that he wanted my people to help bury his trash and provide added security while his troops took care of things before we moved out.

I thought it was fairly selfish of him to ignore the fact that his company had been sitting in the same location for the better part of two days while we had made the trip out by sea, walked to and up the hill, spent two nights on more than a fifty-percent alert, and then made the only contact in the whole operation. But while I was feeling that way, I didn't complain because I wasn't really sure if it would sound like I was whining.

He added insult to injury by calling me to his CP just before dark and telling me that he had decided that the Tigers should take the point to give his company a bit of a break.

I filed the incident away in my mind for the day when I could do something about it. I had no idea when that would be, but seat-of-the-pants told me that I was being jerked around because he was a captain and I was a second lieutenant. And if you weren't in the army in those days, I can only tell you that the distance between those ranks was substantial. The fact that he was a company commander was a special anointing that made his status greater than any other captains not so blessed.

Picking the route, being responsible for the direction, the pace and the speed of movement was a fairly complicated set of balls to balance on my first day in a leadership position. So my unhappiness with the company commander took a back seat to my being worried about getting an entire reinforced rifle company lost in bad guy territory.

I tried to do the best job I could, staying aware of exactly where we were and what to expect to our front. All of those days and nights of map reading and land navigation classes at the NCO academy and in OCS were finally paying off. By dawn on the next day we were exactly where we needed to be and well ahead of our schedule to make the rendezvous. I'm sure happy that we didn't make contact during that night. It was hard enough to navigate without any distractions—like a firefight.

And by dawn the Tigers were very tired. They had not really had any sleep for going on four days. For me it had been a bit longer than that since I hadn't really slept the night before we departed. I was working on raw nerve endings by the time we got to the trucks.

The company commander never so much as said thanks or told me that I did an okay job of piloting his company to the pickup point. As a matter of fact, he never said anything to me.

Still, I wouldn't forget the treatment of my patrol by someone who had only suffered through the boredom of the operation.

CHAPTER 16

·

Coming home to Phan Rang from my first combat patrol, I was a different soldier than the one who left. I had seen some of what Vietnam was about and I had reached the far end of my acclimatization to the water and the heat. Though I was dead tired I felt good about being the patrol leader on the final leg and just being a Tiger.

Once I got back in the headquarters company area—where we were quartered—I found out that our contact had been a fairly significant one. I had assumed that the battalion had experienced plenty of enemy contacts during the months that they had been there before my arrival. That was not the case. Sure, they had had some small actions, but not many and not large and not often.

The number of VC that we had encountered in our artillery ambush was an unusually large element to find at all, much less in the open, in the daytime. On top of that, the prisoner we had captured just poured out a stream of information that made the brigade headquarters happy and put a star next to the Tiger Force's name on their mental charts.

Jim Gardner and the remainder of the Tigers were there to meet us on our return. We were hailed and there was back-slapping all around. Phil Belden had not wasted any time since he had returned. He had been able to scrounge some cold San Miguel[55] beer and some chicken for us to cook up and eat while we unwound from the operation.

I don't know what made me expect any time to sit and rest on our laurels, but I was wrong in thinking we would get some time off in the base camp. The second thing Gardner said to me after congratulations on the contact was to get ready to move forward in thirty-six hours.

Forward for us was no longer the relative term used in earlier wars. Forward in Vietnam meant that area where your higher headquarters was conducting combat operations—provided that you weren't there. It was especially true if you were in the base camp—referred to as *the*

[55] A beer brewed in the Philippines.

rear. So all those linear references from earlier wars, measured relative to the enemy's front lines and your front lines, were revised for Vietnam. Nevertheless, the word "forward" was enough to ratchet in your sphincter muscle a notch or two when you were told you were headed there.

Forward for the 1st Brigade of the 101st was the Tuy Hoa area in Phu Yen Province. The Tuy Hoa rice bowl, only half a mile from the ocean in the northern half of South Vietnam, was a critical area. For hundreds of years the paddies west and south of Tuy Hoa city provided most of the rice that fed much of the southern half of Vietnam. The control of Tuy Hoa and its rice was crucial to the survival of South Vietnam as a sovereign country and as a fighting force.

The 101st was sent there to help protect the rice harvest. Before they arrived the VC were ripping off the local farmers for their rice and running back into the hills with it. The rice and the money they were able to extort from the locals was sufficient to feed and equip the local guerrillas and also provided considerable aid to the main force units in the area.

The 101st's job was to put an end to the diversion of the rice crop and to return the huge rice bowl to the control of the South Vietnamese government. While it appeared to be a simple matter, it proved to be frustrating and difficult to pull off.

I got to spend just a few more hours with Jim Gardner before we had to move out for Tuy Hoa beach. I found him to be an incredibly confident leader and an example to follow. He was comfortable with the troops, gregarious, and approachable. He was nothing like some of the lieutenants I had met during my days as an enlisted man. They were standoffish and distant. Any thought you might have had about approaching them quickly disappeared when you sized them up. It was as if they didn't want to be bothered. I now suspect it was because they didn't want to be discovered as not having the answers to the questions and not being prepared to admit it.

This was not the case with Jim Gardner. During the few hours we spent together he told me he was leaving the Tigers because of his upcoming promotion. He estimated that he would be leaving within ten days and hoped he could give me everything he knew in that time.

In those early days there were no exceptions to the rule that platoons were led by lieutenants—not captains. And since the Tiger Force was a complete bastard outfit with no legitimacy on the books— we were assigned by the books. The organization chart only allowed for two lieutenants in the two real headquarters platoons that made up the Tigers.

It was very unusual for a lieutenant to get a chance to overlap with the officer he was replacing. More often than not, the lieutenant would arrive in the battalion and would go to a platoon that already had a NCO temporarily holding down the job. Overlap was a luxury that I appreciated—however short it was.

Outloading to a new tactical location with an Airborne unit is one of the most complicated operations you can experience. But I was impressed with the battalion's ability to size up its airloading requirements and match air assets to needs. I wouldn't find out until later that the reason was because it was a particularly well developed skill of Major Hackworth's. The battalion staff could not make a mistake in air movement with him checking their work. His ability to estimate loads, weights, and cube requirements was the best I ever saw in any airborne unit I served with.

Thus, the move itself went smoothly. In less than a day and a half we had cleared out of Phan Rang and closed on Tuy Hoa.

For reasons that escaped me, the brigade decided to set up the 1/327 on a ribbon of sand that ran for a few miles south of Tuy Hoa city. Bounded by the South China sea and Highway 1, the beach was a strange combination of sand and very dusty dirt. It was the only place I have ever been where you could swim or take a shower and before you had walked a hundred yards you were covered with a fine dirt up to your knees.

It was also hot and devoid of any terrain features or vegetation. But for us it was home—for a while. We were given an area and soon found out just how difficult it was to be put on a sandy beach. When we had heard we were going to be on the beach, all of us thought that would be a terrific idea.

On a beach, besides the obvious problem of having sand in everything you owned all the time, there were several other peculiarities that were bothersome. Tent stakes didn't want to stay put, sunburn was a constant problem with the added reflections off the sand, walking became difficult when you had to do lots of it in the battalion area, vehicles got bogged down in the loose surface, and everything you ate had a gritty crunch to it.

The only thing that was easy was sandbagging.

Security on a beach had its own unique features that we had not anticipated, and the Tiger Force was given a local security mission as soon as we turned off the highway and drove to the battalion command post.

We were required to establish lightly armed and thinly manned positions around the perimeter of the battalion area. Our first problem was that there was virtually no defensive terrain. Everything was flat and sandy. There was no deviation in the elevation that could offer better observation and fields of fire, and there were no obvious positions to consider along likely enemy avenues of approach—the entire beach was avenues of approach.

Vegetation or terrain features to help conceal the friendly positions didn't exist. So sandbagged emplacements for the machine guns and other crew-served weapons stood out on the beach like olive-drab pimples. We weren't kidding anyone.

Local security extended to patrolling. The first night there I took out a patrol to check the terrain outside our field of view from the battalion area. Since we were on a beach, that meant the places we couldn't see were a long hump away, and walking a long distance in the sand at night was more taxing than we had expected it to be.

Navigation became an added problem. There were no trails, streams, hilltops, bridges, hamlets, or roadways to help us identify just where we were once we got out of sight of the battalion. That night out on the Tuy Hoa beach I got as lost as I have ever been as a tactical leader. My only solution was to head east until we found the ocean and then turn south to follow the water line back to the battalion area. I don't know how many members of the patrol knew how lost we were. But I was very embarrassed.

As bad as the beach at Tuy Hoa was, it was better than some places I would later work in Vietnam.

The light security mission quickly ended, and we were relieved by the arrival of the last elements of the battalion. Headquarters company and one of the rifle companies took over our mission and we were told to stand by to move into the Tuy Hoa valley for operations there.

This began a series of changes to our organization. Hackworth's idea of using the Tiger Force as an advanced patrolling unit *and* a fourth maneuver unit kept us in a constant state of flux. While the change in mission was fairly easy to adjust to mentally, the consequences of flipping from small patrols to a single or two light infantry platoons took some adjustments. Each different mission required a realignment of squads to teams or patrols and a change in the distribution of weapons and equipment. An additional problem occurred with communications. We were not authorized to have as many of the kind of radios that we needed. We were authorized several lightweight AN/PRC 6 radios, but they were useless to us at the distances we were working from one another and from adjacent units.

More AN/PRC 25 radios were what we needed. We had too few of them and we had no replacements if one got wet or damaged. To us, radios were everything. Without them we lost our flexibility. Since we were so light in firepower, radios gave us the ability to call for mortars, artillery, helicopter gunships and tactical air support. One or several of these types of firepower were available to us within minutes—provided we could call them up for help. Without the radios to call in supporting fires we were given only two options—take on enemy forces with what we had, or just lay low until they passed by us.

And rearranging the internal structure of the Tiger Force to flip from lengthy patrols to acting as a small rifle company meant the shuffling of radios. Any radio operator can become expert at how his equipment works and what to do to coddle and pamper it into performing when it is sick. But when the radios have to be shifted, their history gets lost and the receiving radio operator is stuck with an unknown entity until it proves itself reliable or not. A patrol or search and destroy operation is not the best place to discover the performance capability of the only radio you might have.

It didn't take long for extra radios to begin appearing in the Tiger Force. I didn't know where they came from.

The alert became a warning order and then an order. We were to move by chopper to the south end of the Tuy Hoa rice bowl to assist in a sweep through the valley. The purpose of the sweep was to search for and eliminate Viet Cong from the farming community. We were tasked to act as a maneuver element, which meant that we had the night to reorganize and shuffle equipment to become a platoon-size infantry unit.

Gardner was going to be the unit commander, and I was to tag along to get my last few chances to overlap with him and pick his brain about how things should work within the Tiger Force. I was just as happy to do it that way since I had never seen a search operation and only had a vague notion of what was required.

Jim put me to work getting the Tigers ready to go and checking on weapons, ammo, equipment, and rations. He had decided to leave a portion of the Tigers at the beach to complete the setup of our area and to receive the few remaining pieces of equipment that were still on the way to Tuy Hoa from Phan Rang. That meant we'd be taking two dozen Tigers with us to the valley the next morning.

Helicopter operations in 1965 and 1966 were primitive at best. We never could count on choppers being available or showing up on time or arriving with the same mission that we thought they had been given. It was not a problem with the pilots or crews. Rather it was the unreliability of the equipment and the kinks that were still in the maintenance and the operations side of the chopper business.

The basic workhorse for us was the UHID that had worked well in the States, but wasn't quite as reliable in the heat and altitude of Vietnam. Our allowable cargo load shifted from day to day based on the fuel load of the aircraft, the temperature, and the altitude. As the altitude, temperature, and fuel load increased, the number of troops we could load onto a chopper decreased.

This unpredictability translated itself into many confusing chopper pickups. It wasn't uncommon to break down the troops into chalks that didn't end up matching the allowable cargo load (ACL) we had planned on. Ultimately, we would end up with extra soldiers running from chopper to chopper looking for one that could take them after they had been bumped from the aircraft they had originally been scheduled to board.

Worse than the confusion was the disruption of the planned crossloading and the separation of troops from their leaders and leaders from their radio operators. Anyone who spent any time in tactical units in Vietnam during the early years could tell many stories of choppers being grounded on the pickup zone after loading up with critical personnel or equipment.

Since we didn't have a radio in each chopper, often the commander didn't know what men had made it to the landing zone until he arrived there himself. Much of this worked itself out by the time the chopper engines were ungraded and the planners and the maintenance personnel were equipped and trained to handle the high use of choppers in tactical operations. But during those first couple of years it was a surprise every time you landed.

I once lifted off of an airfield with two separate patrols of seven men each destined for landing zones several miles apart. Only when we got on the ground did I find out that the other patrol leader had not been allowed to get on his own chopper. The fact that we were already a twenty-five-minute flight away and on the ground before we found out caused us to scrub the other patrol's mission and combine the two patrols. The screwup caused unnecessary risks for the pilots, crew, choppers, and the other Tiger Force patrol.

Any surprise we hoped to have achieved by landing by chopper in the mountainous rain forest was lost while the two patrols moved along the foothills to effect a link up after dark.

Our liftoff from the Tuy Hoa beach was typical. The Tigers had been spaced out in a pattern similar to the landing formation of the five choppers that were scheduled to pick us up. After we had waited in five-man chalks for over an hour, we were notified that there would only be four choppers and we should rearrange the chalks accordingly.

The rearrangement of one chalk to spread out the load to the others meant an immediate loss of the integrity of the chalk that had to be divided up, and would result in similar reorganizing confusion on the landing zone. It was something we just had to get used to because there was no other option.

For me, it was my first time in a chopper. I didn't have any idea what to expect and was somewhere between being excited and concerned that I didn't know what I didn't know about choppers. As it turned out, it was the first of many experiences I would have in choppers and almost every single flight taught me something about them. Choppers were powerful yet delicate in their survivability. I soon came to understand also that their pilots would ask the machines to do things that had never been put into the aircraft design on the drawing board.

After we shuffled and recounted heads, the choppers arrived. Choppers on the dirty, dusty beach at Tuy Hoa caused a visibility nightmare. As soon as they got close enough to the ground for their rotor wash to pick up the dust, the entire flight disappeared into a yellow-brown cloud of it.

The dust and dirt were blinding. Some of the chalks were more distant from their respective choppers than others and had difficulty determining just which chopper was theirs.

That first flight I had no idea how dangerous it was to be engulfed in all that dust. The chopper pilots couldn't see each other or the soldiers on the ground. Somehow, through the skill of the pilots, we were able to get aboard and off the ground.

Leaving the dust and the beach behind was a thrill. It was a wild first ride that I will never forget. We sat in the open doorways of the choppers with our legs hanging out as the pilots made ascending right turns away from the ocean and toward the rice bowl.

* * *

I had not seen the valley floor on the way into the airfield near Tuy Hoa city because there is very little visibility from a C-130 cargo plane unless you are near the open ramp or parachute doors. So that chopper flight was the first time I got a look at where we would spend six of the next thirteen months.

The Tuy Hoa area was one of the most beautiful places I had ever seen. It was a sprawling green farmland surrounded on three sides by mountains and on the fourth by the sea. It was comprised of hundreds of villages and hamlets that looked like they had been in the same spots for centuries. Each little plot of land seemed to be exceptionally fertile and teeming with livestock, children, and hard-working farmers.

As we flew across the width of the rice bowl, the great numbers of streams and small rivers caught the sunlight and reflected the sparkle of the water. It was hard to believe from fifteen hundred feet that there could be anything wrong in the sleepy-looking farming communities. True of all of Vietnam, looks were definitely deceiving.

My first chopper ride was far too short. I was thrilled with the sense of flying that it offered. But I had no idea then how many thousands of hours I would spend in choppers in the years ahead, or the moments of terror they would provide.

Landing in a wide rice field, we jumped out into ankle-deep mud topped by knee-high rice. Our first few steps were very strange because of the fine, silty soil that made up the mud. As we tried to pull our feet out of the mud it tried to hold on to our boots with a sucking sensation, so we had to wait until the vacuum slowly released our boots.

The choppers lifted off and flew back to the beach for the remainder of Task Force Hackworth. Jim Gardner ran off to find the command group to do some final coordination while Belden and I tried to get Tigers spread out and off the landing zone.

What follows is the sequence of events and information as I lived and learned them at the time. The years since have offered up a considerable number of details that I wish we had known then. The important thing that came to me out of that day—February 7, 1966—was that the troops act on what they think is going on and not what is actually happening. The difference was disastrous for us that day.

Task Force Hackworth consisted of a slice of the battalion headquarters, our own B Company, and the Tiger Force minus some who were still at the beach.

The turnaround didn't take too long and Gardner returned with a change in mission. We left the beach prepared to participate in a search and destroy operation. Gardner explained that one of the companies in our sister battalion, the 2d of the 502d, had taken some small arms fire south of our position and we were going to move with TF Hackworth to the flank of that company, to help if we could. It was not much more specific than that, and Gardner's sense of urgency was nothing out of the ordinary.

Our walk to the B Company, 502d's contact area was slow and uneventful. We were neither rushed nor pushed to get there faster. We finally reached the far left flank of Captain Robert Murphy's company in less than an hour of careful movement.

A fast-moving, although small river separated the right flank of the Tiger Force from the extreme left flank of Murphy's company—or so we thought. Due to the light but plentiful vegetation, we were unable to make visual contact with Murphy's people and only had a general idea where he was.

We didn't know at the time that he had taken some substantial fire, and was basically pinned down out in the open and needed our help to relieve the pressure on his company. Instead, we believed that he had just taken light small-arms fire and we were to move to what was assumed to be the flank of the enemy unit facing Murphy's company.

As we reached the river we were held up while Hackworth took a few members of the task force headquarters forward for a closer recon of the enemy positions. At the time there were a few rounds popping in the tree lines ahead of us, but none of the firing seemed to be coming our way.

When Hackworth returned there was another hasty conference between him, his headquarters, and the two unit commanders—Gardner and Captain Al Hiser, our B Company commander.

While he was gone the activity in the area where the original American company had made contact began to heat up. Firing picked up and we could hear the M-16s at what sounded like a few hundred meters from our position. There was also some scattered semiautomatic return fire that was not M-16s. It wasn't a big firefight, but it was shooting and it was making us nervous. I tried to remember Bill Pfeiffer and pretend the circling A1E Skyraiders[56] didn't bother me. I

---

[56] The Douglas single-engine, prop-driven fighter used for close air support. It was armed with four 20mm cannons and could carry 8,000 pounds of bombs. The Skyraider had a top speed of 322 miles per hour.

rather doubt that I was successful. The general anxiety level of the others told me that I didn't really understand what was going on.

Gardner came back to the Tigers and rounded up Belden, the squad leaders, and me. He gave us hasty instructions to cross the river and move to the left of Hiser and Murphy's companies to approach the flank. We were to stay low, keep moving, and not fire until we cleared it with Gardner, because of the proximity of other Americans we could not see.

We moved out and crossed a small footbridge only to step off into the water on the other side. We took small-arms fire as we did. Gardner didn't want the enemy to see us as we moved across their front. The far riverbank was steep and high enough out of the water to conceal our lateral move.

The water itself was swift and very deep. We could barely touch bottom in places as we used our hands to hold on to the roots as we bobbed along, creeping to the left, heads below the bank.

At a point only a few hundred meters to the left of the bulk of Task Force Hackworth and Captain Murphy's company, Gardner signaled for us to come up out of the water and lay low on the bank. We were completely submerged during our watery route and each of us had difficulty getting up the steep banks in our waterlogged fatigues and rucksacks.

Once we got up on the bank it took several minutes for the water to drain out of our clothes and equipment. We were left slick and slippery and carrying a few more pounds of water weight than we had started the day with. Looking to my left and right, I was able to guess that I was somewhere near the center of the single line of Tigers spread out over a hundred meters to my left and right.

I could see Hackworth's command group on the far right of the Tigers, between us and the adjacent rifle company. I couldn't hear Gardner, but he was talking to Hack over the radio.

The sounds of the contact over on our far right flank picked up in intensity as someone adjusted air strikes farther to our right.

As we waited there in the light brush that separated the river from a stretch of rice paddy, a few stray enemy rounds passed over our heads. I couldn't tell how high the firing was. It was the first time anyone had ever shot in my direction, and guessing the particulars took more experience than I had. Still, it was a feeling I would never forget—my first incoming fire.

Gardner finished talking to Hack and motioned to me to scoot over in his direction. He grabbed me by the shirt collar and pulled my face close to his and told me to pass the word to the left to get ready to rush the far tree line. As I did, he turned to the right and passed the word to the Tigers on his right.

Tigers looked up through the short brush and over it at the field that stretched out in front of us. It was easily seventy meters deep and almost half again as wide. There was room for us to spread out and the dash would be short, even though it would be hindered by our waterlogged condition.

I asked Jim what he thought was up ahead of us. He gave me the last war's reality when he said, "Some small-arms fire and at least one automatic weapon. Probably a reinforced squad."

That was the conclusion that many soldiers who had been in Korea might have guessed from the light resistance we thought was in that tree line. We had at least twice that much firepower with us in the Tigers alone. And since we didn't seem to be the target of the enemy element, Jim was hoping that we could dash across the open, plowed rice-paddy field and be inside the next tree line before we were even discovered.

Our other option was to continue in the riverbed even farther around the short axis of the rice paddy and end up where we assumed the enemy's rear was. But that would also put us in the direct line of fire from our sister company.

I can only guess that Jim was hoping to capitalize on the element of surprise. Why he didn't want to leave part of the Tigers in place to lay down a base of fire while the rest of us moved he never explained to me.

I just sucked it up, got up on my knees in a starting stance, stared at the far tree line and then at Jim, waiting for his signal to go.

For the few seconds I had to examine it, the tree line looked like any other that I had seen on that first morning in the Vietnam rice fields. It was an absolutely straight rice-paddy dike, perpendicular to our route and topped by stand after stand of side-by-side bamboo. The stands of bamboo looked to be as much as twenty feet high and were backed by rows of scattered palm trees.

I looked at the Tigers. They were ready. Each man had prepared himself for the move across the open field and waited at a squat or on one knee.

Jim finally stuck the infantry school pose, stepped out in front of the line and yelled, "Move out!"

And we moved without hesitation.

Gardner broke into a half run as he began shooting his M-16 from the hip. We followed suit and kept on line in a perfect skirmish line, a couple meters between soldiers.

The din of almost a dozen M-16s and a couple of machine guns and grenade launchers was almost deafening.

We got almost halfway across the field without taking any enemy fire when it all went to hell. The peaceful-looking bamboo stands turned out to be the tops of well-dug and well-camouflaged enemy automatic weapons positions. In a fraction of a second the far paddy dike exploded in a wall of flames as several weapons opened fire on us.

In those same first few seconds better than half of the two dozen Tigers went down in that open field, felled by the seeming wall of steel that came at us.

CHAPTER 17

•

Few moments in my life have matched what was happening all around me, as we kept moving toward the tree line. I looked to my left and right and saw fallen Tigers everywhere. Even those who were only downed by initial wounds were being hit again and again by the incredible volume of fire coming from the multiple machine gun positions only three dozen meters to our front.

Those of us who were still on our feet and still charging forward were all surprised that we had not been cut down. The level of noise put out by our weapons and the incoming enemy fire made communicating impossible and we all made up our own minds what to do. It was obvious to all that to stay in the middle of that field was certain death. To try to move back or laterally was equally foolish. So, without any coordination or communication among those who were still moving, we all just kept on charging toward the machine guns, firing everything we had back at the source of the enemy fire.

Our efforts to reduce the accurate enemy fire were wasted. They had dug firing positions behind and under the bamboo that topped the paddy dike. Each enemy gunner fired from a port that was no bigger than a six-inch circle. And the dense bamboo above them acted like a shock absorber. Each time an M-79[57] grenade round hit the bamboo, the fragmentation was just sucked up by the incredibly resilient wood fibers. The small size of the firing ports made it unlikely that the wild spray of our M-16 fire would hit the gunners who were cutting us down.

As I ran and fired my rifle, I was desperately trying to figure out what our next move was. What if we did get into the tree line? Then what? What if *I* didn't and ended up wounded in the middle of that field with the others? Some protective process in my thinking didn't offer up the possibility of being dead there with the other Tigers that

---

[57] The 40mm single-shot grenade launcher. It could fire high-explosive, fragmentation rounds out to a range of 300 meters. The launcher weighed 6.5 pounds and the rounds weighed about six ounces.

had been killed in the first burst of enemy fire or the ones that were dropping as we continued that last few yards to the bamboo.

I could feel the burning in my chest running at a crouch, wearing all that wet equipment and taking shallow gulps of air. And around me the world in my field of vision was turning into a nightmare of death and destruction. My heart pounded with a fury that I had never felt before. My legs were beginning to feel like rubber and the distance between me and the enemy positions just didn't seem to get smaller, no matter how many steps I took.

A Tiger to my left stumbled and crossed in front of me as he tried to regain his balance. Just as he reached a point where I had to stop firing to keep from hitting him, he took more than one hit. The impact of the rounds made a loud noise as he became engulfed in a crimson spray of blood that bent him double at the waist—nosediving into the rice field.

Two more strides and I was on top of him. It only took me a glance to know that he was dead. I had never seen a dead man before, and certainly not one I had just shared a cigarette with ten minutes earlier. I felt nausea rising and thought that I was going to vomit. But something told me that if I stopped or slowed or did anything but move forward I was not going to make it out of that field.

I found a last burst of energy and half sprinted, half leaped to a narrow break in the bamboo along the paddy dike. Bellyflopping onto the ground, I realized that I was just inches behind the enemy line of muzzles that had been shooting at us in the field. I looked back over my shoulder and saw the legs of two more Tigers who were channeled into the same break as they ran up and over me.

Turning back to my front, I saw that I was looking into a ditch that had been dug behind the line of enemy bunkers as a communications trench. I kicked one leg up and forward and levered myself off the break on the dike and into the trench. I landed in a pile of other Tigers—two, maybe three more. And just at the moment I tried to take stock of what was going on, we all saw three uniformed enemy soldiers crouching in the trench no more than fifteen feet away. Each of them had a rifle trained on us, and we began to fire on them as they did the same to us. Most of their rounds went wild while ours hit their mark. I don't know how many of them took fatal hits, but they recoiled violently at the intensity of our M-16s firing on full automatic.

As we fired, we scrambled to get up off our butts on the bottom of that chin-deep trough that left us exposed from both directions.

We climbed up the far wall of the ditch and found ourselves in yet another small rice paddy bounded on its far side by a small, man-made irrigation ditch. In that field I spotted several other Tigers continuing forward, still firing and still charging in the original direction.

Three of us who had crawled out of the first communications trench got to our feet and ran to catch up with the others. Our forward progress was stopped dead at the irrigation ditch on the far side of the second paddy field. There I found the surviving Tigers huddled in the shallow ditch with Belden and Gardner. The incoming enemy fire was terribly intense, and we found ourselves in a crossfire.

No one had to tell me the fix we were in. From our front we were taking heavy fire that was coming through a hedgerow close enough for us to reach out and touch. But that same hedgerow kept us from being able to see who was shooting at us and where their firing positions were. To our right there were at least three machine-gun positions firing down the trench we were in and across the field that we had just crossed. Why they didn't fire while we were crossing it had become obvious. They wanted to suck us into that ditch and then close the door behind us.

We didn't know what was to our left, but the feeling was that it was more of the same. And all of the friendly elements we were aware of were to our right and to our rear. So moving left or exploring it as a route out of our box was last on the list.

Gardner slid up onto the slimy forward bank of the irrigation ditch and tried to find a break in the brush to see what we were facing. Enemy rounds snapped through the hedgerow only inches above our heads, while the fire from the machine guns to our right and rear crossed the frontal fire at a ninety-degree angle. We were in a most classic crossfire and had completely lost our momentum and our initiative.

I sat on my butt, half bent over to duck the rounds buzzing by our ears, up to my armpits in the standing slime of the ditch as I gasped for air and looked for some sign from Jim Gardner.

He reached his left hand back toward me and yelled over the firing for me to give him my binoculars. I shifted my gear around and found my mud-covered binocular case and fumbled for the binos.

Gardner moved forward a few more inches to get a better look with the field glasses and we waited. Though he only scanned the other side of the hedgerow for a few seconds it felt like an eternity. Satisfied with what he saw, he slid back and half pitched the binos back at me. He shook his head as if what he saw was not good.

As I twisted back to my right to reach for the binocular case I was suddenly and violently catapulted up and out of the ditch. I felt sharp pain above my left kidney as I tumbled back into the field we had just crossed.

I raised my head and my glasses fell from my face. The right earpiece had been shot away. My helmet rolled to a stop just inches away from me. The lip of the helmet had a bullet hole just over where it would sit above my eye when wearing it. And my back was on fire with pain as if someone had hit me full swing with a heavy baseball bat.

My first thoughts were that I had been hit and that my entire rib cage was blown open. In a panic I pushed out with my arms and forced myself back into the ditch, sliding along on the ooze of mud and slippery grasses.

I looked up at Gardner to see if there was any sign in his face that would tell me what kind of shape I was in. He leaned over and looked me over. He smiled for a second and said, "You're a lucky son of a bitch. You're okay."

I couldn't believe it. I slipped my arm out of my rucksack strap and reached around to feel my back. It hurt like hell, but my fingers couldn't find any break in the skin. What I did find was a six-inch-long slice of shirt missing from just over my left hip to a point almost even with my spine.

An enemy bullet had found its way between my skin and my rucksack and had sliced through the fabric but not me! The high velocity of the round had transferred enough energy to me through the impact with my gear to knock me on my ass and roll me up and out of the ditch. I was almost giddy with the good luck.

Quickly I reached for the second set of glasses that I had taped to the stock of my rifle and stretched out to retrieve my damaged helmet as I pulled myself even lower into the muck of the ditch to keep more rounds from finding me again. I just knew that I couldn't be that lucky twice in the same day.

While I was trying to regain my composure the enemy fire grew worse. Either they had a better idea of where we were and were firing more accurately, or there had been some shifting of their positions and there was just a greater volume of incoming fire. Gardner exchanged a few short messages with Hackworth over the radio, but I was unable to hear the conversation because of the added noise of incoming friendly artillery that was landing just beyond the curtain of the hedgerow immediately to our front.

Gardner turned to me and said something I didn't understand about the machine-gun positions that were placing enfilade fires down the ditch more effectively than before. He held out his hands and yelled, "Gimme your grenades."

I pulled the two frag grenades off my harness and handed them to him. He quickly dropped them down the front of his shirt, his pistol belt keeping them from falling out. Without another word to me he got to his feet and ran up the trench toward the enemy machine guns, firing his M-16 and yelling profanities at the enemy soldiers in the bunkers barely fifty meters away.

The Tigers in that ditch fired around and over Gardner's head to help suppress the enemy fire. It was one of the most incredible acts of courage that I have ever seen: watching Jim charge straight into enemy positions with their return fire chewing up the muddy field in front and along his route to their bunkers.

Although Gardner was taking enemy fire, and being knocked off his feet, he kept on going, singlehandedly destroying the first and then the second enemy machine-gun position. During his charge, one of his grenades was pitched back out of a bunker after he had thrown it in and the blast of the grenade hit him in several places. Still, he charged forward, shooting, throwing grenades and shouting.

But the third interlocking machine-gun position stopped him only moments after he had silenced the second bunker. When he went down it was for the last time. He had given his life to relieve the pressure on the rest of us in that ditch to give us a chance to get out.

Before I could even take in the impact of Jim's death, someone stuck the radio handset in my face and yelled, "It's Hackworth."

I don't know what I said into the mouthpiece but Hackworth didn't give me a chance to say much. He was screaming at me over the incredible noise, telling me that he knew Gardner was dead and that *I was in command now* and that I was to get the Tigers out of the inside of the enemy perimeter.

It was the first time I realized that what we had was a series of concentric circles of bad guys and good guys. We were on the inside of a perimeter of a heavily armed and well-equipped NVA battalion. And they were surrounded by rifle companies from two American airborne battalions. And *I* was holding up the show. Hackworth wanted to blast the enemy battalion with artillery, mortars, air strikes, and helicopter gunships; but he couldn't until the Tigers got out of the inside of the enemy battalion's positions.

If we had not made it across the field and if we had not pushed through the heavily dug-in perimeter, the American efforts might have been more successful. So I had the responsibility for getting the surviving Tigers out. And Hackworth wanted it done immediately.

I tried to explain our situation to Hack on the radio, and he told me to stand by to make a dash back to the communications trench that the NVA had dug behind the original row of bamboo topped bunkers. On his signal we would try to slip out from under the crosshairs of the enemy gunners while he and the two rifle company commanders brought the maximum fires to bear. He told me to expect hell like I hadn't seen before and not to let it slow or stop us. If we lost momentum crossing back over that field we would die there—guaranteed.

I explained it all to Sergeant Belden and he passed the word. If we hadn't been taking so much fire at the time, I would have expected some resistance to busting back out into the open. But the spot we were in was absolutely untenable. We had to move, or die there. The enemy fire was getting heavier and even more accurate.

Hackworth gave me the final *stand by* and I passed the signal. The incoming artillery began to fall to our front and behind the bunkers that Jim Gardner had eliminated. Gunships worked next to the artillery and an air force fighter-bomber dropped bombs on enemy positions he had identified.

We took off in a flat-out run across the field—no deliberate moves, hopscotching over one another, we had to make the smallest target for the shortest amount of time while Hackworth brought the full fire resources to bear to suppress enemy fires.

I'm sure that I was fairly typical of the Tigers crossing that field again. My legs wouldn't move fast enough. The uneven, plowed field made it very hard to keep my footing, and I stumbled a couple of times. My chest burned and my eyes filled with sweat and grime trickling down from my forehead.

As we ran there was no doubt how much incoming enemy fire we were taking. This time the fire was coming from our flank and from behind us. We could see the ground being chewed up in front of us as we ran. We could also see the leaves and small branches dropping in the bamboo tree line to our front, cut down by the unrelenting firing.

After a few steps I felt someone or something hit me and knock me in another direction. I lost my footing again, but recovered after a few faltering steps and got back on course. After two more strides I was in the middle of the field—the point of no return. But again I was nudged and lost my feet under me, tumbling in a sort of roll but getting back to my feet.

Once I got back up from the second stumble, at just about the edge of the commo trench, I just leaped over the edge and fell down into the ditch, crashing into a pile, no grace or control involved in the landing. But I didn't care. I was below the level of the field and out of the enemy line of fire.

One by one, Tigers came over the edge. I counted and cheered as each man made it. Every man who started from the irrigation ditch had made it to the large communications trench.

We didn't wait. The route to our escape from the inside of the enemy perimeter was up the trench—toward Hackworth's command post. That last dash was hidden from enemy fire, but we weren't sure that the trench was clear of enemy soldiers. On the way we ran over body after body. Most of them NVA, some of them ours.

The end of the trench spilled out into a small clearing that we had to cross to make it to safer ground. Every man found the strength for the last push, and we made it out of the perimeter and into our own B Company's position.

I counted the last Tiger through the gap and yelled "Last man!" to the nearby Americans. As I turned to orient myself, I found that Hackworth's small command post was right there in the middle of it all, not back away from the line of contact. He heard my announcement and turned up the heat on the artillery, air strikes, and gunship runs.

Hackworth pointed at an area inside of the American perimeter for the Tigers to assemble, and Belden quickly led them there. Hack then motioned me over.

He was on his belly behind a large log, the paddy field we had crossed to start the assault to his rear, the enemy on the other side of the log. I followed suit and flopped down next to him. He looked at me and shook his head. I was a wreck. I had taken a couple of more hits crossing the last field and my web gear and an ammo pouch were shredded by enemy rifle fire.

Then Hack gave me a smile and stabbed his finger onto the map he had spread out just under his face on the ground. He gave me a quick orientation as to where we were and where the other friendlies were and where the bad guys were. In the middle of all that, he was controlling air strikes himself and yelling instructions to Don Korman, the artillery forward observer, who was adjusting artillery to fit Hackworth's fire plan.

He wanted me to take the remaining Tigers and assume responsibility for a small section of the crescent-shaped perimeter he had established up against the enemy positions.

Hack's smile was his way of saying, Okay, you did a good job. And I learned that it always preceded a new mission. I was to get the Tigers in position, reorganize and redistribute ammo, treat and evacuate my wounded and stand by for additional security missions.

As I listened to him, Hackworth was the model of calm. Enemy rounds kept coming out of the tree line on the other side of the log and hitting it on the far side with thunk after thunk. A chopper came in not more than twenty meters to our rear, taking fire as it landed, and a civilian jumped out and ran up to us.

He plopped down between me and Hackworth and asked where all the action was. Hack raised his hand up and then pointed his finger over the top of the log. The civilian raised his head and took a single round in the forehead. He went out—dead—on the same chopper that brought him in. It wasn't the last I would hear of that dead civilian.

The term *my wounded* didn't hit me until I was running from Hack's position to Belden's across the original rice paddy. They were *my* wounded. Jim was dead and *I* was in charge and *I* had a hell of a lot of things to do. And it was clear that Hackworth wanted them done fast.

If he tasked me to do anything else, I had to have the Tigers ready to go. Looking at the survivors, I saw a really beaten-up bunch. It wasn't the same bunch that had left the beach on the South China Sea only hours before.

Within the hour I found out just how high our casualties had been. The bodies of the dead Tigers who fell in the paddy field on the first assault had already been collected and laid out near us. All I saw as I walked toward them was their boots sticking out of the ponchos that covered their bodies. The other bodies were still inside the enemy positions and would have to be retrieved later.

The survivors had not been spared. With a couple of exceptions, every Tiger had been killed or wounded. By the time I got over to the Tiger position, Belden had organized a triage to evacuate the critically wounded first and treat the seriously wounded who could wait to be evacuated.

Hackworth had setup a medevac landing zone in the same field we had crossed and chopper after chopper made the difficult approach through the enemy antiaircraft fire to pull out our wounded. One of the choppers didn't make it and crashed near our position.

Trying to reorganize in that chaos was the most difficult thing I have ever done. We could hardly hear each other yelling over the noise, and our voices were hoarse from the screaming we'd already done.

Belden seemed to get cooler and calmer as the confusion increased. Within about an hour we had accounted for all of the Tigers, resupplied and redistributed ammo, and replaced some trashed weapons with working ones.

The contact continued with all the fury that Hackworth and the ground elements could bring to bear on the little village. The positions in front of us finally fell to the pounding, and Belden and I took a few men back into the enemy's perimeter to clear out any remaining NVA soldiers from their well-covered bunkers. We found a few and exchanged bursts of automatic fire. Our efforts added to the enemy casualty figures and let us retrieve the remaining bodies.

By dusk we were absolutely exhausted and very concerned about what the night held for us. We had learned from the reports of all the American ground and air elements that what we first thought was a small Viet Cong unit turned out to be major elements of the elite 95th North Vietnamese Army Regiment. We had grossly underestimated the strength and the determination of the enemy forces, and we had been totally unaware how well dug in they were and how well armed they were.

After checking the three positions that we had tied into the rifle company perimeter, I went to the shallow depression in the rice paddy that Belden had chosen as our command post. He was there going over the details of the names and the wounds of the wounded and the list of our KIAs. Battalion was already on our back about reporting casualties.

The place reeked of death and burned flesh. Fires spotted the remains of the structures that used to be the village of My Canh II. I looked from the smoking village back into our own perimeter and saw the row of bodies that had been Tigers. We had retrieved Jim Gardner's body. The poncho had blown back so I could recognize him.

I had never felt so alone in my life as I did that minute. Jim was gone. I had inherited his responsibilities and I couldn't, by any stretch of my imagination, believe that I was trained or prepared to step into his boots. I wanted to be sick.

Just after dark Hackworth discovered that another serious mistake had been made. Green replacements had been sent forward from the beach and they were wandering around in the dark. They must have come in on the medevac choppers and resupply ships. They were looking for who they should report to and where they belonged.

Hackworth, whose CP was only a few yards from my position, asked one of the soldiers who he was and were he had come from. Nervously, the boy said he was from Montana. Hackworth lied and told him he was from Montana too. He squatted down with the soldier and spent a few minutes telling him and his buddies what had happened, what he was going to do with them and what would be expected of them during the night.

He took the time to tell the troops just what the hell was going on and made them feel a part of the whole chaotic situation. Hackworth was instinctively doing what had been pounded into my head at Fort Benning. But, somehow he made it look easy. I will never forget that he found the time to do that for those men.

Hack called me over to his CP and wanted me to take a small recon party just forward of our perimeter to see what our security situation was. For all we knew the entire 95th Regiment could be massed inside the communications trenches that paralleled our positions only a dozen yards out.

The thought of going back over the same ground, through the same trenches that we had crossed twice during the day at such a high price, didn't thrill me. As I moved back to the Tiger CP I realized that we could get out there and not make it back this time.

I asked for volunteers and got too many to use. They were tired, beaten up, and most of them lightly wounded, but the Tigers still volunteered to go.

Half a dozen of us slipped out of our own positions after hasty, but detailed, coordination with the folks to our left and right. We wanted to make absolutely sure that we wouldn't get killed by Americans on our return. We got a promise from our sister units and they kept it.

I don't think I took a breath during the entire patrol. We went out not more than fifty meters, and then took a turn to move along our own front for another hundred and fifty to two hundred meters, and then returned. As we did, we didn't see any enemy soldiers or activity, but we heard plenty. There was clinking and clunking of equipment and the sound of muffled footsteps out to our front. They were still out there and they were doing the same thing we were doing—getting reorganized and licking their wounds.

Coming back into our own positions was every bit as dicey as being out in bad-guy territory. We knew that our folks were plenty jumpy and we made more than one call on the radio, whispering that we were coming back in to a point near where we went out.

As we got within fifty feet of our own position there was a pop and the night lit up like Texas Stadium. Trip flares give off the most intense white light to illuminate the presence of intruders. I must have crawled over one of our own.

We scrambled like hell, yelling and all talking at once to let our people know it was Tigers and we were coming back through the wire. No one fired on us, even though later some admitted that they were a heartbeat away from opening up.

We reported what we heard out to the front, and by the time I got back to my shallow position from the CP, Hackworth and Korman had adjusted the artillery fires to break up the reorganization that we had heard.

Dropping my gear, I was again aware of the bodies of the fallen Tigers who still hadn't been evacuated because of the danger to any chopper coming into our positions. They would have to wait until we had cleared the area of the still active antiaircraft weapons.

Before I had a chance to check the Tigers' positions, the radio blasted again and it was some field-grade staff officer at brigade head-quarters who demanded that I give him the exact details of the death of the civilian who had wandered into our firefight. I told him that I didn't have a clue who the guy was, why he was there, or where he came from.

The voice on the other end screamed at me for not knowing all the details of what was going on in *my* command and asked how I could possibly be in charge of a combat unit and not have a better grip on what was happening. What I didn't need at that moment was a class in leadership and responsibility from some puke who was in a clean and well-lit tactical operations center at Tuy Hoa North. I told him so. And he threatened to have my ass. He would take the matter up with my battalion commander. I suggested he do so and ended the conversation before he was ready to quit. He was hot and I was hotter. I had no idea who the jerk was. I didn't recognize his call sign and wasn't about to pull out a flashlight to check it out in the bloodstained Signal Operating Instruction booklet that I had inherited from Jim Gardner.

I found out later that the civilian was a journalist from a major U.S. magazine looking for a story. And the jerk who was busting my balls was a major, the information officer for the brigade. I also heard that he had tried to register a complaint with Hackworth at one of Hack's visits to the brigade headquarters. For his troubles, Hackworth offered to kick his ass for him if he ever jumped the chain of command and hassled one of his lieutenants again. I never heard another word about it.

It was after midnight and I realized that it was my birthday. I was twenty-two and in command of troops that were the envy of every lieutenant in my battalion. I realized how different my twenty-first birthday had been. I had been excited and thrilled with the successful completion of my first parachute jump and my first plane ride.

What a difference that year had made in my life. I wouldn't find out until several days later while filling out the paperwork on the battle of My Canh II that Jim Gardner had died on *his* birthday.

During the night there was sporadic shooting all along the perimeter. The instructions for heightened alert were hardly necessary. We had been inside the NVA's well-dug-in and well-connected bunker positions and knew that they still had the capacity to move around with little chance of detection.

Sometime during the middle of the night an explosion went off to our rear—near the friendly positions overlooking the river we had waded through. A grenade had been lobbed into an American foxhole, killing the two soldiers in it.

As near as anyone could guess, the NVA had paddled a small boat up the river until they found that particular hole and just popped the grenade into it and then drifted away with the strong current. They picked that hole because the two soldiers in there were smoking. The cigarette was still burning in the bottom of the hole when they found the bodies a few minutes later.

CHAPTER 18

•

The night had only a few hours remaining before dawn, but for me it went on and on. I reflected on what had happened and anticipated what would be expected of me in the hours and days to come. I tried to convince myself that I was up to the demands, but I had had even more confidence in Jim Gardner and he was only a few feet away—under a grimy poncho.

I thought of what I had experienced in the ten days of my tour in Vietnam and thought that if it was going to be a year like that, I could never make it. I thought of my family and how my father, grandfather, and great-grandfather had all served in the wars of their generations without faltering and I knew that there was no choice. I had asked to be a soldier—an officer—and a platoon leader. And I ended up with the absolute cream of the Airborne crop. How could I possibly complain?

I'm sure I said a Hail Mary or two and tried to get some sleep while staying alert—a special place in hell between awake and out cold that distorts and embellishes all that is real and confirms all that is not. It rarely results in rest.

We went to one-hundred-percent alert an hour before daybreak. I greeted dawn with very mixed emotions. The spookiness of night was gone, only to be replaced by renewed efforts to regain contact with the enemy to finally flush him out of My Canh. We had made it through day one; could day two be worse?

I checked the Tiger fighting positions on the perimeter and found some very dirty, very tired Tigers eager to hear what was next. I promised them that as soon as I knew I'd let them know.

Hackworth sent word down that, a couple at a time, he wanted every man in the My Canh area to see the contents of the foxhole where the two dead soldiers were—dead from smoking.

It was an ugly sight. The hole held them in its grip while the grenade had ripped them apart. And, clearly visible, the remains of the cigarette rested on the floor of the hole. The lesson was clear.

Coming back from the hole I had to relieve myself and I walked back to the bushy hedgerow where we had all waited the day before for Jim's signal to charge across the open paddy—but it was gone!

The vegetation had been almost completely chopped down to about waist level by the murderous fire that the NVA had placed across that field to stop us. It made me wonder that much more how any of us had made it across that field. I remember shuddering at the sight of the mowed brush—mowed by enemy steel.

Back at the shallow hole we called the Tiger CP, I lifted my shirt and looked at the spot where I had been grazed. I found a large, ugly, raspberry-colored, basketball-sized bruise. I realized just how lucky I had been. Some of the Tigers made faces at how bad it must hurt; their view of it was lots better than mine. I probably would have been in more pain if I had actually seen the entire bruise. The doc told me that he thought I'd broken a rib, or at least bruised the crap out of one.

I realized that morning that there were three kinds of combat: the combat the army had tried to simulate in training, the combat we saw in John Wayne movies, and the real thing. None of the three resembles either of the other two and the first two didn't help us get ready for the real combat. I knew from that day in My Canh that I would have to spend the rest of my time as an officer remembering how real combat differed from the pretend and preparing and training for the real one. It would be a tall task, for every soldier had many, many more hours of pretend and movie combat experience than the real thing, and on-the-job training was just too deadly.

There was almost no break at all. We were ordered to sweep back through the area we had been in twice before to look for stragglers and to try to get a prisoner if we could.

We saddled up and moved out of our perimeter back into the village of My Canh. But before we took our first step, the shooting began on the far side of our perimeter and the rifle companies were routing out NVA soldiers still dug in.

We knew that we weren't going to find an empty village from the experience of the units on our left and right, and we moved out much more deliberately and with much more emphasis on concealment than we had the previous day.

As we moved away from our perimeter, choppers and more gun-ships and medevacs and forward air controllers cluttered the sky. The thought of being mistaken by the pilots as enemy forces concerned me since we were not wearing the standard green jungle fatigues.

I made a couple of radio calls to the task force CP to remind them to tell the pilots that while the NVA were all wearing uniforms that the Americans had not seen before, so were the Tigers. I was told not to worry.

I tried to take in everything as we moved slowly through the now visible remains of My Canh. None of us had a chance to see much of it the day before, and nothing on the night patrol. The destruction we had brought on that sleepy hamlet was unbelievable. The place had been pounded with bombs, rockets, miniguns[58], and artillery for almost twenty hours, and in places the terrain features had been obliterated. Dikes had become craters and tall trees had become piles of deadfall. Houses and thatched shacks were smoldering ruins, and dazed and wounded livestock staggered about in total confusion.

The evidence of how large a force we had tangled with was everywhere. Sandal prints by the hundreds testified to a battalion- or larger-size unit. Abandoned and damaged weapons—crew-served machine guns, rocket launchers, and anti-aircraft guns—were scattered about. This had been no light infantry unit. The detail that went into the design and the building of the defensive positions, the firing positions, and the communications trenches attested to the enemy unit's advanced level of training and experience.

With each step, we discovered the size of the beast we had met with and were amazed that we had been inside the jaws of that monster and had somehow gotten out. It was one of the more sobering patrols of my year.

The artillery kept coming in, the gunships kept making passes in front of us, and the air force kept dropping 250-pound bombs into the village. I couldn't see how anyone could have lived through the pounding, or if they did, why they would want to stay for more when most of the others were dead or had escaped. Still, during our sweep we made some contact and killed a few remaining stragglers without taking any more casualties ourselves.

By the time we reentered the wire in the early afternoon, it had become a complete VIP and media circus. I remember Hack pointing at me and saying to a cluster of generals and war correspondents, "Here's Foley, my Tiger commander."

I had never seen that many general officers and their horse hold-

---

[58] High-speed helicopter machine guns capable of firing up to 6,000 rounds a minute.

ers[59] in one place. Our brigade commander, Brigadier General Willard Pearson, was there to see how the battle had shaped up. A lieutenant general from Saigon was also nosing around, and the press was interviewing everyone.

Lieutenant Colonel Joe Rogers, my battalion commander, was briefing the assembled crowd. Numbers were being thrown around about how many of us had been killed and wounded and how many enemy bodies we had counted. It was only the second time I had ever seen Colonel Rogers. But there was layer on layer of echelons between my station as a second lieutenant and his as a lieutenant colonel, battalion commander. Low key was his style, and I doubt if I saw him a dozen more times in the few months he had left with the battalion.

There was a lot of picture taking, and generals' aides fluttered about getting names to provide to the photographers. I found the entire zoo uncomfortable and quickly slipped away from the crowd of flunkies trying to get themselves recognized by the general.

I didn't have any problem with the press or the generals, for that matter, but I was just more at home with the Tigers and figured that the press had plenty of folks to interview and photograph. I just wasn't one of them.

By the time I dropped my gear back at the muddy spot we called our CP, I was hit with a long list of messages that had come in by radio from the beach and by messenger from the task force CP. All of them had to do with providing information up the chain of command. Not one message was information on how the wounded Tigers were, when we could expect some new uniforms to replace the shredded tiger stripes we were wearing, or anything else of importance to us.

Since the operation had completely petered out I thought things would quiet down. But the radio never stopped squawking from the moment Jim Gardner waved us forward to cross what the troops were now calling "Tiger Field." It seemed the ongoing mop-up operation of the 95th NVA Regiment was the only combat action in Vietnam. We were getting so many questions the replies would have filled books.

Every time we reported some essential fact that we were expected to call into higher headquarters, it became the catalyst for more questions. I recall one of the more ridiculous ones that came through intelligence channels. It had to do with a report of several fresh foot-

---

[59] Aides. The term comes from the days of the horse cavalry, when troopers were designated to hold the horses while their comrades went into action.

prints leading away from the far side of the enemy positions at My Canh: some boot prints, and some were from Ho Chi Minh sandals. Ho Chi Minh sandals were made from salvaged tires. They were a terrifically functional and frugal way to provide footgear.

The question was, Could the pattern of the sandals be recognized as having been made from American or foreign tire treads? I think I got a small ass chewing later for the flippant answer that I gave to the caller.

For the next five days I took the Tigers out in larger and larger loops, looking for the fading NVA soldiers. During the day we went on foot patrols and at night we set up ambushes. We made some light contact and added only slightly to the body count for the operation. What was important was that the Tigers were still on their feet, still conducting operations, and still effective. And still, without a complaint.

I would find out, years later, the value of Hackworth's insistence that the Tigers be immediately recommitted to combat operations. He felt strongly about never letting a bloodied unit sit and think about it for too long. He was sure that only guaranteed a unit would begin feeling sorry for itself and would soon become a morale problem. Getting them going again was like starting a cold engine on a freezing night. I followed Hack's lead several times during those years and I found it to be true.

During the half dozen patrols we mounted around My Canh we were able to reorganize into two small teams that would either work independently or as one team. We picked up some efficiencies in our combat loads, our rations, our signals, our movement, our light and noise discipline, and our self-reliance. The kinks were working out and each of us was just glad to be alive after the battle, to have something to work out.

Eventually, Task Force Hackworth abandoned the village and moved to a fire support base a few miles to the north. When we were finished with our ambush patrol we were to make the walk to the hamlet of Van Loc to join the battalion there.

Moving through the Tuy Hoa valley was incredibly deceiving. The visibility could be as much as several hundred yards across open fields, and if you stayed in the tree lines and the hedgerows, you could see and not be seen. At least that's what we thought.

In reality, every move we made was being watched by guerrillas whose sole job was to follow us at a distance, figure out what we were up to, and report it up their chain of command. Occasionally, they would take a few shots at us and run like hell. At other times we must have slipped them, or they were unable to pass the word that we were in the area.

We didn't realize the extent to which we were being watched, and when we did start to suspect it, we were decoyed by being allowed to find small enemy units to engage.

But that first long walk from the south end of the Tuy Hoa valley to Van Loc was the beginning of dozens of patrols that would take Tigers from one end to the other of that huge valley—looking for VC or NVA. Often we were out of radio contact with our battalion Tac CP and out of range of our direct support artillery batteries. That pretty much qualified the Tigers to consider themselves *long* in the Long-Range Patrol sense of the word.

Long-range *reconnaissance* patrol had been a term thrown about in other units in Vietnam, but Hackworth would not restrict us to that narrow definition. While he might have used the term a few times, he dropped the notion that our job had to do with just reconnaissance: We were to make contact when and where we could and reconnaissance was considered an added mission, not a primary one.

Van Loc II was a small bend in a river that had been a hamlet sometime before our arrival. What remained were some charred thatched huts and a dirt roadway that ran directly through the middle of the perimeter.

Inside the perimeter was the tactical command post for our battalion and two artillery batteries. Security was provided by one of our rifle companies. The Tigers were given a small area inside the perimeter and a slice of the perimeter to man at night. In the daytime the rifle company filled in for us.

Our mission once we closed into Van Loc was to get reorganized, reequipped, take on replacements and train, train, train. We were also put on standby for any mission that might come up. We weren't on a complete standby but neither were we out of the combat zone.

Fresh food and beer was waiting for us when we got to our own area. Platoon Sergeant Lawrence Smith had somehow arranged to get for us what no one else in the battalion had. We ate, drank, showered, and got mail. It was a bit of heaven. But late the first night back, Hackworth called me to the CP.

I walked into the general-purpose tent that was blacked out from the outside but brightly lit by generators on the inside. He offered me a beer and said we had to talk about the Tigers. I was still not comfortable talking to a major, but he didn't much care how comfortable I was. *He* was comfortable talking to me and that's all there was to it. I tried to look casual and cool as he began going through a list of mental notes he had for me.

Some of his notes were critical. He wanted us to work on *out G-ing the G*. In the pre-Vietnam days guerrillas were often referred to as "Gs" by American forces. Hackworth was talking about the Vietnamese G. He wanted us to move quieter, faster, and lighter than they did. He wanted us to be more independent and less reliant on helicopters and radios to conduct our operations. He wanted us to move through an area and not leave a sign we had ever been there.

These were not the strong suits of American combat units at that time. We had been trained to move quickly, loudly, and decisively when closing with and destroying an enemy force. Hack wanted stealth to be our byword.

I took notes rapidly and tried not to wonder at that point just how the hell I was going to do that.

He continued. He wanted me to recruit more Tigers and pick only the best. He didn't care how many or how few we accepted, as long as they were good. Anyone who couldn't hack it or changed his mind would be released from the Tigers and reassigned without prejudice.

I asked him how we were going to get enough volunteers. He laughed and leaned forward to tell me a secret about combat. He told me that after the amphibious patrol and the battle of My Canh, the legend of the Tigers was growing out of proportion to our actual deeds. But that was good. He went on to tell me that every man in the 1st of the 327th wanted to know if he had what it took to be a Tiger. He said all we had to do was stand in the middle of the perimeter on a small ammo box and whisper that the Tigers were looking for volunteers and they would come.

He was right.

They came and they worked hard. We ran local, short-duration patrols and longer-distance shakedown patrols that spanned several days. It was truly on-the-job training. The wrinkles were worked out of our patrolling techniques by the high number of Ranger school grads we actually had in the Tigers.

In Airborne tradition, everything we did started with the mission and worked backwards. We would get an order for a patrol or an ambush or a stay-behind ambush and organize and equip for that mission alone. Unlike a rifle company that would carry everything with it that it would need for all types of missions, we went as lightly as we could. When in doubt we took more ammo. But the weather was moderate enough for us to not have to carry too much related to surviving weather extremes. Rations were the heaviest problem after ammo.

Hackworth used us as an effective economy of force. We were not only sent out to verify rumors and reports of enemy activity, but he also increased the safety of the firebase and the static rifle company positions by denying the enemy freedom of movement. He knew the value of controlling the countryside. Even if you didn't have someone parked on every inch of the real estate, you could throw the VC off balance by active and vigorous patrolling.

We sorted out some volunteers and sent some back to the rifle companies without any fanfare. Then an extraordinary thing happened. A young black staff sergeant came to my CP and told me that he wanted to join the Tiger Force. He had an engaging smile and a terrific can-do attitude. But I didn't have a job for a staff sergeant.

He was young to be a staff sergeant, but still older than I was. I told him that I just didn't have a job for him. My two platoon sergeants were E-7s and most of my team leaders were sergeants, E-5. I just didn't want to move a three-stripe sergeant down to make way for a staff sergeant after all of the training we'd been doing.

He told me that he'd be a rifleman and wait for a job to open up, if it was all right with me. I took Pellum Bryant on the spot and did just that with him. He went to work for a three-striper, and there was not a complaint out of him.

Bryant took to the Tigers like he'd been there all his life. He quickly got to know every member of what was shaping up to be two Tiger platoons. He was good at everything he was given to do and he was reliable.

About the same time Bryant arrived, Hackworth called me in for another one of his chats. Beers appeared and he beamed. It seemed the reputation of the Tigers and the wisdom of creating them had become an accepted fact, not only in our battalion, but at brigade headquarters. The other two battalions had created similar units: the Recondos in the 2d of the 502d, and the Hawks in the 2d of the 327th. Hack had also persuaded Lieutenant Colonel Rogers to allow him to expand the Tigers to a two-platoon unit with three officers.

The announcement that there would be three officers hit me between the eyes. I was becoming pretty possessive of the Tigers, having inherited command on Jim Gardner's death. New officers most likely meant that I would no longer be the senior one. There still wasn't a lieutenant in the battalion whom I outranked. But our success had caught up with us. Every lieutenant in the battalion was on Hack's back to let him into the Tiger Force. He picked two of his most experienced and most trusted first lieutenants to send to the Tigers.

Johnny Howard and Norm Grunstad were classmates from West Point. I had only met them briefly, but both had been with the battalion for much longer than me and were itchy to get time with the Tigers. The new organization was that I would lead one platoon, Johnny would lead the other, and Norm would be the Tiger commanding officer.

I was pretty disappointed with the news but saluted and didn't argue about it. As it turned out, I got along well with both of them.

My experiences with Norm and Johnny were limited because Hackworth often gave missions to the Tiger platoons directly and not through Norm. We were often working independently, and many times Norm wasn't anywhere near where my platoon was when a hot mission came down to us.

So I scaled my focus down to worrying about the one platoon that I was responsible for, and quickly discovered that not only did I have a terrific bunch of troops to work with, I had two completely qualified platoon sergeants—Belden and Bryant.

Still, we stepped off on operations with little trouble. There was so much momentum built up in the core of the Tiger Force that the introduction of new officers and a dozen or so new volunteers didn't do anything to retard the spirit or the bravado of the Tigers.

With the new organization came a backtracking of patrolling missions. Instead of working in the far-off hills, we returned to the valley floor and the surrounding small hills to revisit the hamlets, trails, and streams for any signs of rebuilding and returning NVA units.

At the same time we began to experiment more with new techniques and new methods of patrolling. We also found ourselves as guinea pigs for the new equipment that was arriving in Vietnam.

As to the techniques, we began by saturating the valley floor with patrols during the daytime and establishing small ambushes at night. We tried stay-behind ambushes. We'd make a point of setting up before dark and then moving. Our assumption was that we were being watched by villagers and VC sympathizers, if not directly. There was no way our ambushes could be successful if the enemy knew where we were, and it proved to be very risky for us if they wanted to hit us after dark.

We tried finding remote observation posts where we could keep likely routes under constant observation, to be able to drop artillery and air strikes on enemy patrols. The technique didn't work all that well in the daytime, but at night we had an advantage—the Starlight Scope.[60]

The arrival of the experimental Starlight Scope in Vietnam was a major breakthrough in leveling the playing field. The VC and NVA were masters at working at night, and they had spent their lives walking the trails that we were hard-pressed to find on our maps.

The Starlight was heavy and awkward but terrific when it worked. But it was a constant worry for me. I was cautioned that to lose one or even talk about it could cause grave repercussions. The item was to stay hidden and remain classified as long as possible. There was no sense in letting the VC know that we could see at night.

The Starlight was a clever application of physics to create a single scope that accepted and amplified low, ambient light levels, projecting a green image onto the eyepiece at the rear of the scope. Looking through it at night was much like looking at a daylight scene through a dark green piece of glass. Everything was monochrome green and very contrasted. Still, images ranged from easy to not-so-easy to recognize. At its worst, the Starlight was a wonderful device that probably saved far more American lives than we can ever estimate, and cost the enemy an equal or greater number of casualties.

But for us the Starlight came with extra demands: we had to carry it in a manner that would conceal it, we had to provide reports on its effectiveness, and we had to account for it as a controlled item.

On one patrol to the south end of the Tuy Hoa valley, we were tasked with climbing up what was a nearly vertical slope that took five or six hours to climb. Our mission was to confirm intelligence reports that there was an enemy base camp located on or near the top of the very steep hill. Once we got there, we found little evidence that there had been anyone there since prehistoric times. We spent the night setting up an ambush without contact.

By midafternoon the next day, we were back down on the valley floor and headed back to the firebase, some fifteen kilometers away. But I was alarmed to find that one of the Tigers had set down our Starlight Scope on a rock, thinking that his partner was going to spell him by carrying it down the hill. It was never picked up.

I called the battalion CP and reported in doubletalk that we had left the "item" on top of the hill. I don't know what I was hoping to hear.

---

[60] The AN/PVS-2, Night Observation Device. It magnified light from the moon and the stars 50-60,000 times and could see things at ranges out to 1,200 meters.

What I got was a message from Hackworth to find it or not bother coming back—ever.

I had a real leadership problem on my hands. Send a portion of the dozen-man patrol back up the hill to retrieve the Starlight—if it was still there—or take the entire patrol. I discussed it with Pellum Bryant and decided we would *all* make the trip back up the hill, even though only two of the Tigers were at fault for the screwup.

Morale hit an all-time low on the second trip up. But we broke into the clearing we had left early that morning and found the Starlight still sitting on the rock. If anything proved that there was no VC activity on top of that hill, the recovery of the Starlight did.

Still, with all its extra weight and battery problems, it was great to have.

As the weeks wore on we received new test ammunition for the M-79 grenade launchers, different types and sizes of canteens, and even tested a large hot-dog-shaped container for water that could be dropped from a chopper. While it was interesting and encouraging to get new items that might help us operate better or might help save lives, the added burden of slightly modifying operations to test the items was a pain, as were the subsequent evaluations that I had to draft and forward.

But the real topper was the Manpack Personnel Detector, Chemical, quickly nicknamed the "people sniffer."[61] I was picked by someone up the chain of command to go to a nearby Special Forces camp to get the short course on the new gizmo. When I asked, I was told that my name was selected because I had retainability and because I worked in reconnaissance. It sounded like a weak excuse to me, but I had little to say about it.

Trying to describe the people sniffer is fairly simple. It was a mechanical nose that could be carried by the foot soldier in the bush. Its principle of operation was based on the theory that all mammals give off minute amounts of ammonia, and the sniffer could detect them. The selling point was that people were supposed to give off so much more ammonia than other animals that the sniffer would be able to detect the presence of humans at great distances.

Did it work? Sometimes. But it depended on a large number of variables. First, the operator would have to carry the rucksack-size metal box on his back. That was a problem. Then there was a vacuum

[61] The XM-2, also know as Olfactronic Personnel Detector. There was also an Airborne version known as the XM-3.

cleaner–type hose that extended from the box to a sample-collecting device that attached a couple of inches behind the flash suppressor of the operator's rifle. Finally, the sniffer operator had to be the first person in the direction of march, or he would detect the troops in front of him.

To these physical problems was added the complications created by the shifting weather and wind patterns in the bush and in the open. And there was the reduced vigilance on the part of the point man– sniffer operator. Because he had to watch a readout needle on the gauge mounted to the front of his rifle, he was unable to keep his eyes on the area to his front.

The weather considerations were so important to the operation of the people sniffer that the instruction included a complete mini-course on micrometeorology. Great care was taken to acquaint the operator with the different airflow up and down hillsides, canopied and bare, at different times of the day.

Once I returned from the people-sniffer training I had to give the same training to selected operators from the three infantry battalions in the brigade.

I don't mind saying that my heart was not in the job and I didn't much believe in the utility of the device. It worked, and the physical sciences involved were sound, but the tactical application of a device that displaced combat gear and diverted the attention of a point man was just not workable.

Just after sniffer training, the personnel turbulence picked up. Many were moving into short-timer's status since they had come over with the earliest elements of the battalion. Belden was one of them. I told him that as soon as he got his orders he could plan on going, because I had Bryant to replace him. The announcement made both of them happy.

CHAPTER 19

·

In early March we had been working north of the firebase at Van Loc when one of our rifle companies bumped into a dug-in enemy emplacement near a village named My Phu—not more than five thousand meters from My Canh. The company was coming back to the firebase from an unsuccessful sweep and we were patrolling in the hills, looking to drum up business since the rice bowl had gone fairly quiet.

The rifle platoons that made the initial contact immediately wrapped around the enemy firing positions and tried to develop the situation into a favorable chance contact. What started out as simply the exchange of a few rounds became a significant battle.

The NVA unit turned out to be near their own pre-dug positions, and they quickly scampered into them and began returning highly effective fire against the Americans. The contact developed quickly enough for Hackworth to divert all of the battalion's resources to bottling up and destroying the enemy battalion.

When the fight began the Tigers were at the battalion's firebase at Van Loc. We had only been there overnight to refit and send out more ambush patrols and to provide security for the artillery battery in the perimeter. We were immediately alerted to reinforce the fight at My Phu. That meant an immediate reorganization to a maneuver unit again. So with one ear on the radio crosstalk we reorganized our teams, redistributed weapons and equipment, and prepared to be committed to the fight.

Hackworth wanted us at My Phu right away, but the chopper resources of the brigade were not that flexible. We stood by anxiously waiting to be thrown into the fight while we heard of the staggering casualties on both sides. My concern grew as the sun waned but the fight didn't. If things didn't happen soon, we'd have to make the move by chopper at night. Up until that time there had been no night chopper combat assaults into hot landing zones—we would be the first.

Around an hour after sundown we were picked up by a flight of choppers capable of handling half of the Tiger Force in one lift. That didn't make me happy either. If we were going to be thrown into a fight, I wanted us to go in one lift and be an integral unit once we hit the ground. The thought of going in with the first lift, and then having to secure the LZ and wait for a turnaround to bring the second half of the Tigers in while under fire, seemed to me like giving the enemy a better second chance to blow our choppers and Tigers out of the sky. But I was a second lieutenant and my opinions on how best to commit the Tigers were not worth much that night.

None of us had gone anywhere by chopper at night short of administrative flights. Night heliborne assault just hadn't been developed as a standard technique. I was told later, by some chopper pilot friends, that the reason for limiting night chopper operations was that there were few reaction forces and plans in place to handle the contingency if a chopper got shot down. In all probability the survivors would have to wait for help until first light.

I had my radio headset pressed tightly to my ear to hear the latest developments as we lifted off the PZ at Van Loc. The fighting continued and so did the list of mounting casualties. I was told by Hack to expect to land on a hot LZ and to be careful not to shoot up troops from A and B Companies. We would not be landing inside a secure area, he said, so be ready to defend ourselves as soon as we jumped out of the chopper.

"Chopper?" I asked for more details and discovered that I was the only one who had not been told that we would only be able to get into a small landing zone one chopper at a time, and that we would be going in with no navigational lights and no landing lights to make us harder to hit. As we flew the short hop to My Phu, my pucker factor went up. I had no idea what the ground situation was, only a vague idea where the friendlies were, no ground reference points to orient myself, and no idea what to expect—beyond trouble.

One of the pilots turned around and gave me a hand signal that we were five minutes out, to let me pass the word to the others on board. I nodded okay and kept on trying to pass the word to the leaders in the two choppers behind mine. It was at that point I realized just how tense everyone was. I had been smoking a last cigarette in the darkness of the chopper cargo compartment, and I absentmindedly flipped the lit butt out the open doorway. The cigarette went out into the slipstream, got caught by the wind, and zipped by the doorgunner. The gunner must have thought it was an enemy tracer because he opened up on full automatic with his machine gun, spraying everything below with snaking tracers.

I quickly explained to him that I had flipped the butt and we were not taking ground fire. I have to admit that I was terribly embarrassed by the stupid move, but no one saw any humor in it. Neither did they say anything about it—then or later. Everyone was deep in thought as we lost altitude on our approach to our first hot night LZ.

The descent was agonizingly slow, and all of us searched the pitch-black paddy fields and clumps of dense vegetation for some sign of friendlies or enemy forces. Tracers zipped in all directions and the sky was streaked with smoke trails from the dozens of flares that had been dropped by the air force, circling at a much higher altitude.

We slipped out of the slight illumination of a distant flare that was slowly drifting diagonally across the sky over the battlefield.

The six Tigers and the door gunners leaned out, stepped out on the skids, and searched the ground below for some sign—anything. No one was sure we were landing at the right spot, or if we were even close to our own A and B Companies.

As we got within several dozen feet above the landing zone, I was able to make out what looked like the weak beam of a GI flashlight. It flickered on and off and then stayed off. Since I couldn't talk to the pilot over the intercom or get his attention while he was on short final, I just had to hope that he knew more about what was happening on the LZ than I.

The first chopper in, we landed on a hard, dry rice paddy. The Tigers with me bailed out and ran out from the chopper just far enough to let the pilot maneuver up and out of the LZ without worrying about killing someone. The noise of the chopper turbine and the blades covered the first few rounds of enemy fire directed toward us. I think each of us heard or felt the presence of the small-arms fire, but we were all looking for someone else to confirm it. The level of confusion, landing blind on a black LZ while taking fire, was new to all of us. No one in the 101st had ever made a night combat assault on a hot LZ before, and we just had no experience, no right way to do it.

The chopper lifted off and left room for the second ship to follow him in. I pulled the few men I could muster off to one side of the landing zone to start counting heads. I probably should have tried to establish some kind of perimeter for the choppers to land inside of, but I thought that there was a greater chance of a chopper injuring a Tiger than there was of a Tiger providing any kind of protection for the choppers. Even if we knew where the fires were coming from, we were hesitant to return fire for fear of hitting someone in A and B Companies—wherever they were.

Between the first and second lift, while I was trying to get a headcount and a feel for the landing zone, all I heard was shooting—at us, around us, and near us. I didn't have a clue where I belonged and where the Tigers were supposed to link up with friendlies.

Suddenly I heard my name being called. It was a voice I recognized immediately. Soft-spoken, but forceful, Hackworth was trying to get my attention. He was standing in the middle of the paddy repeating his call. As I turned around and crouched down to see if I could silhouette him against the skyline, I fully expected to find him surrounded by some security.

But that, as I was beginning to understand, was not Hack's style. He stood alone in the middle of the paddy, ready to guide me and the Tigers into our positions.

Reaching him, we talked as we watched the second chopper land—it too taking enemy fire. He wanted me to assemble my platoon and help seal the circle of troops that he had wrapped around the enemy battalion that they had bagged. He also made it quite clear that A and B Companies had been badly chewed up, and if anything went sour during the night, he was counting on me to take up the slack. My Tigers were fresh and he would expect them to be flexible and ready.

Assembling the Tigers in a clearing that I couldn't see well, while under fire, was something that I would never like to have to do again. The confusion factor was almost as high as being in a firefight. And the ability to communicate was hampered by the fact that we were receiving sporadic incoming fire. In a better situation, we would have called for supporting fires on the locations we could identify as the source of the incoming. But since we hardly knew where we were, much less the other friendlies, we just had to try to avoid the incoming and get to our assigned position on the perimeter.

Hack lead us through the light vegetation to one side of the unconnected circle and let me know where he wanted me to place the Tiger Force. He told me to come back to his CP after that for more instructions.

It was a completely unnerving experience, trying to move into line while the shooting was still going on, not knowing exactly where the good and bad guys were. The Tigers didn't make the job more difficult. They understood the confusion, waited patiently while I established contact with the rifle companies on each flank and then moved quietly into their two-man fighting positions.

During the movement, the sky was filled with snakes of red and green tracer fire. And the entire battle area was bathed in the gently rocking light provided by high-candlepower flares.

I went back to Hack's CP only to find him in his usual unprotected headquarters that consisted of him and his radio operator, Daryl Nunnelly. He was talking on the radio. He didn't even say anything to me directly. He simply reached out and grabbed my sleeve and gently pulled me down, closer to the map they were looking at.

His gesture was a mixture of his wanting to include me in the instructions and a concern for my safety. Just because it was command post didn't mean it was safe by a long shot. He finished his radio conversation and traced his finger in a tiny arc on the map. He explained that he was sure that it was better than a battalion—or what remained of one—and that the plan was to close the loop and pound the crap out of them all night with air and artillery.

My job: don't let them out. He then dropped his grease pencil on the map case and grabbed my shoulder and told me that he wanted no heroics out of the Tigers. He wanted me to make sure that I understood that all we had to do was sit tight and let them try to squeeze out of the circle. "Let them make the moves and we'll drop 'em from good firing positions," he said, and followed it up with, "You got that?"

It was clear. He didn't want another My Canh II, and I could feel the anguish in his voice from the heavy casualties that the battalion had already taken that day. He wanted to take care of the NVA battalion with no more casualties. His priorities were clear to me—the troops came first.

For a man who had garnered a reputation for being ruthless on the battlefield, I was never confused about his priorities. He wanted the small-unit commanders to be absolutely sure that he was interested in body count—but his body count was about how many healthy American soldiers we brought back from the field. Good training and solid leadership would result in plenty of enemy casualties. We didn't need to make any more charges across any more fields, like My Canh II, to be successful.

To this day, his priorities have never changed and he remains the strangest combination of aggressiveness and concern.

While I would spend many, many more bizarre nights in Vietnam, that night of the My Phu battle will always stand out. It was well after midnight when I finally got the Tigers' positions adjusted, areas of responsibilities assigned, and coordination made with units to my left, right and rear. During the entire process I could feel and hear the movement of the NVA in our encirclement. They were scraping things on the ground, digging, clanking metal against metal, and signaling to one another with whistles and bird calls.

During the same time, we were dropping an unending stream of artillery and mortar fire into the perimeter and lighting up the night with a nonstop string of parachute flares.

We fired at each other sporadically, not sure if we were seeing movement or shadows from the oscillating flares. No one slept. No one ate. We just watched and waited for the muffled sounds of the far-off artillery tubes to deliver the deafening crack of rounds on target in our circle.

Occasionally, we would see the NVA carrying their wounded by their arms and legs or on homemade stretchers. When that happened not one of our people fired at the images. I found out later that A and B Companies were sending recovery teams forward (into the encirclement) to retrieve their own wounded. They, in turn, were not fired upon by the NVA.

It was as if there had been an unwritten contract to fire on combatants only and to allow each other's recovery teams to move unharmed.

It was a very long night. The smell of death hung in the still air, and the acrid smoke from the hundreds of mortar and artillery rounds burned our eyes. I don't know how many casualties we inflicted that night. I do know we only took light casualties, as did A and B Companies.

Dawn came and painted a completely different battlefield than I had assumed was around me in the darkness. I was upset to find out that I had made some very unwise choices in positioning the Tiger Force. Some positions were looking up at slightly higher ground. Others were oriented the wrong way, and still others were too far apart to be mutually supporting.

The lack of understanding of my sector led me to fill the blanks in my mind the way I thought the ground lay rather than the way it actually did. I'm glad that the NVA didn't make a break in force to try to punch out through us. It would have been very costly for us, defending the shaky deployment that I had designed in the dark.

After first light our battalion lifted the artillery and mortar fires and continued the medical evacuations of the wounded that didn't get out from the previous day, as well as the new casualties during the night.

The enemy firing had stopped.

What we saw in front of us was an incredible scene of destruction. What had been a cluster of small hamlets making up a village on generally flat rice-paddy land was churned earth and smoking leveled structures. The eighteen to twenty hours of continuous small-arms fire, air strikes, artillery, and mortars had pockmarked the tiny village over and over again. Bombs destroyed gardens and sent the earth flying several times over—each time a new one landed. The effect was the repeated violent relocation of large chunks of earth, trees, hedges, and thatched houses.

With the firing stopped, the rich black earth smoked from the explosives and the few pieces of remaining thatch and wood flickered with small flames. And among the loosened earth were bit and pieces of bodies, equipment, and uniforms that we could see from our positions.

I was again summoned to the CP. Hack and Lieutenant Colonel Joe Rogers were preparing the battalion to sweep through the battle area. The plan was to develop the contact if there were remaining NVA forces in the circle. We were to do so by probing the enemy positions to determine the remaining strength, with the caution not to act impulsively since we had them surrounded, and the village that concealed them under constant observation from the air.

By seven o'clock the air was filled with circling choppers, bird dogs,[62] and medevac ships. The rifle companies sent out small patrols and I did the same with the Tigers.

I led one of the first patrols out into the center of the circle. I was prepared for some enemy casualties and some remaining resistance, and moved the small patrol cautiously in a widely dispersed formation. I wasn't prepared for what we found.

As we got into the bunkered and camouflaged areas of the village, we found large concentrations of enemy dead. But they weren't just dead. They were dismembered and scattered all over the area. The continuous pounding had blown them apart and then continued to blow pieces of bodies all over the area. The level of violence that we witnessed was extraordinary. The trauma inflicted on the NVA was so thorough that it was often difficult to identify body parts. It was a field of collapsed bunkers strewn with meat, bone, flesh, hair, and uniforms. That was about as precise as we could be in our identification of the damage done during the night.

It was horrible and chilling. Though I had seen dead men before in

---

[62] The L-19 light observation airplane, also designated 0-1, was widely used in Vietnam for artillery spotting (forward air control or FAC) and surveillance. Its civilian counterpart was the Cessna 170.

my first few months in Vietnam, I had never seen so many bodies so dismembered or so widely scattered. I'm sure that none of us will ever forget the degree of destruction we witnessed that March morning.

As soon as it became clear that there was not much chance of significant enemy contact, Hack called me and told me that he was pulling most of A Company and some of B Company out of the search for stragglers. The mop-up would be the Tigers' job, and he was going to relieve and reorganize the battered rifle companies.

We spent most of the morning walking cautiously the length and breadth of the enemy positions, surveying the extent of the destruction and searching for any remaining NVA stragglers. We found none, though we continued to find more and more body parts exposed and half covered by loose dirt.

We found out what the scraping noise was during the night. The NVA had slipped small figure-eight lengths of rope over the feet of the dead and dragged them off somewhere. Some of them must have been wounded or interrupted by the subsequent fires, because we found a few bodies that had been dragged short distances and left behind with the ropes still attached to the ankles.

The other noises must have been the survivors trying to dig out others who had been buried under the mounds of dislodged earth. We found several small entrenching tools where their owners had been using them to help their buried buddies.

Without exception, it looked as if all of the hundreds of dead had died horrible and terribly frightening deaths. We buried as many as we could and doused the others with diesel fuel and burned the bodies to cut down on the risk of infection in the area. By the end of the day we were exhausted and terribly depressed by the experience.

The Tigers weren't any more hardened to the job than I was. And before it was over there were more than a few of us who lost our breakfasts doing the job. We talked little and stayed cautious—ready for the odd survivor, but there was none. The dead were dead, and the living had made it out during the night.

But where did the survivors go? Where they always went in Vietnam —they slipped away in the night. I suspect that there were some holes in the encirclement that we, as a battalion-sized force, failed to plug. To this day I am amazed at how successful the VC and NVA were at breaking out of what we thought were tight encirclements. But they knew the terrain and we didn't.

Our first few months of existence was hard. We learned every lesson the hard way and had no one to compare notes with. The

Tigers didn't operate at all like the rifle companies and didn't know what to expect with each coming day. So we kept on taking on new missions and trying out new techniques to outdo the VC and some worked. But each new discovery cost us dearly.

Not long after we returned to the firebase at Van Loc, we got a new battalion commander. Walter Meinzen was a no-nonsense West Pointer who had little or no sense of humor. I got the feeling that he didn't much like me from the minute we met. He was the first officer I ever worked for that I just didn't get along with.

His first appearance in the Tiger Force area was an unannounced inspection of the Tigers as we waited to be outloaded for operations to the north of the firebase. Meinzen told me to assemble the Tigers so that he could inspect them. This didn't go over well with the troops. Each of them had rigged their rucksacks and web gear to carry the maximum amount of ammo, water and rations to take us through a ten-day operation. We were pack-mule heavy and hardly able to stand without bending at the waist to compensate for the loads. Trying to stand at attention for Colonel Meinzen was nearly impossible. And I think he detected the negative attitude that the normally gung-ho Tigers were giving off. They felt it was chickenshit to inspect them after they had been inspected by Tiger NCOs and by me. But they didn't say anything.

Wearing telltale new fatigues, boots, and light web gear, Meinzen found small things that he wanted corrected. His criticism wasn't well received by the Tigers. But I was a second lieutenant and he was a lieutenant colonel, and I had little footing to argue with him over it. I let it go. As soon as he finished the inspection he strode off to his tent without so much as a customary thank you.

We all brushed it off and mounted our choppers to head off to the foothills of the Vietnamese central highlands.

That operation began a true test for us. We were patrolling a wide variety of mountainous terrain types and operating at great distances from the battalion. Our overall mission was to develop more enemy contacts for the rifle companies to exploit. Our days consisted of humping the hills that were often near straight up-and-down climbs. Our nights were ambush after ambush. We got little sleep and learned to be very self reliant. Our contact with the battalion was by radio and occasional ration resupply.

It was very hard to tell just where we would find enemy forces. We could not count on them working in a certain type of terrain or avoiding certain areas. They were equally comfortable setting up their small base areas in the triple canopy rain forest as they were concealing them in small caves or tunnels.

I suspect that we avoided many contacts at their option without ever knowing it. It was months before we discovered the extent of the damage that we had inflicted on the VC and NVA forces in the Tuy Hoa valley in the My Canh II and My Phu battles. They weren't ready to tangle with our battalion again until they could replace their losses and retrain their units. Had they been at the strength they were at those two battles, I suspect that we would have been in deep trouble on some of our long and lightly manned patrols.

The patrols themselves were extremely unforgiving and were the best classrooms for learning small-unit techniques. We discovered just how hard we could push ourselves without sustaining crippling illnesses and injuries. We could almost tell when we were overdoing it and would pay for it with a drop in security, lack of dexterity on the move, and failing resistance to the array of illnesses and diseases that looked for the chance to invade our bodies.

As the hills got steeper and the patrols got longer, the number of losses went up in direct proportion. I had to find time to pull Tigers out of their jobs—sometimes for just a few hours to let them sleep or just clean up and lay down in a sunny spot beneath the canopy. They just needed some small breaks to recharge from the constant demands on their bodies and the strain on their minds.

When we failed to do this it would result in compromising our positions as we called in medevac choppers to take away our sick and wounded. Malaria, dengue fever, chronic boils, dysentery, and infected cuts and bruises were as crippling as gunshot and frag wounds.

Then, after each evacuation, we'd have to move harder and faster to put distance between us and our evac site to regain our security. That backfired on me. Every man knew the cost of calling for medevacs and wouldn't speak up if he had a problem until the problem was so far advanced that there was little option but to evacuate him. I never did figure out how to make them say so when they were hurting. I just tried to watch them. But I was no doctor.

We tried ever more daring patrols designed to flush the reluctant VC out of their strongholds in the many hiding places throughout the huge Tuy Hoa valley. We tried to act as bait. The concept was to walk trails and hope to spring an ambush. At first blush the idea seemed foolhardy. But when you are really prepared to be ambushed, there is not too much more danger in it than making a chance contact. We were feeling fairly confident that the VC and NVA remaining in the area had broken down into very small elements to avoid being detected by American patrols saturating the area.

So to look like we were doing the same and tempt the enemy to fire on us, we struck out in patrols of ten to fifteen men. We carefully selected areas we had become familiar with, and we had reaction forces staged nearby in choppers waiting to pounce on whatever contacts we developed. Thus, we didn't have to sustain a long contact. We only had to survive a short and violent one. We upped the ante by having almost every man in the patrol carry a machine gun.

On the few occasions when we did make contact, it usually happened with us spread out in an extended file along small trails with close vegetation. We would take fire from small or hasty enemy ambushes, and return such an overwhelming volume of heavy fire that they were often overcome in the initial volley.

While the technique never proved to be too costly for us in casualties, it was terribly costly in how it tied up other reaction force troops and choppers that could be out searching for contacts themselves.

I suspect that the high demand on manpower and machinery, balanced against the few enemy casualties we produced when contact was made, caused the tactic to be dropped.

After one such operation we were instructed to move to the battalion base camp on the South Tuy Beach. As we approached the battalion encampment, I got a call over the radio that a chopper and crew had just been shot down a few miles down the coast and just inland from the ocean. I was to take my two chopper loads of Tigers to the site, evacuate the pilots in my choppers, secure the downed aircraft, and wait until it could be recovered or for further instructions.

My only response was, "Wilco."

We landed in a fallow rice-paddy field next to a sugarloaf hill that ran parallel to it and to the sea on the other side of the field. At the base of the hill were *two* downed choppers, not one.

We found out that the two gunships had been returning to the brigade when one took accurate ground fire. The pilot wrestled the crippled gunship to the ground, and the second chopper landed behind it to pick up the crew. As he attempted to take off, the pilot of the second ship meshed rotors with the crippled ship, downing his own chopper in the process.

So what we found was two three-man chopper crews and two completely loaded Huey gunships.

* * *

The first part of the mission was only complicated by the fact that I had no radio contact with the downed crews and had to try to pass information back and forth through the pilot of my chopper. No one on the ground knew if there were any VC in the area or where the initial fire had come from, but they suspected the sugarloaf hill next to the choppers.

, We quickly landed the two Tiger Force choppers in the middle of the wet rice field and unloaded. As Pellum scattered the Tigers around the choppers to set up a perimeter in the less than optimum terrain, I waved frantically for the chopper crews to hurry up and get into our ships.

As soon as the extraction choppers cleared the area it got pretty quiet. It was a clear day, bright and sunny, and our visibility was excellent. But we still didn't know what the enemy situation was.

I radioed back to operations to find out what the plan was to lift the choppers out. I got the runaround—no one knew the exact answer. I was told to stand-by by one of the battalion TOC RTOs.

Pellum and I were both concerned by the fact that we were in the worst possible position. We had nothing to provide cover or concealment for the Tigers, and our presence in the bottom of a hole surrounded by hills on two sides had to be known by everyone for miles around.

Then Pellum came up with a good idea to equalize the odds a bit. He found that each of the choppers had two working M-60 machine guns on board, extra barrels, and thousands and thousands of rounds of belt ammo. We dismounted the machine guns and added them to the eight we had already brought with us. We couldn't have been more heavily armed if we each had a tank.

While Pellum was working on distributing plenty of ammo around our feeble little perimeter, I tried to plan some artillery fires on the hill to our west and the one to our south. I knew that I could easily direct lots of accurate artillery on positions on the hill because I was sure of my position and sure of the hill's locations. That's when I got the bad news—no one could fire for us.

We were on the end of the gun-target line. Our target was to the west of us and the artillery batteries were also to the west at the maximum effective range of the tubes. The concern was that if they fired for me, there was a real good chance that a round could go a bit long, clear the top of the hill, and land on us. And there was nothing we could do to change our positions or dig in for protection. We were tied to the choppers with our bellies in three inches of stagnant water.

Before I could report my problem to the battalion headquarters, we began noticing movement all around us. Not much, just a glimpse of a fleeting figure on the hilltop and a couple of fast-moving, pajama-clad images darting between clumps of bushes on the southern approach to the hill. We were sure that we were in some trouble, and soon began taking small-arms fire from the hilltop not more than three hundred feet above us.

I called for gunships and was told that there was another contact going on and they had priority. Whoever answered my call at the TAC CP suggested that I use artillery. I tried to explain that I couldn't get artillery when the enemy fires started getting more accurate, and a strange voice overpowered my reception of the TAC CP's.

The voice asked me if I needed some help. I said yes, but I had already been told that I was in the wrong location for supporting fires. He told me to look up and to my rear.

There, lazily rolling flying figure eights in the sky, was a navy bird dog. He was an ANGLICO pilot, Army-Navy, Ground Liaison, or the navy's equivalent to an army forward observer. He was trained to bring naval gunfire onto ground targets in support of the army and the Marines.

I told him that I needed artillery and couldn't convince the army that they should fire the mission for me. I could use all the help I could get, but then I had a sudden sinking feeling. I remembered that all I knew about calling for naval gunfire procedures was from a short classroom exercise back at OCS.

He told me to stand by while he did a little looking and a little checking. He flew over the target area and took some ground fire. After telling us to button up, he fired some artillery on the far side of the hill, safely away from us. From there he must have convinced someone to fire the mission for us. I didn't know who was firing or where the fires were coming from, but he delivered.

He then told me to pass the word to my troops to put our heads down. I thought that was unnecessary since he knew we were taking fire and that we were down as far as we could get. After all, we were taking plunging fire from the hilltop, not fires that we could hide behind something to avoid.

Before I could tell the observer that I wasn't too sure that we were far enough away from the target he called to tell me that the rounds were on the way. A split second later I heard the report of the guns. Rounds plowed into the exact spot on the hilltop we'd selected. The ground rocked and our ears rang with the incredible noise the three exploding projectiles made.

Without waiting, the pilot called for three more rounds in the same location. They too impacted with deadly accuracy, and we all waited for some response from the hidden enemy positions on the hill.

The plopping of flying debris into the paddy water stopped, the smoke cleared, and it was silent except for the ringing in our ears. We waited for the enemy fire to resume. It did not. We scanned the surrounding hills for any sign of movement. There was none. And the sun was setting.

I thanked the navy observer for his accurate and effective fire and let him head back to his airfield for the night. He gave me a frequency and call sign to use if I needed any more help during the night.

The thought of calling for more indirect fire at night, that close to the target, didn't thrill me, so I just thanked him and told him I'd let him know if I needed more hilltops rearranged.

Another call to the TAC CP told me that there was no chance of recovery before full dark, and the aviation battalion didn't intend to attempt a pickup at night. I was instructed to sit tight and wait for further instructions in the morning.

Pellum and I huddled next to one of the choppers and tried to figure out what to do during the night. We knew that any enemy unit in the area was absolutely sure what we were doing, where we were, exactly how strong we were, and what kinds of weapons we had. There was nowhere we could move to, no more help to call for than what we had already tried, and no idea just what the enemy intent was. We decided to take advantage of the machine guns to keep any enterprising enemy forces from sneaking up on us by using them to fire harassing and interdicting fire.

So in the closing light of the day, Pellum and I set out to create range cards for each of the gunners. We moved from position to position and selected the most likely approaches to the perimeter, and set them as priorities for the gunners to aim at in the dark.

Throughout the night we would fire random bursts of machine-gun fire along the approaches we had identified. With as many machine guns as we had and a high density of tracer rounds, the night was filled with ricocheting machine-gun fire every few minutes until dawn.

During the night we took no enemy incoming fire. Still, I was worried that they might think we were worth the effort, move some mortars within range, and lay some rounds in on us. That would have been very costly for us since we had no cover to hide behind and had brought no entrenching tools to dig in with.

* * *

By first light I had received a call from the aviation battalion that they were going to send a Chinook[63] to rig and lift out the two choppers—one at a time. While I was glad that they were going to recover the choppers, I was disappointed that they were only going to send one Chinook to do the job.

I really don't know what I expected. Chinooks were the workhorses and just finding one to recover the choppers was hard enough. But even if they had two of the large choppers available, there would have been no way that they both could have worked at the same time since the two downed choppers were less than twenty feet apart.

My concern was that they would first send in a Huey to drop the rigging crew and wait for them to finish before bringing in the Chinook, and then have to make a turnaround to pick up the second chopper. Then there would probably be a second Huey to pick up the rigging crew. Still later there would have to be other choppers to pick up the Tiger Force.

I saw it as plenty of time for any remaining enemy snipers to try to bring down one of the four flights that would be overhead.

While waiting for the rigging crew I called in a situation report to the TAC CP, and asked what the plans were for extracting the Tigers. I was told to stand by for a reply. That bothered me: there didn't seem to be any plan to get the Tigers out as soon as they were no longer needed at the crash site.

The recovery of the choppers went off without event, and by early afternoon the slicks came in to take us back to the battalion base camp.

I sent Pellum with the Tigers to the Tiger Force area to clean up and get some chow while I reported to the TAC CP to find out what was on tap for us.

As soon as I entered the CP, Colonel Meinzen gave me a puzzled look and asked where we had been. I was confused. I wasn't sure if he was kidding or not. My experience with the man had been that he was not the type to kid with second lieutenants.

I said that I had just returned from the chopper recovery down south of the battalion's base. He didn't even know we were out there, that there were choppers down, that we had taken fire, that we had to scramble for support—nothing.

Now, *I* was dumbfounded. It seems that during the relocation of the

---

[63] A medium transport helicopter that could lift up to four tons of cargo or thirty-three troops. Cargo could also be sling-loaded underneath and carried that way.

battalion from the firebase to the beach, and with the turnover of personnel in the TAC CP, I simply had been lost in the shuffle. And while I was out at the crash sites thinking the brief reports I was sending into the CP were informative enough and were being passed on by operations to the battalion commander, nothing was happening.

The realization that we could have been in very big trouble out in that paddy and not have been able to raise some help bothered me plenty.

As a junior officer I learned a very valuable lesson that day: Communication wasn't just exchanging radio traffic. If your commander doesn't know what your situation is, there is every chance that you could be the cause of a disaster for your troops. I filed that little near calamity in my brain and promised myself that it would never happen to me again—no matter now much of a pest I had to be on the radio.

CHAPTER 20

•

After several more weeks of moderately successful patrols in the hills to the south and west of the Tuy Hoa valley, things quieted down and we returned to the firebase at the Tuy Hoa beach for a few days' rest. While we were there we began shuffling short-timers to other jobs in the Tiger Force headquarters and we also lost a few who were sent back to the rear to help teach at the brigade SERTS—Screaming Eagle Replacement Training School.

Because the bulk of the brigade would be rotating back to the States in the summer, a large number of individual replacements were arriving to fill in the slots vacated by death, wounds, illnesses, and rotation. Since they all came from different training experiences and there had been some unfortunate events after replacements had been fed into manuever units, a standardized orientation course was created.

At the same time we were doing some readjusting within the Tiger Force, we lost Johnny Howard to malaria. Then we lost David Hackworth to a new job. The brigade executive officer moved to a battalion to assume command and Hack replaced him. Turmoil trickled down to the Tigers and we did as we had always done—we adapted.

No sooner had we made these personnel changes than we were alerted to move from the Tuy Hoa rice bowl to the coastal town of Phan Thiet, south of Tuy Hoa.

Phan Thiet was a particularly ugly patch of red dirt on the South China sea with a runway that had an unusual dip in the middle. Any soldier who landed there didn't need to look outside the aircraft to know he was at the Phan Thiet runway. It headed downhill for the first half of its length and uphill for the remainder.

Far to the west of Phan Thiet was the southern stretch of the central highlands we had worked west of Tuy Hoa. Intelligence held that there was considerable enemy activity in those mountains but they weren't sure just where. Those reports had brought our brigade and some other allied units to find the elusive VC. The large stretches of relatively flat terrain west of Phan Thiet would have to be checked out along with the mountains.

The Tigers were dispatched to the mountains to develop contact. I mounted a heavy patrol of about a dozen Tigers and lifted off from our new Phan Thiet base camp, headed for the heavily forested mountain chain.

That patrol was one of the most distant we had ever conducted. We were well out of artillery range—ours or any other friendly unit's. We also suffered from a loss of radio contact. We had to rely on a scheduled bird dog to act as radio relay. Twice a day the tiny plane would fly out of Phan Thiet to a midpoint where it could relay our radio traffic back to the Phan Thiet base.

I expected the mountains to be similar to the ones we had become accustomed to in Tuy Hoa, but I was wrong. The Phan Thiet mountains were much more heavily covered in thick vegetation and were much steeper. They also were a lot rockier. The streams that flowed out of the Tuy Hoa mountains had flowed gently down the hills to the valley floor. In Phan Thiet the streams had cut deep paths through the rocks, creating streambeds with very deep, steep sides. It wasn't unusual to encounter a hilltop stream only to find that to cross it required climbing down several hundred meters to its bed and then back up the other side. As we crossed one of those streams, I was unaware that the torrents of rushing white water and large boulders would soon take their toll on me.

We humped the hills for days and found little to convince us that there was or had been any enemy activity in the area. Each time I called back a dry hole, I would get new instructions to move to another part of the mountain range to look for trouble.

I'm not sure if not making contact wasn't more stressful than making it. As patrol leader I was constantly worried that the lack of contact would result in a drop in alertness and a false sense of security. And in the back of my head I was convinced that *they* were really there and keeping us under observation, until they could pick a time to obliterate our small patrol so far from help.

One night we were moving along the steep slope of a hill, contouring it. We had to get to a point along a route that paralleled the length of the hill's axis. But rather than walk the spine of the hill, I elected to stay just off the top, for more security.

After a few hours picking our way through the dense growth on the hillside, we began hearing noises behind us. We would stop and the noise would stop. We would resume our march and the noise would resume. After stopping about three times, Pellum Bryant and I were convinced that whoever was following us didn't care if we heard them. The crashing and crunching of deadfall grew louder and louder, and I moved the patrol up to higher ground and set up a hasty perimeter to defend against whatever enemy force was approaching.

My readiness to make contact at three in the morning, with no radio contact with my higher headquarters and no way to call for artillery, was weak. But the noises continued and the stalkers kept approaching without concern.

Suddenly, the noise stopped. Pellum tugged on my shirtsleeve and handed me the Starlight Scope. I raised it to my eye and scanned the nearby hillside for the source of the noise. There, not two hundred meters away, stood the largest tiger I had ever seen, his leg raised as he pissed on the base of one of the huge mahogany trees.

No wonder he didn't care who heard him. It was *his* rain forest and from the looks of those hills, he had never seen humans before.

I relaxed for a few seconds and then wondered what I would do if he decided that we should be his breakfast. I wasn't too keen on shooting a tiger. Neither did I want to give away our position by shooting if we didn't have to. Before I could make a decision, Pellum put something in my hand. I held it up in the slight glow of the night and realized that he was way ahead of me. It was a CS or tear-gas grenade.

But as quickly as we had the solution, the problem went away. The tiger must have lost interest, or he got a real whiff of how gamey we were and turned and walked away from us.

I was glad we didn't have to have a showdown with that beautiful animal. I was also glad that he stopped following us. I had conjured up all manner of explanations in my head as to why some enemy unit—a large one in my mind—would be following us and was unconcerned about our knowing it.

A few nights later we came to grips with nature a second time. We had been moving up a particularly steep hill for most of the evening and were exhausted. After several nights of moving all day and setting up ambushes at night I elected to take a night off. I found a spot in a terribly dense thicket. I posted the two machine gunners at the only two approaches and allowed the remainder of the patrol to go to thirty percent alert to get some rest.

About an hour before dawn I was shaken out of my sleep by the thundering clap of two claymore mines[64] detonating and the rattle of machine guns. Before I could even orient myself as to what was happening, there was a loud, high-pitched trumpeting. Then, as I tried to get up on one knee to see what was happening, I was knocked back on my butt by another Tiger who fell into me.

After a few moments of confusion, I was able to find out that one of the machine gun positions had thought we were being probed by an enemy force, and when the noise immediately in front of them became too suspicious, they detonated their claymores and opened fire.

What they did was spook and slightly wound a baby elephant that took off toward us instead of away from the firing. He ran through the center of the thicket, knocking Tigers aside as he did.

While no one was injured by the four-foot-tall elephant, we were pretty shaken up and I elected to move to a new location for the rest of the night, feeling that one had been compromised.

The next morning we found small blood trails that told us the elephant had been hit. The incident made me more aware than ever of the wide variety of threatening events that can befall a patrol operating at a distance from support. I shuddered to think what might have happened if someone had been killed or seriously injured and we needed to conduct a medevac from that thicket. I also realized what a bad choice the thicket had been. I had chosen it because of the concealment and the early warning it gave us, but failed to consider the difficulties it could pose.

The last few days of the patrol were more of the same. We were getting more fatigued by the demands of the extremely rough terrain and the smothering heat of the lush triple canopy. To that was the added strain of the length of the patrol and the diminishing rations.

On the last morning we walked up a streambed trying to find any sign of life in the area. It was a technique we had learned in Tuy Hoa. All enemy forces eventually came down to streambeds to fish, get water, and wash clothes and gear. And they usually didn't cover up their footprints and the damage they often did to the soft stream banks. It was easy to backtrack from a point on a stream to the enemy positions.

We were so desperate to turn some sign of enemy activity that I

---

[64] The M-18A1 directional, 3.5-pound antipersonnel mine. It contained 600—700 metal balls and a 1.5-pound charge of C-4 explosive which when detonated created a kill zone of about 50 meters in a 60-degree arc.

elected to put security up on the high sides of the mountain stream and walk the streambed looking for tracks.

After a couple of hours of fruitless tracking I leaped up on a rock and lost my footing on the slippery surface. My feet went out from under me and I landed in a pile on still another rock—knee first. The sharp pain in my knee was unrelenting. I wasn't sure if I had broken anything, but I was sure that I was in real pain.

The fall provided a few moments of humor for the patrol since it is always fun to watch the boss bust his ass. The medic looked at my leg and suggested that I stick the knee in the cold running stream for a cold soak and gulp down a Darvon. And after a few minutes I was able to get up and walk. The knee was very stiff and ached quite a bit. But I was mobile again.

By the middle of the afternoon my knee had swollen to the point where my fatigue trousers were cutting off the circulation. I had to cut the seams on both sides of the trouser leg to allow enough room for me to bend the leg and get some blood to my lower leg. And the pain was returning with a vengeance.

As we moved to a pickup zone for extraction, I was happy to know that I would be able to get back to the base area at Phan Thiet and get the combined weight of my body and my combat load off the knee for a while, to allow the swelling to subside.

I reported to the operations tent at battalion and gave an extensive but empty report concerning the long patrol. We had learned a lot about patrolling in Vietnam, but still not much about the elusive enemy that was supposed to be secreted in the hills. I didn't appreciate that even that information was useful to higher headquarters. Knowing where they *aren't* is almost as good as knowing where they *are*.

I was grungy, hungry, and very tired when I came out of the tent, on my way back to the Tiger Force area. I took a few awkward strides when I heard Colonel Meinzen's voice. He wanted to know what was wrong with my leg. Approaching the tent, he had seen me limp and noticed the swelling and the rips down the sides of my trouser leg.

I told him that I had bumped my knee and that I'd be all right. He quickly brought me up short and questioned me about my qualifications to determine the extent of damage. He then instructed me to immediately report to the battalion aid station to have it looked at.

After my trip to the medics I ran into Meinzen again in the mess tent. He smiled, asking me if the medics had fixed me up. He was not happy to hear my reply. The battalion surgeon had pulled me from duty and I was being evacuated to the 8th Field Hospital in Nha Trang for more observation and care that evening.

At the hospital they ran me through the usual tests and X-rays. I was then allowed to take a shower, and then assigned to a bed in a ward between a soldier who had broken both feet by dropping an artillery round on them, and another who was recovering from a circumcision.

A doctor saw me later that night and told me that I was to stay in bed and that he would diagnose my injury after he read the X-rays. In the meantime he prescribed pain medicine, put bags of ice on either side of my knee, and inserted a small drain in my leg to draw off the collecting fluid that had swelled the whole joint to at least twice its normal size.

I don't know if it was the drain or the medication, but I was relieved of much of the pain within the hour and I laid back to enjoy the supreme luxury of fresh sheets and a real bed in a clean, airy ward.

By lights out I was aware of the tension easing out of my neck and shoulder muscles. I hadn't had a single moment to do nothing since the day I arrived in the battalion. The sensation was welcome, but at the same time I felt guilty that I was eating fresh food; wearing clean, fresh GI pajamas; and simply resting. I wondered what the Tigers were doing and if they were okay. I probably could have enjoyed the break better if I had known that just hours after I was evacuated, the battalion had begun a move from Phan Thiet on the eastern II Corps-III Corps border to Nhon Co, on the western border with Cambodia.

The second day in the hospital, my doctor came to my bedside and announced that he had consulted with another doctor and they had decided that they needed to operate on my knee. He explained that the kneecap was fractured and that the tissues and cartilage needed some minor cleaning up. The fracture of the knee cap had trashed some of the soft tissues underneath.

The thought of an operation on what just felt like a very sore knee didn't thrill me, and immediately I remembered that I had never met a jock who had ever had a knee or shoulder cut who ever had full use of it again. I also felt a flash of panic run through my mind about the consequences of being laid up for recovery after an operation. I couldn't see any scenario where my job with the Tiger Force would remain unfilled while I laid around a hospital in Nha Trang. I also thought of the multitude of unpleasant jobs that I might be shifted to after returning to my battalion—if I was even lucky enough to go back to my battalion. In a hasty moment, I told the doctor that I thought I could get by without the operation.

He laughed and told me that if he didn't operate on my knee that it would continue to swell, hurt worse, stiffen up, and I'd soon be begging him to cut. I asked him to give it a chance. I suggested that he let me go back to my unit on light duty for a few days to see if it would heal itself.

He laughed again. He bet me that if he let me go back to my unit I'd be back in his ward within a week. I asked him if fifty was a good bet. He took the bet.

The next day, after pulling the drain out of my leg, he put me on orders back to my unit with instructions for thirty days light duty. I was given my tiger-striped fatigues back, cleaned and with a couple of large safety pins some kind soul had attached to them. I also got a pair of crutches. That bothered me. The last thing I wanted was to go back to the battalion looking for certain like I was useless.

I passed the smiling doctor at the nurses' station, and he told me how easy it was going to be to take that fifty dollars off of me. I smiled back and tried my best to look like walking on the crutches didn't hurt. As soon as I got out of the ward I found the first medic I could and told him a big lie. I said that I had been instructed to turn my crutches in but that I wasn't sure where the doctor told me to go.

The medic directed me to a supply room not too far away. Once there, I told the clerk that I was supposed to swap the crutches for a cane. The clerk was a patient who had been given the job and didn't much care about anything other than having a great, rear-echelon *get over* job that kept him out of the field. He didn't suspect that I was trying to put anything over on him, and gave me the cane.

It took me two and a half more days to catch up with the battalion. I had to hitch rides from Nha Trang on the South China Sea to Nhon Co on the Cambodian border. I was able to thin out the paperwork that the hospital had sent back with me to avoid as much restriction on my return to the Tigers as possible. I didn't want the battalion surgeon to put me on ice. From my first night out of the hospital, I found that sleeping with my leg elevated as high as I could get it was helpful in relieving the pain and reducing the remaining swelling. I babied the leg and did everything I could to disguise as much of the limp as possible.

Just before arriving at the battalion base camp off the Nhon Co airstrip, I lost my cane.

* * *

There were a few more days of delay while the battalion closed on Nhon Co before its full strength was committed to the battle that had developed. The extra days allowed me to do a lot of sitting and plenty of healing. The swelling went down, and all that remained was terrible stiffness, some pain, and extreme tenderness. But looking at my leg in trousers you could no longer detect any swelling.

The first week of combat operations took us to a nearby village called Bu Gia Map. What we found there was the start of the monsoon season followed by the first new contact for the brigade. A rifle company made light contact and the Tiger Force was spun around to investigate the possibilities of finding more enemy elements.

We spent the next three weeks humping through dense rain-forest cover that blanketed the low, rolling hills. But unlike the rain forest we had experienced before, the Nhon Co area was thick with bamboo. Much of our movement was interrupted by hacking through bamboo or taking wide detours to avoid it. And the rains made the job slippery, and swelled the streambeds to hard, rushing brown rivers that we often found difficult to cross. The area had its own special breed of ground leeches that were everywhere and into everything we wore and carried. We found ourselves rotting from the constant dampness and the heavy rain showers. The weather slowed our pace and cut our visibility and drained our energies. It ruined our ammunition and interfered with our radio communications. We had to adjust our combat loads, rations, and goals to accommodate the dramatic complications that came with the monsoon season.

We saturated the area around Bu Gia Map with patrol after patrol and ambush after ambush, but made only occasional contact with small enemy units. Meanwhile, a sister battalion discovered a large but abandoned headquarters and POW camp. Occasional stragglers were captured and revealed that the massive artillery strikes and the repeated B-52[65] strikes that the brigade had been dropping on the suspected sites were working. The NVA units massed just inside the border with Cambodia were forced to break up and cross back into Cambodia to reorganize and refit from the damage.

They were also successful at springing a large, multicompany ambush after being tipped off by an NVA prisoner about his regiment's

[65] Boeing Stratofortress strategic bombers. These aircraft could carry 66,000 pounds of bombs, which they dropped from high altitudes on targets in North and South Vietnam. A typical bomb load might consist of eighty-four 500-pound and twenty-four 750-pound bombs. The B-52s flew their raids from Thailand, Guam, and Okinawa.

location and plans. When the smoke cleared, the NVA had left several hundred of their number dead in the killing zone as they fled to the protection of "neutral" Cambodia.

By the end of the Nhon Co operation, the contacts were getting fewer and the terrain was getting more difficult to traverse. Choppers were frequently grounded, and supplies were stacking up somewhere in the pipeline. They sure weren't getting down to rifleman level the way they had in Phan Rang, Tuy Hoa, and Phan Thiet.

During the operation I had been lucky enough not to aggravate my knee injury. And by deliberately going out with a very pared-down combat load, I was able to reduce the strain on the knee joint. But it cost me rations, risky ammunition loads, and extra gear to keep me warm and dry. I just didn't have a choice. I had to travel light to allow the knee to heal.

Pellum quickly figured out what I was doing but kept my secret and said nothing directly to me. He complained about bringing too much chow with him and made a small scene out of deciding what to throw away, casually asking me if I wanted whatever it was he was pitching. I had never met a man as generous as Pellum Bryant. It was no surprise to me why the troops all loved him so much. He was a rock wrapped around a huge heart, something rare in a macho organization.

The one positive thing that came of the Nhon Co operation was the completion of the rebuilding and retraining of the Tiger Force. The splitting and shifting of platoon members and the incorporation of a handful of replacements had given way to enough field experience that they were working better than ever—the weather notwithstanding.

Colonel Meinzen and I had a couple more discussions about just what my mission was, and he didn't like the tone of my voice. He reminded me that the Tigers' mission was whatever he decided it was and I would be smart to drop my attitude about standardizing the organizational configuration, equipment, and missions.

That was the last conversation I had with him. He had not been lucky during his short tenure as battalion commander. He had fallen ill a couple of times before, and not too long after our talk about the Tigers, he was evacuated, too ill to continue in command of the battalion.

* * *

We soon got alerted to move again, this time to a small airstrip in the center of II Corps[66] called Cheo Reo. There we took on more new replacements in the battalion and waited for our new commander. I was called in by the battalion executive officer (XO) and told that I would be in temporary command of headquarters and headquarters company,[67] until they could find a captain to replace me. It would be in addition to my duties with the Tiger Force.

The job surprised me, but the announcement that I would be replaced didn't. There were plenty of captains in Vietnam qualified to command an Airborne battalion headquarters company. There was just no way to expect that I be allowed to command a company at the rank of second lieutenant. I assumed that the temporary assignment was prompted by the expected arrival of a new captain and the courtesy that is normally extended to an incoming battalion commander— to put off pending major assignment decisions until he arrived. And since I was already on the books of headquarters company, I was the likely candidate to hold down the fort until a replacement became available.

We were all surprised when the new CO turned out to be our old XO, David Hackworth. So decisions concerning officer assignments would be something he could do with little or no deliberation: he knew us all, and as brigade XO he knew what and who was projected for assignment into the battalion.

Hack arrived and everything changed. All of the plans he had privately held for the 1/327 and had been unable to sell to Joe Rogers, and then Walter Meinzen, were suddenly on the front burner. He was the new bear in the woods and he didn't have to clear any of his decisions with anyone.

At the same time we received word to move again—this time to the northwest to help a beleaguered Special Forces camp at Dak To, on the Laotian border.

My job as headquarters company commander was to get the battalion headquarters and the headquarters company to Dak To. As a second lieutenant it was a real eye-opener. I had never appreciated the complexities involved in moving a large number of combat troops

---

[66] The Vietnamese II Corps area. South Vietnam was divided into four corps areas: I in the northernmost part of South Vietnam where the Marine Amphibious Force was responsible for operations; II Corps, in the central highlands; III Corps, around Saigon; and IV Corps, in the Mekong Delta.
[67] This is the administrative element of a battalion or larger tactical unit, responsible for administration, intelligence, communications, and other activities.

and their equipment and supplies from one location to another without losing their combat effectiveness, their ability to communicate, or unit integrity. And the entire process was complicated by the monsoon and the strict number of cargo aircraft assigned to us for the job. I can only assume that while we made the move, Hackworth was watching me to make sure I didn't screw something up and leave an important segment of the battalion headquarters stranded at some godforsaken airfield.

Dak To was truly a forbidding-looking place: A shabby little airstrip with a shallow clearing on one end and a Montagnard[68] town on the other, covered by lush green vegetation and surrounded by steep mountains.

We closed on Dak To, set up our temporary base in the clearing off the runway, and immediately moved out to relieve the beleaguered Toumorong outpost. During all the turmoil, Hack called me to his CP to speak with him. He began by telling me that there was more than the normal confusion going on in such an operation because of the loss of so many of the original Stateside group who were rotating back home, and he was having to make assignments accordingly. I fully expected him to tell me that since a few new captains had arrived during our move, I would be relieved of headquarters company command to go back to my platoon in the Tiger Force. Instead, he blew me over with the announcement that he wanted me to turn over my job in the Tigers to a new lieutenant and that he wanted to pull me up to battalion headquarters.

At first I was confused. I wasn't sure if I had done something wrong or what. But before I could even sputter a reply he slapped me on the shoulder and told me that he wanted me in his operations shop. I would become an assistant and the battalion S-3[69] liaison officer. He went on to tell me that he was happy with my performance and thought I could learn something in the "three shop."

I walked out of the CP tent unsure about what had just happened to me. I wanted to go back to the Tiger Force but was flattered that Hack thought enough of me to put me in the nerve center of his battalion.

---

[68] The nomadic tribes of the central highlands region in South Vietnam and Laos. The name comes from the French for "mountaineer." There was always great animosity between the Montagnards and the lowland ethnic Vietnamese, but both sides sought their allegiance during the war.

[69] Operations. Army staffs are divided into general (G) (division and higher) and special (S) (brigade, regiment, battalion). They are: personnel (G-1/S-1); intelligence (G-2/S-2); operations (G-3/S-3); logistics and transportation (G-4/S-4) and (sometimes) civil affairs (G-5/S-5).

But I felt a sudden loss in the pit of my stomach about leaving the soldiers with whom I had spent half a year and had shared so many long dark nights.

But in those days it was considered extremely bad form to question or complain about assignment decisions made by the commanding officer. The assumption was that all assignments were made for the good of the unit, and personal preferences were not considered or solicited. So I swallowed hard and walked back to the Tiger Force area to say goodbye.

I only had a few minutes to say my goodbyes and they weren't very serious since I wasn't leaving the battalion, only the Tigers. I could immediately sense the anxiety that my departure generated. I had not been that long away from the platoon level to know what happens when reassignments start happening. The status quo is disrupted and the rumors start immediately.

For good or bad, they had gotten used to me, and now I would be leaving and an unknown face would replace mine. Every soldier in Vietnam first worried about the officer in his immediate chain of command. He had the most direct influence on what happened to them, and was the first line of resistance to protect them when the system began making unreasonable demands on them. Until a new officer showed that could be counted on to be fair with them and come to their defense, it was a shaky time around the unit.

I didn't know my replacement, just his name. I couldn't promise them anything and they all understood. I was extremely pleased to meet and get to know John Carey. If I had to build my own replacement out of new parts I couldn't have built a finer one than John. He and Pellum Bryant hit it off immediately and the anxieties of the Tigers quickly gave way to the real worries associated with the extremely heavy combat that they saw in the next month.

I would be lying if I said that I missed the Tigers and the job right away. Hackworth threw me into the middle of the swirl of activity that was the constant state of affairs in the battalion command post. It was my job to do as much of the face-to-face coordination with higher, lower, and adjacent units for Hack and the S-3.

Stepping into a fight with a tough new NVA regiment and changing over virtually every officer in the battalion due to rotations was tough. But I soon realized that one of the reasons Hack had moved me into the S-3 shop was for continuity. I quickly went from being one of the newest officers in the battalion to one of the few remaining old-timers.

The job was exhausting and frightening. I was asked to operate alone to coordinate very important details of fire support and operations coordination. I was often in a chopper all day long carrying messages to and from companies and the brigade headquarters, not to mention coordinating with the Special Forces and the South Vietnamese units in the area. And while I was out carrying the mail, I was expected to stay up to speed with the quickly developing fight that went on for days without letup. Then I would end up back at the CP at night and be expected to pull long shifts as the duty officer.

I have to admit, at Tiger Force level the thought of being on the battalion staff looked like a really easy job. Again, things weren't quite what I guessed.

At the very beginning of the battle at Dak To, Hackworth replaced Grunstad with Lewis Higinbotham in the Tigers. I had known Higinbotham for several months in his other assignments on the battalion staff. I found him bright, courageous, and combat savvy. He was a new captain and had been bugging Hackworth for some time to get into the Tigers. For my money, the Tigers were in good hands with Lewis Higinbotham and John Carey at the helm.

What followed our arrival at Dak To was a month of continuous combat operations. It turned out to be the most intense fighting of the original 1st Brigade's year. A day did not go by when at least one element of our battalion wasn't in contact with elements of the 24th NVA Regiment, fresh out of Laos.

What we had been committed to was the North Vietnamese Monsoon Offensive, designed to overrun allied outposts in the central highlands. It just turned out that the tiny Toumorong outpost and the Dak To area were their first objectives. During the month, the battalion covered miles upon miles of near-vertical mountain terrain making company- and battalion-size contacts. After the initial contacts were broken—usually at the enemy's initiative—we'd pursue them in small groups to their rally points. Once we had confirmed the location of those sites, we would strike them.

The number of artillery fire missions, air strikes, gunship missions, B-52 strikes, and airmobile operations was far larger than any previous operation the brigade had experienced. The enemy force was well trained, well rested, and well equipped. And unlike our earlier experiences, when the enemy broke up into small escape parties and disappeared into the bush never to be seen again, this time they fought hard until their positions became untenable, and then they would withdraw only to mount more attacks in very short order.

During the battle, Hackworth commanded the battalion from a very mobile command post that consisted of hardly much more than himself, his chief RTO, Daryl Nunnally, and a couple of radios. He had little use for a command-and-control helicopter except as a means of transportation to move to another ground location. Anything else that needed the C & C to get done seemed to fall on my shoulders.

I spent my time on the move. I would frequently get involved in replacing lost platoon leaders and senior NCOs with fresh ones, delivering overlays and maps, picking up prisoners, and writing pieces of the after action reports.

The days started early and miserably. My duty station was wherever Hack wanted me to be, and my rack was wherever I ended the day. I would spend some nights in a shallow sleeping hole in the driving rain. Other nights I would find myself in the cargo compartment of a chopper or the back of a truck, trying to write up the day's combat summaries by the light of a weak GI flashlight.

No nights were quiet and the casualty counts on both sides were high. I cared about all of them, but my ear was especially tuned to word about the Tigers. They were thrust into the heat of the battle and they rose to the demands. They endured multicompany battles with none of the heavy, crew-served weapons that the rifle companies had. The heaviest thing they carried was the M-60 machine gun while they had to face enemy mortars, rockets, recoilless rifles, and command detonated mines.

Still, the Tigers fought on and took some very heavy casualties during the operation. During the first week of the battle they were down to sixteen men, and nine of them were wounded. Hack pulled them out of the battle, refitted them with more volunteers, patched up the walking wounded, and put them back into the fight. They were a remarkable bunch. They took it and went back in for more.

The stories of the Dak To battle got to Saigon quickly, and suddenly we were the place to be. Reporters and television film crews descended on us in great numbers. Most of them were too timid to come to the actual battlefield and were satisfied to remain in the rear—at the brigade CP on the airstrip.

But some had more guts and wanted to be where the fighting was. Ward Just came from the *Washington Post*, humped the hills, and got wounded while covering the Tiger Force. He went on to write some chilling stories about the battles the Tigers fought in field reports and later in books.

One morning I was tapped to take the C & C back to the airstrip to pick up some operations orders, overlays, and a long list of things like batteries and cigars. At the airstrip I was instructed by the battalion executive officer to pick up a news crew and take them back with me to the battle.

After finishing my scavenger hunt, I found the three-man crew sitting on their gear on the runway and introduced myself. The reporter told me he wanted to go forward to get it all on film.

I pulled out my notebook and asked for the particulars about each of them, name, news organization and such. Ron Nessen, later to become presidential press secretary, asked me why I needed to know all that. I told him the story about the journalist who had arrived unannounced at the My Canh battlefield only to get killed, and how later I got my ass chewed over it.

Nessen laughed and said, half joking, "You aren't going to let that happen to me are you?" All I could tell him was that I was sure I wasn't going to get my ass chewed again for not knowing who he was. He didn't see much humor in my reply.

On the flight forward to a rifle company position, Nessen's crew said very little and watched the large number of air force and army aircraft filling the skies over the battle area.

Nessen wasn't daunted by the proximity to the battle. He met the company commander and immediately asked to go out with a patrol preparing to leave only minutes after our arrival. It was okay with the company commander, and the film crew attached themselves to the small patrol.

In a matter of minutes after they left the company perimeter the patrol was hit by an NVA ambush, and Nessen took a serious wound in the chest.

CHAPTER 21

•

I thought I'd seen the last of the visiting firemen when Nessen got wounded and evacuated. Several days after the Nessen incident, the battalion was still in contact and I was with Hackworth at one of his rifle company command posts. He liked to tag along with the rifle companies and leave every unit in the battalion available to maneuver. He had little use for setting up a command post and then draining off combat troops to serve as a palace guard.

We had just made a small contact, and the shooting was just about over when a small observation chopper approached our position. The pilot picked out a small clearing near us and put it down, only to let out a single lonely figure.

Hack was giving us the plan for the day, and as I looked up to see who was getting out of the chopper I spotted the round, short figure of an elderly man wearing a khaki uniform covered by one of those see-through plastic raincoats. On his head he wore an army green baseball cap, and on the cap was a large black star. I knew immediately who it was—General S. L. A. Marshall. His face had been on the jacket of every one of his books that I had to read at OCS.

Hack also recognized Marshall and told me to go get him. I ran up the hillside to the landing zone and saluted the general, introducing myself. He was gentle and jolly and glad to be there. As we walked down the hill I asked him what he wanted to see. He told me that he had heard the company we were with had a contact and that's where he wanted to go.

I told him that the smoke hadn't quite cleared yet and he might want to wait before going down to the side of the perimeter that had made the contact. With that he stopped, put his arm round my shoulder, and said, "Let me tell you something about soldiers, Lieutenant. In battle as soon as the shooting is over every man has to decide if he was a hero or a bum in the skirmish. It's my job as a historian to get there before they decide so I can find out what actually happened."

I didn't much appreciate what General Marshall said until years later, when I tried to recall the details of my own performance in battle, and while listening to others recount common experiences from different points of view.

Through my own experience I was surprised to find that you felt like you had been a hero on some days and a bum on others. The magnitude of your courage fluctuated from day to day and from moment to moment. At any given time you were thrust into situations that would flood your bloodstream with adrenaline, and your response would vary. The first time you found yourself hesitating, it was a frightening experience. You had been confident and aggressive only a moment before only to find yourself hesitating. It wasn't until many more intense moments had passed for me that I realized that it was probably a natural response.

During my months with the Tiger Force, courage or bravery had only been an issue once, and I should have recognized it then for the danger it presented, but I wasn't experienced enough at the time and I was confusing John Wayne movies with the real battlefield.

I had a young staff sergeant in the Tigers who constantly spoke of doing something heroic to win the Medal of Honor. I dismissed the conversations as just beer or bravado talking when I should have found out what was behind the talk.

During the months that the sergeant served as a squad and patrol leader I had never had any real problems with him. After I left the Tigers he was killed. The story I got was that he was leading a small patrol in search of the NVA who had broken contact with the battalion when he spotted an enemy element. He lost sight of his responsibilities as patrol leader and struck out after the enemy force, instructing his charges to stay put until he returned. He left them without a patrol leader and disappeared into the thick hillside growth.

He was killed by the very NVA soldiers he stalked. Luckily, the patrol had other qualified leaders to recover the body and avoid further contact until they could get new orders.

He never got the Medal of Honor, and I'm sorry I never said anything to him while I commanded the unit. It's hard not to feel somewhat responsible. I can say that I was extremely critical of that kind of boasting and bravado in my future assignments and never failed to tell that story to future braggarts.

The end of the Dak To battle signaled the end of the old 1st Brigade of the 101st as I had come to know it, and ushered in virtually all new faces. The original Screaming Eagles who left Fort Campbell, Kentucky, for Vietnam had all been replaced.

Hackworth had stayed way beyond his original tour of duty and was getting heat to return to the States to an important job in the Pentagon. He didn't want to go and he didn't want to end up in the Pentagon, but like all soldiers, he had to follow orders.

Before he left he had a ceremony to pin first lieutenant's bars on my collar and Jon Every-Clayton's. Jon had arrived in the 1/327 only hours before I was assigned to the S-3 shop, and earned his Combat Infantryman's Badge in the heat of the Dak To campaign. I never envied him that experience. But he came through just as I knew he would.

I didn't know then how much of an impact working for David Hackworth would have on my life. But I don't know what I would have done differently if I had. It would be a while before I would find out that to have been one of his warriors would carry with it a reputation that was just as likely to help you as hurt you. It all depended on how the people involved felt about Hackworth.

On Hack's departure we got still another battalion commander, our fourth in my tour over there. And, like all commanders, he had his way of doing things and made sure in short order that we implemented his policies and procedures. So while we wrapped up a mop-up operation in the Dak To area, we outloaded for a return trip to the Tuy Hoa area.

I didn't appreciate it then, but soon thereafter I understood the ripple effect on the soldiers in the Tiger Force of changes in battalion, company, and platoon commanders. They were whiplashed by the changes that came with each new commander and said very little about it beyond the normal bitching that is a soldier's right.

The remaining months in the 101st were not a Ranger's experiences, yet they were filled with the kind of stuff that a young officer needs to develop a better understanding of how the entire picture works. Not all of my experiences were pleasant, though all of them were useful.

My first unhappy experience came in regard to the level of jealousies and bitterness that a unit like the Tiger Force generated in an otherwise proud brigade. During the months that followed, I often ran into folks who would know that I was from the 1/327 but not the former commander of the Tiger Force. Many were not shy about telling me that they thought the Tigers were a bunch of prima donnas, and that in their opinion they weren't any better then any other unit in the brigade.

I was surprised at the comments and the attitude, because I knew of no occasions when the Tigers had bragged about being better or tougher or special in any way other than the fact that they often had unique and difficult missions.

What I came to discover was that their reputation was distorted all out of reasonable proportion and the stories exaggerated by the jealousies created by the simple fact that they wore distinctive uniforms and headgear. I found out that being different meant that you were treated differently, whether you knew it was happening to you or not.

I found staff officers and NCOs at the brigade headquarters who made it clear that there was no love lost for the Tigers, implying that they would do a little equalizing when an opportunity arose to do something to or for the unit or its members.

I was terribly disappointed by what I heard and wondered if it was just unique to the Tigers, and if I had done something to cause that negative attitude to drift through the brigade.

I spent the next few months working in operations, learning plenty about the planning and supervising of battalion operations, and was often called upon to provide input to the plans. It was in this capacity that I became intimately familiar with helicopters—their strengths and weaknesses.

We were lucky enough to have our own aviation battalion. So more often than some of the other units in Vietnam, we were able to work again and again with the same pilots. This was very good news for the troops. Pilots who were familiar with the troops they lifted in to landing zones were quick to respond when things went sour and needed far less briefing to come to the rescue.

As the junior officer in the operations section I was often given the battalion commander's command-and-control chopper to make my rounds and conduct recons confirming details that the maps didn't show us.

During all of this flying time I became friendly with the same small group of pilots who flew for us and asked plenty of questions about just what made helicopters and pilots tick. My curiosity was simply that I wanted to know about them even though I knew that there was no chance, because of my poor eyesight, I could ever qualify to fly.

They all picked up on my interest and often allowed me to take the controls of gunships, slicks[70] and light observation choppers. I learned to do a better than decent job of takeoffs and landings, and even had a

---

[70] UH-1D helicopters, so called because they did not carry the externally mounted weapon systems of the gunships. Slicks were used to transport troops on assaults.

few classes in autorotations.[71] I was thrilled to learn and they were happy to teach me.

During the discovery of choppers, I realized how we could use them better as an asset to patrols like the Tiger Force. We had used them all wrong and I had never appreciated what they could do if we each knew more about the others' needs—in the air and on the ground.

Then there were some of our more screwball inventions. One day late in the summer a pilot arrived with a jerry-built contraption in the side door of a C model Huey. Someone had come up with the idea of making a high-powered, night-capable gunship that could fly at an altitude that would allow it to see a large piece of the operational area and be able to fire on targets spotted.

The conventional M-60s and rocket pods didn't allow them to do this well, so someone cobbled up a series of cargo aircraft landing lights on a frame in the open cargo doorway that could be flipped on to focus an incredibly bright, powerful beam of light that would illuminate anything on the ground at a slant range of a few thousand feet.

Then a .50-caliber machine gun, topped with a Starlight Scope, was attached to a large piece of plywood and slipped into the chopper. The theory was to fly around the Tuy Hoa valley at night at an altitude that would lead enemy forces on the ground to believe that the chopper was not a threat. The gunner could scan the ground below with the Starlight Scope until an enemy patrol was spotted in the open. Once spotted, the gunner could turn on the lights and fire on the patrol with enough range and cyclic rate to do some damage.

All of the technical details had been worked out for the test run. When I asked the pilot why he had come to our battalion to show it to us, he admitted that they needed a gunner. I couldn't understand why finding a gunner would be a problem. They had plenty of good, qualified door gunners in the aviation battalion. He said that they were looking for someone who knew the valley and could help them distinguish between friendlies and bad guys, somebody who knew the rules of engagement and the details of where friendlies were operating: someone like an operations lieutenant who might be able to fly with them on the nights he wasn't pulling duty officer.

I was drafted. The concept sounded interesting and challenging. It

---

[71] A helicopter pilot's emergency landing maneuver when rotor power is lost. Even without power, a helicopter's blades will continue to rotate due to centrifugal force, and this creates enough lift to permit the aircraft to glide steeply earthward. Just before the aircraft glides into the ground, the pilot changes the pitch of the rotors, causing the chopper to settle relatively calmly to the ground.

was also filled with some cautions. I was going to be taking it on myself to clear the firing by having my finger on the trigger of the fifty. And flying around with the huge landing lights blaring would make us a tempting target for eager VC gunners on the ground. Still, I was up for it and cleared it with my boss, the S-3.

The first flight was a loose check ride to see if we could even get all the elements to work. We had to test the scope, test fire the weapon, see if the lights worked, and set up communications that would be working when we needed them.

We started by flying to an area far to the east of the valley—over the South China Sea. There we dropped an empty wooden ammo box into the water and tried to find it at altitude with the Starlight Scope.

The scope worked well and I turned the lights on to flood it with the intense beam before firing on it. As soon as the pilot looked out his left door to see what I was going to fire on he was able to setup a steady left turn to keep the light on the target. I could operate the light in terms of the diameter of the beam, but not the direction. That took the pilot's practiced hand.

I fired a few bursts of .50-caliber rounds at the target and hit close enough to confirm that everything was working all right.

With that, we moved back into the valley and alerted all of the nearby units that we would be flying a gunship over the area and to let us know if we got too close.

We flew the area for over an hour and found nothing. My neck got tired peering through the Starlight Scope. We ran short of fuel and batteries and went back to the chopper's home base for refills of everything, including hot coffee.

On our second trip up over the area, we spotted a dozen-man VC patrol walking in a single file in a wide-open area—between two very distant tree lines. I started shooting at the same time I threw the switch on the lights. The skies between us and the target lit up with the column of white light that cut through the layers of night mist and light fog over the paddies.

The enemy patrol immediately took hits and I was helped out by the left door gunner, who fired his M-60 down the same column of light. His fires were not as effective due to the distances involved, but the extra firepower helped add to the confusion on the ground.

I was focused on firing and didn't pay much attention to what was going on around me. The fifty kept cranking out round after jarring round and the inside of the chopper got brighter and brighter until the gunner on the other side of the chopper grabbed me. I heard him yell, "Cease fire! Cease fire!"

I let up and looked up and realized that the recoil of the 50 had caused the plywood board everything was mounted on to walk its way out the opposite door, causing the beam of the light to flood the inside of the compartment. A few more rounds and the extra boxes of ammo on the plywood panel behind me would have fallen out the other open door. It was possible that I might have been next if we hadn't noticed the flaw in the system.

It was back to the drawing board with what was tabbed the "Lightning Bug."

After several more test flights we worked the bugs out of the system and it went into regular use in the brigade. I spent many nights and drank plenty of coffee pulling my night shifts in the left door of that gunship.

From my staff job at the battalion headquarters I kept a mother hen's eye on the Tiger Force and did what I could to help make things work more smoothly for them. One of the things I was particularly sensitive about was making sure that the normal commotion in the Tac CP didn't overshadow the fact that they were out there somewhere and needed to be monitored.

The months that followed the battles of Dak To were taken up with still another rebuilding for the Tigers. They had to fill in the spaces left empty by the killed, wounded, and ill Tigers lost in the central highlands fighting plus those lost through normal rotation.

While all of their losses were sad, they took a particularly hard one not long after we left Dak To. On an otherwise routine operation, Pellum Bryant was lost to a land mine. One of the Tigers detonated a mine by stepping on it. Without concern for the presence of other mines, Pellum provided immediate first aid to the severely wounded soldier only to set off another mine while helping the wounded Tiger.

The gain and then the loss of Pellum Bryant was the largest single morale factor in the first year of the Tigers. He was a remarkable soldier who was loved by every man in the unit. His manner was gentle and his smile ever present. He was tactically proficient and a natural leader. At a time when growing dissatisfaction among the black community was tearing at black soldiers to support demands and extreme actions, Pellum was color blind.

It was my good luck that discrimination still existed even in a largely black Airborne brigade. After a few months of getting to know Pellum and spending night after night sharing bits of food, scraps of toilet paper, and stories of home and dreams, I asked him why the Tiger Force. He was surprised at my question. I asked him why he would want to come to the Tiger Force when I had no job for him and he'd have to take a rifleman's job. He tried to put me off but I pressed.

He explained that he had been assigned to one of the rifle companies in our battalion before volunteering to come to the Tigers. There one of the senior NCOs in the company pulled all the new black soldiers together and gave them a warning. He explained that because their faces were black that they would eventually prove to be cowards because that was their nature. He threatened them. He would be watching them and as soon as they turned yellow he'd make sure that they were sent to the stockade.

Pellum told me that to his mind, he thought life as a rifleman in the Tiger Force had to be better than being a senior NCO in a company where that attitude prevailed. He said he was sure he would end up in the stockade over a fight with the NCO long before he would ever get a chance to show cowardice.

I'm terribly sorry that Pellum and the other black soldiers in his company had to suffer that slur. But I will forever feel lucky that Pellum came to the Tigers. His spirit and his leadership made the Tigers who and what they were. He became the heart of the Tigers and his spirit infected each of us. Of all the losses I suffered in Vietnam, it is Pellum's death that causes me the most pain.

After months of light contacts in the Tuy Hoa valley, the brigade was moved to Kontum City to operate in fresh turf. During the move we lost the battalion adjutant, and I was slipped from the S-3 shop to the adjutant's job. I thought I was over my head when I arrived in the S-3 job, but paperwork and personnel was a nightmare land that defied organization. The staff section was in a state of chaos because it had been a holding area for one good captain after another. They would arrive in the battalion and be assigned to the adjutant's job only to leave shortly thereafter to take one of the coveted company commander's jobs.

Privately, I didn't take the news well. I had no interest in being the battalion adjutant, and knew that it would only be a temporary job until the next qualified captain got off a chopper. But I kept my feelings to myself and reported for duty.

My world was a tent filled with folding field tables and piles of gritty paperwork. My first official responsibility was finding five hundred lost paratroopers. I was completely mystified at the charge of lost soldiers when the executive officer made finding them one of my priorities. But once I got into it I discovered it was a huge bookkeeping problem.

In earlier wars the evacuation of an ill or wounded soldier happened in echelons. As the soldier was transferred back to battalion he was dropped off the company's morning report[72] and picked up by the gaining unit. The transfer of accountability happened at the same time the evacuation did.

But Vietnam was the day of the medevac chopper, and soldiers were often picked up in the field and flown to a field hospital and then evacuated on to general hospitals in the Pacific region. More often than not, the soldier might be admitted to a hospital in the States before his rifle company started begging for documents from the gaining unit, to release them from accountability for that soldier.

So I walked into the job with a tall order already on my plate. In addition to taking care of the mounds of paperwork normally associated with an infantry battalion in combat, I had to find every single lost warrior.

I felt a little guilty about the relative luxury of the adjutant's office. My days in the cockpit of a chopper had come to a halt and my frequent trips to the rifle companies diminished greatly.

I had become a headquarters rat and was looking at combat from the other end of the spyglass. Sure, there were mortar attacks and occasional ground probes of our headquarters. And there were losses suffered by headquarters personnel associated with the dangerous jobs in support of the combat operations. Jeeps were blown off the roadways, aircraft flying to the brigade rear were downed, and headquarters personnel suffered. But it wasn't like waking up in the bush, looking for trouble all day, then setting up an ambush and waiting for it to come all night.

Still, the job was filled with its own unpleasantries. By the time I went to the S-1 section, I was one of the very few old-timer lieutenants in the battalion. As a result, I knew more soldiers in the battalion than most of the other officers. So each time we had a casualty evacuated to the brigade clearing station, I would drive or fly there to meet the incoming choppers.

I soon came to dread the job. Each medevac call brought with it the horrors of the battlefield. From throughout the battalion casualties would funnel into brigade and I would see each dead and wounded soldier. As often as not, I would recognize the casualty on sight as

---

[72] Department of the Army Form 1, a daily report of each army unit's personnel and organizational status, accounting for the whereabouts and status of each soldier assigned, as well as any significant changes in the organization such as new commanders, unit redesignations, etc.

soon as I would step into the triage section or the receiving section of the graves registration unit.

Every trip was about pain and death. I saw the faces of soldiers I had served with and come to know. And within weeks after going to the S-1 section, I was also seeing the faces or bodies of boys who had just processed through on their way to companies and platoons.

There is no way I could ever decide which part of the job was worse: saying goodbye to the wounded and maimed soldiers, or identifying the bodies of those who were finally and forever out of the war.

I regretted the day that I said goodbye to Jon Every-Clayton, who sat shivering in an OD blanket on a warm sunny day. Malaria had taken Jon down and he became just another casualty as I watched him get evacuated.

On another day I went to the holding tent where they kept the bodies until they could be identified and forwarded to the mortuary in Saigon. The NCO in charge told me he had parts of one of our soldiers that he was having trouble identifying. I steeled myself for what I would find in the tent and entered.

Inside, several bodies were laid out on wooden pallets to keep them off the ground. On one pallet there were the legs and parts of the shoulder girdle, chest, and throat of a headless soldier. Even before I could recognize what body parts I was looking at, I recognized a tattoo in the pale, blood-drained skin that was the name of the soldier's wife. It was a simple paratrooper's tattoo that had jump wings and a ribbon threaded through the insignia. On the ribbon were the words Carrie Ann. I knew the owner of the tattoo even though I couldn't recognize any other part of his body or uniform. Though I identified many bodies before and many after that day, it was that boy's body that stands out vividly in my memory. The inhumanity of war was there, just pieces of a boy who had left a widow and a small child and wouldn't even be sent home whole to be buried and remembered. I swallowed the pain I felt and put it on top of earlier pains and under many more to come.

Being adjutant was one of the easiest jobs in the battalion and I grew to hate it in very short order. I started thinking more and more about going home and getting out of Vietnam. I was growing tired and I was different than the boy who had arrived more than a year earlier, wondering if he would be able to keep up.

My orders finally came and I was thrilled to discover that I was going back to Fort Benning. For all its unpleasant training memories, I still liked Benning and what it stood for and what it aspired to. It was something familiar, and to my thinking at the time, unthreatening.

Working in the 1/327 was like trotting with thoroughbreds. I was thrust into the midst of fine soldiers, NCOs, and officers who would go on to prove themselves again and again in peacetime and future wars. Our battalion turned out handfuls of general officers and command sergeants major, many of whom are still serving in the highest levels of today's army.

It was an incredible stroke of luck that I ended up in the 1/327 and in the Tiger Force, and it changed my attitude about the army as a career and myself as a professional soldier.

CHAPTER 22

Fort Benning in the spring of 1967 was clearly a different place than I had left only two years before. Everything was expanded in multiples. The three officer candidate companies that filed in rotation to graduate new second lieutenants had expanded by several more. The Sand Hill basic-training barracks were filled to a capacity not seen since the Korean War. And new courses were being added to the curriculum, including a special one to provide replacement NCOs for the ones being lost to war.

That course took promising young soldiers from basic training and advanced individual training and sent them through intensive instruction on becoming an NCO. At the end of the course the best of them were given the sergeant's stripes that had once taken soldiers years to earn. The effort took plenty of criticism from the army's oldtimers, and the NCOs were quickly named "Shake 'n Bake"[73] sergeants.

The basic officer course where ROTC graduates got their introductory training in infantry subjects and techniques was also bursting at the seams.

And since the Vietnam War was an infantryman's war, Fort Benning, Home of the Infantry, was the focal point for all things related to Vietnam. The post teemed with visiting government dignitaries and journalists.

Only the real estate on post looked familiar. All the activities were geared up to a near-frantic pitch. And I was dumped right in the middle of it. Though the war in Vietnam had been going on for six years by then, there had only been army troops on the ground for about eighteen months and a very small number of the experienced veterans had returned to Fort Benning. Of those who did, most of them were senior NCOs and officers of captain and above. There was a shortage of lieutenants who had served in Vietnam.

As a result, I found myself immediately assigned to the platoon

[73] After the commercial product of that name, because they were considered "instant" NCOs.

tactics committee of the company operations department. I would become a *platform instructor*, teaching officer candidates and basic officer students about what would be expected of them in Vietnam.

But first I had to go through yet another course on being an instructor. It seemed my fear of public speaking was going to be scrutinized still another time. I was still a little shaky about the Instructor Training Course (ITC,) but knew that it was unavoidable and put myself into it. Like my experiences at the 7th Army NCO Academy and OCS, I was put through all the classes on techniques and training aids and then critiqued on my performance. But by the time I went through the course, they had added television to the curriculum. I discovered that the presence of a television camera and use of a replay critique can really add to your anxiety.

Still, after a few weeks of ITC I was issued the blue enameled FOLLOW ME pocket badge that marked me as a platform instructor. I still recall the morning that I attached the insignia to my khaki uniform. I remembered the image of that tall lieutenant outside the mess hall at Fort Dix and how amazed I had been then. That lieutenant hadn't been a person to me any more than the two sergeants on that stage, but they were what I fell back on when I put a uniform together or walked through a troop area. If I was going to do the job, I was going to look the part and project the attitude. It made no difference how unsure I was inside, I wasn't going to show it. And that from Bill Pfeiffer.

I was assigned to the traditional courses to cut my teeth—first as an assistant instructor on "The Rifle Platoon in the Night Attack." It was a hangover from the Korean War. And I assisted in other classes like "The Rifle Platoon in the Live-Fire Attack." The live fire was a class that took plenty of supervision, and the last thing any of us wanted was to be wounded or killed in a practice attack after surviving Vietnam.

The course that really got my attention was "The Rifle Platoon in the Defense." Once I got to that problem area I became acquainted with the simulated defensive position that the committee had set up. It was a life-size training aid to teach candidates and basic officer students how to deploy a rifle platoon on the military crest of a small hill overlooking a long shallow valley. The importance of coordinating and tying in the elements of a rifle platoon with its adjacent platoons was so clear to me, after that morning at My Phu, when I realized what a poor job I had done.

I must have done a fairly decent job there because I was given my own class to teach: "The Night Attack." It was a matter of pride to be tabbed as a principal instructor (PI) for a class. That meant that everything that happened there was your responsibility. You had to worry about schedules, lesson plans, assistant instructors, equipment, safety gear, radios, pyrotechnics, chow schedules, timing, and most of all *pitching* the class. Pitch was the verb used to describe the act of getting out in front of hundreds of students and presenting the formal part of the class from memory. You had to stick to the written script and use all of the correct instructional techniques. It required a performance of very high standards and caused every PI more than a few restless nights.

I was newly married to my high-school sweetheart after five years of waiting for her to finish college and for me to get back from Germany and Vietnam. Living in the small army quarters on post was a whole new world for me. I was used to years of being with bunches of other soldiers around when I ate, slept, or took a leak. Having a home and a wife, and lots of homework to do at the dining room table, was a real change.

The hours involved preparing for instruction, rehearsing on site, and actually giving classes that started at dusk and went into the wee hours, were very long. But after Vietnam and prior assignments it didn't seem all that unusual. At least when I did get home I could wash up and sleep between clean sheets.

Being back in an academic environment, I was very conscious of the nagging obligation to get my college degree. I had enrolled in a couple of night-school classes at American University only to find that I had to drop out once I took over as PI of the night-attack class. I kept telling myself that something would shake loose and I would be able to work around the demanding schedule, to get into a class and stay there.

But that didn't turn out to be my experience. After a few months teaching out on Red Diamond Road, I was promoted to captain. I was thrilled to get my tracks,[74] especially since I had just turned twenty-three. Within days after making captain, I was called by my boss and told that I was moving to a new problem (class) as PI.

Vietnam had finally changed the face of Fort Benning and the content of the curriculum. Every class on post was reviewed for how it

---

[74] The two parallel silver bars of an Army captain's insignia of rank are often called "railroad tracks," for obvious reasons.

had to be updated to reflect the realities of Vietnam and the platoon tactics committee was in the forefront of the revisions. My committee converted a class into a comprehensive lecture and practical application of the kind of operations most common in Vietnam. It was to be the showpiece of the post and a place to bring every visiting fireman, congressman, and journalist. I was to give the class with a co-instructor.

My partner turned out to be Captain Richard Stilwell, a veteran of Vietnam and the 173d Airborne Brigade and one of the finest soldiers I've ever known. He was competent, pleasant, positive, and a joy to share hard work with.

We were handed a thick script and told to memorize it. Our job would be to teach a four-hour lecture-demonstration and then to supervise the execution of a twenty-three-hour practical exercise for the students. The class was designed to demonstrate and allow the students firsthand experience in village and tunnel search operations, convoys, counter-ambush, and night movement.

Dick and I were at first overwhelmed with the scope of the instruction. We had to commit to memory the exact words to the four-hour lecture. Variance wasn't permitted because we stood in front of a huge set of bleachers pitching about what was taking place in a demonstration area behind us. As we spoke, certain words were used by the assistant instructors in the control shack to cue helicopters to lift off, vehicles to start rolling, soldiers to move through precise routines, explosives to go off, and weapons to fire.

We narrated as the students watched an infantry platoon cordon and search an authentically recreated Vietnamese village. They watched soldiers making good and bad moves, and saw the consequences of falling for booby traps and turning their backs on innocent-looking "villagers."

After the search was finished, an American convoy moved across the front of the bleachers and was ambushed by enemy soldiers expertly hidden in spider holes and well camouflaged positions. They watched the soldiers in the convoy attempt to execute counter-ambush techniques while helicopters rolled in to make simulated firing runs on the ambushers.

The class was a nonstop spectacular of the most common actions conducted on a daily basis in Vietnam. For the students it was suddenly a visible reenactment of what they had studied in theory, and what they had only seen clips of on the evening news.

For the visiting firemen it was something they took back to Washington to add credibility to their arguments about the Vietnam War, regardless of their position.

For the journalists it was a chance to get some pictures of Vietnam operations without actually having to get shot at.

For me and Dick it was a chance to screw up. The standards for instruction were very exacting, and before we could even pitch the class we had to rehearse it to perfection and then present it to virtually every colonel in our chain of command up to the two-star general commanding Fort Benning.

Our murder board was a grueling day of pitching the class with full demonstrations and hundreds of support troops going through their paces and then walking the VIPs through the practical phase of the class. I know how Dick Stilwell made it through; he was really a class act. But for me it was really a tough day.

Looking back, murder boards were what made Benning Benning. They set a standard of excellence that explained why I got the high quality of instruction I did as a student—maybe not cutting edge, but high quality. When I was a student in OCS and jump school, I had no idea what the instructors had gone through before they were turned loose on the students.

How different it was on the other end of a Fort Benning pointer.

The class was officially called "The Rifle Platoon in Counterguerrilla Operations." The common name for it was Higley Hill—after where the class was taught. As we got better at giving the class, we added up-to-date combat examples of successes and failures right out of Vietnam. It was the one time in my experience at Benning that virtually no effort had to be made to get and hold the students' interest. They were motivated to pay attention and sucked every bit of information out of the dozen instructors and assistant instructors it took to run the twenty-seven hour problem.

We ran the problem two to three times a week and that meant we would frequently be up for thirty hours at a stretch. We would come home, clean up, change uniforms, grab extra ones, and head back to Higley Hill to meet the next group of students. It was then that I realized why Fort Benning instructors always looked so good. They changed uniforms several times a day and even in the middle of classes.

If Dick and I began a class and it was hot and we perspired even the slightest bit, we would hurry to the range shack to change. While the students got ten-minute smoke breaks every hour, we were usually up on the shack breaking starch again. Every time we stepped out into the gravel pit in front of the massive bleachers we would look fresh, shined, and polished or we'd have our committee chief to answer to.

During the night phase of the class we were all very demanding of the students. They were tasked with putting together an operations plan to move by truck and armored personnel carrier from the bleachers to a dismount point where they would have to move through the Georgia kudzu to a simulated hamlet. Their movement would take them almost all night, and by dawn they had to have the hamlet under observation and then conduct a cordon-and-search operation at first light.

The move by convoy was complicated enough and the night movement was filled with its own problems for the students. We didn't cut them much slack, knowing the consequences of carelessness firsthand. Every student platoon had at least one Vietnam veteran with it to critique each false step and risky move.

By the time the problem ended the next afternoon the students had been through the full variety of Vietnam operations.

I felt we were doing something important at Higley Hill. It was one place at Fort Benning where instructors could spend enough time with the students to impart some important techniques that we had learned the hard way. We were teaching them what they needed most and wanted most to know about: Vietnam. How I wished there had been a class like Higley Hill when I had been an officer candidate.

The months flew by and I saw very little of my new wife, and gathered exactly zero college credits. There was just no class offered in the Fort Benning-Columbus area that fit around my schedule.

In October I was summoned to Washington to take part in an award ceremony. Jim Gardner's widow was to receive the Medal of Honor on behalf of her fallen husband. The army invited those of us who were close to Jim at his death, and I was able to catch up with old friends—Belden, Hackworth and others.

The dignity of the ceremony was marred by the coincidence of it being the same weekend that the Yippies had decided to descend on Washington. Tens of thousands of them arrived to show America and the White House how they opposed the war in Vietnam and demanded its immediate end.

Being a uniformed infantry officer in Washington that weekend did not garner any well wishes or even a passing thanks. But neither did it provoke any confrontations. I was surrounded with Yippies on the flight up and in the airport and in the streets. But not one of them made a remark or even said a word to me.

The low point was at the Pentagon. As the ceremonial party arrived in a small convoy of army sedans, we found the Pentagon surrounded by Yippies being held back by a smaller circle of armed soldiers.

As we got out of the cars they chanted insults directed at us in general and Jim's widow in particular. When they screamed at us it wasn't too bad. But when they went after a young girl who had lost her husband in a moment of true heroism to save others, it showed me how low people can go to pursue a goal. Jim's widow was a lovely woman from Tennessee who didn't deserve her loss. Neither did she deserve the insults. I never asked her if she heard the ones specifically aimed at her and she never said. While they were an angry mob, she was a lady.

Back at Fort Benning all we talked about was Vietnam, what was happening there, who we knew there, and what they were doing. I picked up the habit of keeping a television or radio tuned to the news. And in the background we all heard a clock ticking, getting louder every day. Every official-looking envelope, every call on an army phone line might be the one alerting one of us for return to Vietnam.

For me it came barely eight months after my return to Fort Benning. The colonel on the other end of the phone asked me if I was ready to head back to Vietnam. There was no other acceptable answer than, "Yessir. When?"

He said that I would be getting orders to return to Vietnam in the next three months. I asked what kind of duty. He said the words I dreaded: *advisory duty.*

All of us at Fort Benning had heard the horror stories from the old Vietnam hands who wore the MACV[75] patch on their right shoulder —to be an advisor was the worst possible assignment. The stories were replete with examples of unmotivated South Vietnamese soldiers, risky combat operations, poorly maintained equipment, graft, political shenanigans, worthless leadership, and sheer incompetence.

I looked for some way around it and asked the assignments officer if there was any way I could get back to an American unit. He said I could generally have my pick of a unit assignment if I volunteered to go early.

So that's what I did. A few months later I got a call from the same

---

[75] Military Assistance Command, Vietnam, the primary U. S. military headquarters in Vietnam. The U.S. Army, Vietnam (USARV) was its major subordinate tactical element.

colonel at infantry branch[76] in Washington. He said that my application for early reassignment requesting an American unit was on his desk. He was going to approve it and put me against a vacancy projected in the Americal Division. But then he said that he noticed that my personnel file had several applications in it to go to Ranger school.

I had long given up going to Ranger school once I had already gone to combat and served as a platoon leader specializing in the very skills they taught. In my mind I had OJTed my Ranger training.

Then he asked another question that left me with only one reply. He asked, "You still want to go to Ranger school, don't you, young captain?"

To which I replied, "Oh, yessir."

He said, "Good. There's a class starting down there a week from Monday and I'll slot you into it. You'll get your alert orders in a few days."

Ranger school in a little over a week?! A fate worse than death. Soldiers spent months and months preparing for Ranger school, running and climbing and toughening up for the extraordinary demands that are placed on a Ranger student's body in the nine-week course.

I had been going to work, teaching, humping the Georgia countryside at night, and starting all over again the next day. I hadn't done that much physical conditioning and needed some time to get into Ranger-school shape. But there wasn't going to be any time. I had less than a week to get my life in order before I reported in to Harmony Church and the Ranger Department.

The news was not the best for my wife either. We had seen very little of each other while I was at Benning and all of a sudden I came home and started packing. But she didn't complain and she quietly prepared to be uprooted again.

I hadn't even gotten captain's bars sewn onto all my fatigue uniforms when I was ripping them off again. At Ranger school there is no rank, only positions. During the course you are either a patrol leader, an assistant patrol leader, or one of the other members of a patrol. Administratively, the student class was organized into a company of over two hundred students. So we were also assigned to rotating responsibilities as acting squad leaders, platoon leaders, and company staff jobs.

On the first day I was tabbed to be the student company com-

---

[76] The office in the Office of Personnel Operations that assigned infantry officers throughout the army. The other branches had similar assignment offices.

mander. In addition to attending all of the training and passing all of the tests in the course, I had to be responsible for the care, feeding, bedding and accountability of the two hundred and fourteen students. That meant that whatever went wrong in the daily running of the student company, I caught hell for it. That included Ranger students showing up late for formations, riding the sick book at the dispensary, losing equipment or even flunking out—I would hear about it in a big way.

Ranger school was everything I had heard it was and more. The three-phase course covered hand-to-hand combat; gruelling physical training; complex land navigation; airborne, air, land, and amphibious operations. The actual instruction and practical application took place at Fort Benning; Dahlonega, Georgia; and Eglin Field in Florida.

While Ranger school had been around for decades and had refined and improved the exacting demands of the curriculum on the students, Vietnam added a special twist to it. The focus was quickly shifted to emphasize counterguerrilla operations in jungle and mountainous terrain, and air mobility by helicopter.

The daily training schedule made every army school I had been to seem like a vacation. We began instruction in the dark and were still at it into the early hours of the next morning. And when we weren't getting formal presentations and demonstrations, we were out all night running patrols to ambush, recon, raid, or snatch prisoners.

It didn't take me long to realize that I was right in my personal assessment of my readiness to attend the course. But there was just no way that I would quit or fall out of a run or fail to keep up with the younger, fresher Ranger students.

From the first morning in Ranger school we started losing students. They fell out of runs and quit. They failed the high-standards physical training tests, and they just walked up to the tactical officer and said they wanted out.

The quitters and the ones who couldn't hack it were pretty much gone by the time we left the Benning phase for the Mountain phase. The remainder of the losses we sustained were from illness, injuries, and a couple of compassionate recycles for family reasons.

We had some unfortunate accidents during the course that cost the lives of some of the students and seriously injured others. I don't know how it could have been avoided. It is always a problem when the effort to provide realistic combat training results in training accidents.

*   *   *

The Mountain phase was exciting for me because there was so much new for me to learn. I had never had any mountaineering instruction before, and the Ranger instructors were expert at quickly teaching us what we needed to know to feel at home on sheer rock faces, overhangs, and rappelling in free space.

When we arrived at the Mountain Ranger Camp in Dahlonega I fully expected to have some of the load lifted from my back by being replaced as student company commander.

It didn't happen. No new student was given the job, even though the other jobs in the company were routinely shuffled by the tactical officer who supervised all of the administrative needs of the student company. I was ready for the break, but didn't complain when the change didn't come through. It would have been bad form.

The strain of Ranger school was cumulative. By the end of the first week you were sore and exhausted. By the end of the fourth you were nearly a zombie from lack of sleep and the constant demands of training. But by the end of the course you were completely surprised that you had made it without being hospitalized.

The hours of near hallucinations brought on by lack of sleep that I had grown to hate in Vietnam were part of every day in Ranger school. It wasn't as dangerous as spacing out in Vietnam, but there were all the same sleepwalker-like events. Ranger students, myself included, would think they were someplace else, making imaginary phone calls to their girlfriends while in ambush on the side of Hawk Mountain. Others would think they were standing in front of Coke machines and would kick and pound on large tree trunks, wondering why no soft drink dropped from the tree after they had put a quarter into it.

We lost students and we lost equipment. I was reminded of the lost Starlight Scope but just couldn't impress on the others the importance of keeping an eye on their equipment. They just didn't appreciate the consequences involved. I resigned myself to the conclusion that they would each have to lose their own Starlight Scope in Vietnam to get the big picture.

By the time we got to Eglin Field in Florida we had lost even more students. The five original platoons we started with had whittled down to four very thin ones. We had all lost plenty of weight. Many were suffering from one upper respiratory infection or another and no one was spared all manner of rashes, blisters, and a multitude of insect bites.

However small the breaks were in your skin when you arrived in

Florida, they were guaranteed to blow way out of proportion after prolonged immersion in the Florida swamps.

The swamps were a shock for everyone of us. We had heard of the swamps and seen beautiful Florida tourism brochures with cypress trees dressed in hanging mosses, rising elegantly from the black water. The beauty of those scenes was lost on us when we spent night after night wading through the armpit-deep swamp water, unable to see the sky through the trees.

Everything about the swamps threw us. We were unable to find solid reference points and landmarks to navigate. We were unsure of the distances we traveled because we couldn't accurately count our pace in the squishy swamp bottom, studded with cypress trees that found our shins time after time.

The already strained patience of the students was stretched by the accumulated exhaustion and extended training in the last few weeks we spent in the Florida swamps.

There was also a feeling of diminishing opportunities to graduate and receive the coveted and much respected Ranger tab. Those students who didn't satisfactorily perform in the job of patrol leader on an unspecified number of patrols would not get the tab. Some would not graduate at all, and others would graduate but not be awarded the tab. The thought of finishing the grinding weeks of Ranger school and not getting the tab was just unacceptable.

Still, even the Ranger students with the poorest marks on patrols charged on and pursued the tab. Unfortunately, many of them were grossly disappointed at graduation.

Ranger school had made the adjustment to Vietnam faster than the rest of the infantry school because all it took was a decision passed to the instructors concerning the change in curriculum rather than an evolving academic process with extensive murder boards. The Ranger school quickly filled with Vietnam-veteran instructors, and there seemed to be almost no problems associated with making the instruction directly applicable to Vietnam.

They were particularly good at introducing rapidly changing battlefield situations to the execution of otherwise simple patrols. As a student patrol leader, you were often given a mission to go from point A to B and conduct a reconnaissance of a possible helicopter landing zone. Before Vietnam the mission might have been to recon a parachute drop zone.

During the movement to the recon site, the Ranger instructor was likely to detonate an artillery simulator and declare the patrol leader dead, the radio knocked out, and the patrol compromised. The instructor would designate a new patrol leader and give him virtually no time to get moving, but to get the patrol moving, nonetheless.

I thought the rapidly changing situation scenario was particularly effective as a Stateside training method to prepare students for Vietnam. Flexibility was so often tested in Vietnam and survival and success were directly related to quick responses and innovative field expedients. Ranger school emphasized flexibility and teamwork.

We fought the whole concept of change during the first few weeks of Ranger school, but those who survived the course learned to adapt to every requirement for change that the instructors threw at us.

In a career's worth of army schools I have to say that the two finest and most useful to me were the 7th Army NCO Academy and Ranger school. I had admired graduates of Benning's Ranger school for their self-confidence and proficiency as combat infantrymen long before I went there myself. I probably appreciated what they taught far more after having first been to Vietnam than I might have had I gone right out of OCS. And the Ranger-qualified Tiger Force members were the best of an already well-qualified and highly motivated collection of volunteer Airborne infantrymen.

It was both surprising and highly gratifying when I was called out on graduation day at Eglin Field to receive the award as Distinguished Honor Graduate of my class. I was presented with a plaque and an engraved fighting knife from the Ranger Battalions Association and the Association of the U.S. Army.

Just graduating and earning a Ranger tab was my highest aspiration. But ending up at the top of my class was a thrill and a moment I am very proud of.

CHAPTER 23

I hated leaving Benning a second time. I had enjoyed the short assignment there even though the hours were long and the duty taxing. My mindset was quite different about going back to Vietnam than it had been on my first trip.

Since I had returned from Vietnam many things had changed. The opposition to the war had become a staple on the evening news and the weekly casualty figures were insinuated into every piece of analysis done on the government, the army, the White House, and the economy.

The draft resistance had grown from a series of widely scattered protests to a cottage industry. And the spinoff of the draft deferment standards spawned new community colleges up and down the east and west coasts of the United States.

Listening to the whining and the harping about getting out of Vietnam was a luxury that I didn't have the time for while it was happening. And catching up when I got out of Ranger school and went on to Vietnam was something I knew not to do. Instinctively, I knew that I didn't want to leave for Vietnam with the meat of every argument against the war in my head. It would change nothing for me and only be massively depressing to know that I was going back to a war that kids in the street didn't want to participate in, and many others not even subject to the draft had jumped on as a cause du jour.

If the war was wrong and our country had made a mistake, it was up to our country to change policy and pull out. Nixon was promising to get us out and I fully expected that we would soon cease fire and withdraw, win or lose. It was my duty to return, do what the job required, and let people far more qualified than I take care of the disengagement. In a sense I held simultaneously a head-in-the-sand attitude and a realistic appraisal of what my bitching about it would *not* accomplish.

At the time my head was filled with the demands that I knew would be facing me in a matter of a couple of weeks. The war had escalated, the number of experienced NCOs and officers had dropped, and I was fully expecting to be assigned to the Americal Division as a rifle company commander.

To an infantry officer, then and now, commanding an infantry company in combat is the highest aspiration and one of the most respected jobs in the army. The responsibility for the lives of over a hundred soldiers and the accomplishment of the missions given a company put its commander in a squeeze that could only be well executed through leadership and training.

Those demands on me were foremost in my mind as my plane touched down at Cam Ranh Bay. And, like before, I prayed that I wouldn't come up wanting.

When I last saw Cam Ranh it had been a deep-water port with a few Quonset huts scattered around the sand dunes. Stepping off the plane this time, I saw the first hint of the massive changes that had taken place in Vietnam. One of the first, and most disturbing, was the choke point they put us through. Before we were allowed to proceed with our in-country orientation, we were funneled into a room and a sergeant recited a list of contraband items we were not allowed to bring into Vietnam. The list covered a multitude of items from switchblades to drugs.

He told us that we were allowed one chance to drop anything on the list into the large red plywood box near the stage. It was called an *amnesty box*. He then told us that he would leave us alone for a while and on his return the amnesty was off. If we were caught with any of the banned items from that point forward, we'd be prosecuted under the Uniform Code of Military Justice.[77]

The amnesty exercise, while somewhat understandable, put me off in the first few minutes I was back in Vietnam. But that wasn't the end of changes. And true to my six years of experience, there was change. As soon as I checked into the processing detachment in Cam Ranh, I was told that my orders to the Americal had been cancelled. A flash of low-level panic seized me at the thought of being assigned to an advisory job after the effort I had gone through to avoid one.

I wasn't surprised either when the clerk told me he had no idea where I was going but that I had to get to Long Binh to report in to II Field Force[78] for further assignment.

The thought of being assigned to a huge American headquarters

---

[77] The uniform code of laws governing the conduct of all personnel of the U.S. Armed Forces. It is published as an appendix to the *Manual for Courts-Martial*.

[78] This was a corps-level headquarters established to exercise tactical control over the U.S. forces operating within its area of responsibility. The others were I Field Force, in

wasn't much more appealing than an advisory job. I could only hope that once I arrived I would be assigned to a conventional maneuver unit under the command of II Field Force.

What happened was even more surprising. I stepped off the plane at Bien Hoa Air Force Base to find the smiling face of an old friend, Captain Peter K. Laisik. Peter and I had been in the 1st, 327th together in II Corps.[79] A fine officer and a combat-experienced platoon leader, there he stood—head to toe in a type of camouflage uniform that I had never seen before. On his head he wore a floppy hat similar to the ones we wore in the Tiger Force and commonly worn by the Special Forces. His jungle fatigues were cammies, but the pattern was new; it was the now common woodland pattern that is the standard issue in today's army and worn by just about every police agency in America.

On his left shoulder he wore three arced tabs over the camouflaged II Field Force patch. They read: LONG-RANGE PATROL, RANGER, and AIR-BORNE. He smiled broadly, shook my hand, and welcomed me to F Company.

F Company? What the hell was F Company? I'd never heard of it. Peter ushered me to a jeep and explained as we drove from Bien Hoa to Long Binh to in-process me.

F Company turned out to be the II Field Force Long-Range Patrol Company. During my absence from Vietnam and in part due to the successes of units like the Tiger Force, each of the two Field Forces had decided to create their own long-range patrol companies. And, like the Tiger Force, F Company was assigned to the staff supervision of the operations section (G-3) of II Field Force rather than the intelligence section (G-2), as were some other long-range patrol units. The difference was very important and set the whole tone of the unit's attitude.

Long-range patrol companies and detachments had popped up in virtually every American maneuver unit. The ones who were responsible to the intelligence effort were usually designated as *LRRP* units, and those who were under the supervision of their headquarters operations sections were more often designated *LRP*. The difference in the abbreviation was the extra *R* for reconnaissance. At the risk of

---

Nha Trang, in the South Vietnamese Army's II Corps Tactical Zone, and XXIV Corps, in Phu Bai, in the I Corps Tactical Zone.

[79] That is, the II Corps Tactical Zone of the Army of the Republic of Vietnam, generally the central highlands area.

overgeneralizing, LRRP units were primarily in the intelligence-gathering business and the LRP units were in the enemy contact business.

Intelligence and contact missions were conducted by both types of long-range patrol units. But the primary missions of intelligence collection or making contact set the stage for what was most likely to happen to a team once it was on the ground. The doctrinal philosophy of intel versus ops has raged on since Vietnam and I don't see any day when it will end.

For me, there was no philosophical contemplation. The decision had been made before my arrival and the missions for F Company (Long-Range Patrol), 51st Infantry (Airborne) came from the operational side of our higher headquarters and that's the way it was.

F Company had been set up to operate in the southern half of South Vietnam for almost nine months by the time I got there, and it already had a terrific reputation. If the Tiger Force was a new car with all the accessories, F Company was a Cadillac. It had four patrol platoons of up to seven patrols each; a communications, mess, maintenance, and headquarters section; and an array of attached assets.

In addition to the organic resources, F Company had a dedicated Huey lift platoon to insert and extract teams, a gunship platoon for fire support, a full ground cavalry troop to act as a reaction force, a forward air controller (FAC) to coordinate and deliver air strikes, and an artillery liaison officer to coordinate artillery support.

On any given day there would be as many as five hundred men focused on the F Company operations either conducting patrols, supporting them, or preparing to launch them.

In essence, F Company was a very light Airborne-Ranger infantry battalion, capable of emplacing and supporting multiple small combat patrols with immediate air, artillery, and maneuver elements to exploit enemy contacts.

For a Ranger this was the big time. This was ideal assignment if you were going to be in the Ranger-LRP business in Vietnam. The more Peter talked, the more I relaxed about my worries over ending up in a headquarters or an advisory job.

Somewhere in the middle of his enthusiastic briefing I stopped him long enough to ask him how I ended up going to F Company—half the length of Vietnam away from where I was supposed to go—and what I would be doing. He smiled smugly and told me that he had heard I was due in-country and had put the bug in the ears of the right people at II Field Force. They tracked me down and got me diverted to F Company where I would be the operations officer.

Operations officer? In a company? He explained that F Company was set up much like a battalion, with staff-officer responsibilities divided up into operations, intelligence, supply, and administration. F Company had an operations officer, intelligence officer, and a communications officer, and Peter was a combination of adjutant, supply officer, and executive officer.

I said, "Great!", relieved by the details and excited by the assignment. Then I asked who the commander was. He told me that I didn't know him and that I'd be meeting him later. It was the first statement out of Peter's mouth that didn't spill over with enthusiasm.

II Field Force Headquarters was a complete surprise to me. When I had left Vietnam, various high-level headquarters had commandeered existing Vietnamese buildings to adapt to their needs. But while I was with the Tiger Force, and after my departure to the States plenty of construction had taken place.

II Field Force Headquarters was a long, narrow set of buildings that paralleled the road to Saigon and sat a short jeep ride to the south of the sprawling Bien Hoa Air Force Base.

As Peter took me to all of the usual spots I had to hit to in-process, I was able to see the size and complexity of the headquarters whose primary function was to control the combat and administrative operations of up to five full infantry divisions, several separate brigades and regiments, and a plethora of assorted support units.

The headquarters had every creature comfort and even some that troops didn't have in the States. The buildings were all newly built tropical structures with fans, screens, and cross-ventilation. Clubs of all sorts dotted the compound: Enlisted men's clubs, NCO clubs, senior NCO clubs, officers clubs. Theaters, basketball and tennis courts fought for real-estate space with large post exchanges, swimming pools, gymnasiums, snack bars and Class VI[80] (liquor) Sales stores.

And to top the whole facility off, general officers had fully air-conditioned, gleaming aluminum Airstream-type house trailers to live in.

It was truly a Disneyland in Vietnam.

As surprising as the appearance of the headquarters was, my first look at the troops should have warned me about what a different war they were in than the soldiers who laid in wait on night ambushes in F Company.

---

[80] There are ten classes of supply in the Department of Defense supply system, VI being "personal demand items," which includes alcoholic beverages, but in garrison the so-called "Class VI Store" is actually a retail outlet operated by the Army and Air Force Exchange Service.

Their uniforms were all fully appointed with all authorized patches, badges, name tapes, and headgear. Every uniform swished with the scratch of freshly ironed starch, and their boots gleamed with spit shines. When the young LRP driver caught my reaction to the appearance of the troops he said, "Hootch[81] maids."

Hootch maids? He explained that they all paid Vietnamese girls to come clean up their barracks, make their bunks, wash and starch their uniforms, and even clean their latrines for them. For the headquarters rats at II Field Force there were virtually no unpleasant duties.

I hadn't missed the presence of the civilians either. Everywhere in the compound there were Vietnamese men and women doing all of the menial tasks that soldiers had traditionally done. They were washing vehicles, pulling KP, sweeping streets, digging ditches, hauling trash, cutting grass, painting rocks, and policing the area.

What a wonderful place to be assigned! That is if the war was a fairly low priority for you and proximity wasn't much of a problem either.

After checking in at II Field Force and meeting all of the staff officers and NCOs I'd soon become familiar with, Peter took me back to Bien Hoa to the F Company base camp. As we drove through Bien Hoa Army—the section of the base area reserved for army units—I noticed another distinctive change. Black soldiers congregated in distinct groups. Gone were the gatherings of mixed colors. There was an unmistakable tension in the air and a confrontational attitude in the walk and the look of the black soldiers.

In addition to the visible attitudes of the blacks was an open effort on their part to modify their hair and uniforms to accentuate their segregation. Afro hairstyles were everywhere. Wide, dark leather bracelets and watchbands were worn by many, while others wore thin black gloves in the middle of a hot Vietnam day. And passing black soldiers were quick to exchange what I would come to recognize as a black power salute of solidarity.

It was all new to me. The same signs were nowhere at Fort Benning, nor had they been in the 101st before I left my earlier tour in Vietnam. It was disturbing but I didn't even know why, I just knew that it would lead to some kind of trouble.

---

[81] Since the Japanese occupation, American soldiers stationed in the Far East have used "hootch" (sometimes "hooch") to mean any kind of temporary billet other than a tent, or any kind of native house or sleeping place. The word is a corruption of *uchi*, Japanese for "house."

Before I could talk to Peter about it, a thirty-four-foot jump tower appeared down the roadway, in front of our jeep.

Now, no paratrooper ever sees a thirty-four-foot tower without remembering the days of agony he went through making qualifying exits from the door of such a tower. I asked Peter whose it was and he said, "Ours."

We came closer and stopped at the barber-pole gate of our own compound, marked by a large black, red, and white plywood scroll. With the jump tower prominent near the front gate, the camp took up several acres of former rice-paddy land—flat and manicured to military standards. It was nearly as plush a base area as the headquarters I had just left at Long Binh. Several long, low team barracks stood neatly arranged next to a company headquarters, mess hall, and a tactical operations center. Just inside the compound's gate stood the officers' quarters complete with its own club.

But except for the solitary soldier standing guard at the entrance gate, there seemed to be no one in the large compound. Peter explained that the company was *forward*. For F Company, forward meant any temporary launch site used to base the combat and patrolling activities. Late in the summer of 1968 it was out of Cu Chi, the base camp of the 25th Infantry Division, near the Cambodian border. I would be going forward as soon as I got settled in.

Peter took me to the orderly room where the basics took only minutes. The clerk helping Peter run the rear detachment got all my particulars, and I was quickly on my way to the operations section. It consisted of a heavily sandbagged building surrounded with large rolls of concertina wire stacked in rows on top of other rows.

Inside was just about everything you could expect to find in a working infantry battalion tactical command post. Radios stood on solidly built wooden benches and shelves to monitor every frequency necessary to run the air and ground operations of the company. In a place or two there was a hole where some of the equipment had been taken forward to Cu Chi, but would return when operations were again launched from that room.

Maps of the entire II Field Force operational area and the bulk of eastern Cambodia covered all of the available wall space. Provisions for batteries, supplies, expendables, backup radio equipment, and a number of field telephones took up the remaining space.

It was clear to me that my predecessors had thought out the needs of the company and filled them. It was reassuring to know the extent to which they had gone to be deep in resources and redundant in many. But the place was manned by one RTO who was there to relay information to II Field Force from the company—forward.

Peter and I grabbed something to eat in the mess hall while I waited for a ride forward. He ate and worked and tried to give me bits and pieces of the setup in the company. But mostly he tried to fill me in on what he expected of me to help him help the company. It was right and appropriate for him to prioritize that way. He didn't know when we'd get another chance to speak.

It began to rain and the chopper that had been expected for a milk run didn't show up. I had planned to take the chopper back to Cu Chi to report to my new boss.

I was eager to find out more about the company, its mission, its commander, and its troops from Peter but he was really swamped with calls to take and make, wearing the many hats that he did. He promised me we'd get time to talk, and suggested that I relax for a while since he was sure it would be my last quiet night in Vietnam.

I found my room and stowed what gear I was sure I would not be taking forward with me. The thought of having my own room with a sink and a shower was nearly enough to make me feel guilty. But I would soon find that I would spend very little time in it while in F Company.

Peter's duties didn't allow for much more discussion, and it was obvious to me that he was beat by the time he finally turned the light off over his desk. I decided not to push it. I wanted to do something to thank him for saving me from the possibility of a terrible assignment somewhere else in Vietnam. The least I could do was let him get a few hours sleep.

Sleep that night was hard to come by. It was like any first night in a unit filled with unknowns and the promise of plenty of enemy contact. I wondered just how complex and how difficult my job would be and if I had the skills and the talent to pull it off. I cursed myself for not having paid more attention on my earlier tour to just how the operations section of my battalion had worked. I was sure that I could have gleaned something then that would prove useful to me later.

I got up from my rack and went outside to the two-holer latrine that stood several yards from the officers billets. The sky was filled with stars, the sounds of choppers were everywhere, and I realized that I had at least another year of such nights ahead of me. It's as difficult a feeling of yearning as you can get, knowing you are as far away from home as you are going to be.

I looked around the compound, named for two of F Company's soldiers killed in action—Lindsay and Lattin. Though the place was empty and quiet, I could just feel the presence of the men that had left there for battle to come back victorious or bloodied.

It was a long night.

After breakfast a chopper arrived carrying broken equipment and weapons parts, two LRPs headed for R & R, bundles of paperwork for Peter, and a rucksack filled with captured documents marked for G-2.

The pilot put me in the right seat and we took off for Cu Chi. I had never seen the huge flood plains of the Mekong and its tributary rivers from anything less than eight thousand feet before. Flying along at seventy knots at fifteen hundred feet was a real eye-opener for me.

The area was heavily populated for as far as I could see in every direction. Even the rivers and large streams were busy thoroughfares for boat traffic.

The central effort seemed to be divided between going to and from local markets and tending the fields that supplied them. With the exception of a very few light industrial districts clustered in the small towns, everything was oriented on agriculture, fishing, and the military.

South Vietnamese Army compounds, firebases, and outposts dotted the terrain every few thousand meters of our flight path and as far as I could see on either side of us. It occurred to me that if I could pick them out from fifteen hundred feet in the air that they shouldn't be hard for the VC to find.

What had not changed was the South Vietnamese soldiers' approach to the war. Even from the chopper I could see them crowding the roads, clustering in the marketplaces, lounging in hammocks, and sleeping in the backs of parked trucks. There was just no sense of urgency in their daily routine.

I could see Cu Chi from a long way off. It sat on the western edge of a wide band of partially abandoned rice farms. A solid strip of swampy reed plains separated the farms from the Cambodian border. The terrain was flat and the concealment offered by vegetation was almost non-existent. That was the first thing that bothered me about operating west of Cu Chi.

Cu Chi itself was a moderate-size town next to which the 25th Infantry Division had placed its base camp. The camp's most visible feature was the red laterite dirt that defined all of the damage that could be done by posting a partially mechanized infantry division in farmland. It looked dirty—everything the same reddish color. The dust kicked up by all of the truck, track, and chopper traffic had covered the base with a thick layer of red powder.

During the course of the division's history in Vietnam, it had been augmented by some and then lost other units and had sometimes been split up into separate brigade-size base camps. These changes left a large portion of the huge Cu Chi base camp abandoned. One such area was known as the Old Warrior area, named after the mascot of a unit who had once been billeted there.

Operating along the Cambodian border was just too far for F Company to be supported from Bien Hoa. So II Field Force moved F Company operations to the Old Warrior section of the Cu Chi base camp.

As we approached the large, worn landing pad with the Indian-head insignia painted on it, I got a look at the shabby buildings and facilities. It was clear that the area had been abandoned for quite some time before F Company moved in, and the elements and the red dust had taken a toll on the tropical buildings, roadways, and walkways. It looked pretty sad.

As he shut down the chopper, the pilot pointed me toward what looked like a onetime supply building. I grabbed my gear and headed for the company TOC. Looking around, I could tell where the troops were living and where the company had taken over old buildings to serve its feeding, bathing, and supply needs. The rest was left in its original shabbier condition.

LRP gear hung from the eaves of the building, drying in the sun. Boots sat on crumbling barracks steps, crusted with drying mud and slime from the marshy terrain they had just walked through, and rock-and-roll music came from a couple of the hootches.

I could see a few of the team members just back and teams preparing to go out in a few of the ramshackle hootches. And as I approached the TOC I had to step around an older soldier, wearing only shorts, stretched out on a folding cot just catching some sun. He was sound asleep and I assumed he was catching up after a patrol.

On the ground, next to the cot, was a mess hall cup and a bottle of Pernod. I winced at the thought of the sickening French liquor and assumed that it was not a problem for an off-duty LRP to have a drink if he wanted to. It made sense to me, considering the hours they spent in the bush.

* * *

Inside the TOC I was greeted enthusiastically by the man I was replacing, Captain Tom Meyer. Tom was on his way home after a hard tour of duty with F Company. I remembered how thrilled I was to meet my own "turtle" when I left Vietnam the first time. "Turtle" was the term we used for the guy who replaced you because he was always so slow in coming.

After some short pleasantries, Tom got me a cup of coffee and began briefing me on the job. He made occasional references to Zummo, the commanding officer, but focused on the operations and the intricate process that he had developed.

Tom explained how the teams prepared for inserts, how long they could be expected to stay out in the AO, what happened when they were compromised or made contact, and how they were extracted. He was very proud of the operation and the teams. He had plenty of good things to say about their professionalism and their state of training.

I asked about chopper support, remembering how hard it was to come by for the Tiger Force, and how we could never count on them not to be diverted. He smiled and told me that I would be very happy with the slick and gun support that F Company had. They were part of the family and could be counted on down to the last pilot.

While Tom was briefing me I kept one ear on the small speakers that sat in the spaces between the radio equipment mounted on a bench and on the wall. Teams were calling in situation reports and progress reports. There was plenty of crosstalk from the pilots about swapping shifts of standby choppers, refueling, and maintenance.

At first it sounded very confusing, but I was most impressed with the tone of all the message traffic. There was not a trace of friction among the voices and not a hint of confusion about what they were doing. It sounded like men all familiar and comfortable with one another. I don't mean by that that they were casual or not focused on what they were doing. They were serious. They just didn't have that manner about them normally associated with confusion on a battlefield.

Tom assured me that I'd be very pleased with the army and air-force pilots and the artillery support personnel.

I asked again about the CO. Tom motioned out the front door. Out on the cot—that was the boss, Lieutenant Colonel Joe Zummo.

CHAPTER 24

•

It only took a few minutes for me to dump my gear and get to work alongside Tom Meyer. Our overlap wasn't going to be long and I had to pick his brain as fast and as well as I could. Since the TOC was filled with radio operators and other company personnel, I thought it was the wrong place to ask Tom what the story was with Zummo. I decided to focus on the most obvious questions related to the company's operations SOP and my job.

I never got a chance to ask Tom about Zummo before meeting him. Tom left the TOC to fly out to the AO to pick up a team and Zummo walked in, still groggy and sweating from the hot sun. He looked at me in the darkness of the TOC, squinted and asked, "Who are you?"

I told him that I'd been assigned to F Company. I thought I'd better not tell him that I thought I was to be the new operations officer. Over the years I had discovered that all commanders jealously guard the privilege of making their own decisions about who gets assigned to what. It was a good way to get off on the wrong foot, telling a commander his business.

He scratched his stomach in a most unmilitary manner and grumbled something about remembering that I was supposed to be Meyer's replacement. I nodded in agreement and fully expected to get some instructions from him on my job and what he expected of me. I got nothing. He just shrugged and said, "Meyer'll take care of you," and walked back to the sleeping area of the large building. I didn't see him for the rest of the day. It was the most unusual welcoming I ever got to a unit.

Tom got me started that afternoon. I began by getting a copy of the organization chart to get a feel for how many operational teams each patrol platoon had and what their status was. Some were out in the AO west of Cu Chi, some were just back and standing down, waiting for a warning order for their next mission, and others were prepping to go out.

Still other teams had been zeroed out as too short in manpower to field a full six-man team. The status of a team changed from day to day, and at any one time a team could be in any one of these states of readiness or deployment.

Radio calls filled the radio net and there was a constant stream of LRPs entering and leaving the TOC for various reasons. Each time someone new would come through the door, I would be introduced. While I was glad to meet each new face, it made it difficult to concentrate on absorbing all of the new information that I would be expected to master.

I tried to get some time with the map of the operational area, but the interruptions continued and I was eager to get up to speed. Tom Meyer returned and I met our command and control pilot and the platoon leader of the slick platoon that routinely supported F Company.

Michael Reitz was an artillery officer by training but a helicopter pilot by divine right. Of all the chopper pilots I have known in my life only three, in my opinion, were born to fly. And two of them were with F Company.

I explained to Mike that I was trying to get a handle on our operational area and was not very successful at it. His suggestion was to get on out there and see it. I agreed.

The AO was a complete surprise to me. I had never seen an area quite like it. It was flat. At least it was flat by central highlands standards, and it was often wet or marshy. Its most dominant characteristic was the clumping of little thatched huts into large farms, hamlets, or small villages. Each of these areas was marked by little squares of trees that broke the wind and shaded out the sun on all four sides. From the air they looked like scattered little blocks of green with structures inside them. From each of the little squares a spider web of foot trails led off and eventually joined other trails, which would become dirt roads.

In turn, the dirt roads would eventually lead to the few hardtop roads—all of them leading to marketplaces and some of them leading to the larger cities, including Saigon.

Mike flew the C & C with the grace and effortless motion of a sailboat captain. His moves were almost automatic and his control of the chopper was smooth. As he gave me the tour of the AO he kept me oriented on the map I had on my lap. His mental bearings were so well fixed in his own head that he could tell me where something we were looking at from the air was on my map by just reaching over and tapping the terrain feature.

Mike's map was in his head, and it was more accurate than the one I had stretched across my knees. He could point out features of flatland life that it would have taken me months to discover by myself. I was most impressed with the fact that he had a ground-oriented tactical sense about everything. He would point something out about the terrain or the rivers or the weather and then explain its impact on the teams. He understood the teams and what they needed to survive and do their jobs on the ground.

I quickly realized how much we had missed in the Tiger Force by not having the same chopper support dedicated to us. But in those days there just weren't as many choppers, the priority was placed on the infantry battalions first and the Tiger Force later.

Mike Reitz showed me everything. He flew the chopper so that the visibility was best from the right seat, and we hit it off right from the first minute. I knew I was going to like him and I had a hunch that I was going to be able to trust him and his judgment. What I didn't know, at that moment, was the importance of the role he played. F Company was entirely dependent on good, solid, and predictable chopper support. The terrain and the weather in III Corps was much more suitable for chopper support than it had been in II Corps.

There was also an added piece of good news—we had H-model Hueys and no longer had to rely on the B, C and D models that we had in the 101st. The difference was in payload size and weight. An H model could lift more weight than earlier models and could hold larger cubic loads than the B or C models. It boiled down to an increase in the reliability and the lift capacity to support teams on the ground. And having Mike to consult about the differences and the capabilities was great.

I returned from my first flyover of the AO with plenty of notes to absorb. My day had been filled with good news—except for Zummo. I had decided not to ask Mike about Zummo since I thought it would put him in a spot. I just didn't feel right about arriving in a new unit and then asking everyone to explain just what the problem was with a commander who seemed to be completely out of place.

That evening I kept working on gathering information and sat in on a briefback that Tom conducted with one of the teams going out the next day. I was impressed with the attention to detail, the professionalism, and the focus. Everything in the operations section of that company was about the teams. Nothing else mattered and no other business was done there but team business. That was good.

Late in the evening, I was sitting at an improvised desk when Zummo came back. He was still in his bathing trunks and was wearing his floppy hat. He asked me what the status of the teams was, and I did a fairly good job of briefing him. But as I was briefing him I got the feeling that he really didn't care about the teams. He was sizing me up. I didn't know how to handle briefing a half-naked lieutenant colonel, so I just kept on doing what I was doing.

He grumbled something about one of the team leaders having a tendency to complain and wandered back out of the room again.

Later, I wanted to jot a few words down on paper, to let my wife and family know where I was and that I was okay. My stuff was in the sleeping area, which was nothing more than a large room with a plywood floor, some folding cots and a single bare bulb down near Zummo's bunk.

Zummo didn't notice me entering. He was on his bunk, reading a paperback book, sipping more Pernod. The scene bothered me and I didn't know what I was going to do about the distance the man had kept between us and the chill I got from being around him.

I didn't feel comfortable approaching Zummo. So I simply got the envelopes I was looking for and went back into the TOC to finish writing.

The next day started early with me sitting in on a team getting a warning order. We then took the C & C out to the AO a few minutes before the lift ships.

As we lifted off the Old Warrior pad, Tom Meyer made one more call to the first team scheduled to come out that morning, to make sure they were ready. He gave them an estimate on the pickup time and promised to get back to them after the first scheduled insert.

Tom coordinated the insert of the fresh team from the back of the C & C like it was the easiest thing in the world. He identified the landing zone from quite a distance, and called the lift ship to bring on the team to be inserted while he put the gunships in a high orbit to be ready to roll in on anything that threatened the inserting team or the supporting aircraft.

The radio traffic was thick, but effective. Choppers coordinated their every move to avoid trouble. Tom kept the inserting team and the pilots abreast of what he wanted and when he wanted it. There was no wasted effort and no needless orbits.

The lift ship came into its landing zone barely skimming along the ground on its approach and touched down in the wet paddy, heels of its skids first. The chopper gently rolled forward from the momentum of the stop and the team burst out of one side. As they sprinted for the nearby tree square, the chopper rolled up on the toes of its skids and lifted off the ground.

Then it was silent. Everyone listened and watched the ground for signs of shooting. The silence was dramatic after the non-stop chatter that had filled my headset during the setup and approach to the landing zone.

The slight hiss in the headset was finally broken by an out-of-breath whisper. The team leader reported the team in and safe—no opposition. Everyone in the chopper exhaled, and Tom gave the choppers a new heading to the team coming out.

The next few days were a blur of activities. I followed every move that Tom made until he jumped on a chopper and headed back to Bien Hoa to out-process. He had done a great job and deserved to get home and get some rest.

Zummo and I were not warming up to each other, but I was too swamped with my job to worry about it. He seemed either to avoid me or he would just sit in the TOC and watch what everyone was doing. Occasionally, he would make some remark about what we were doing right or wrong, or just remain silent for long periods.

I got a lot of help from the pilots and from the young and very experienced assistant operations officer, Lieutenant Al Snyder. His radio call sign ended in the suffix of *3F*. As a shortcut he became known as Three Fox not only on the radio, but in person. No one referred to him by his real name. Instead, everyone knew Snyder as Three Fox.

I found Three Fox to be just about the most efficient lieutenant I had ever worked with. He was capable of handling many things all crowding in on him at the same time without rattling. He knew the capabilities of all the teams. And he knew all the personalities. He was a strong right arm and I was very happy to have him there.

After a few nights on the job, Zummo came in and watched while I handled the incoming transmission from a team that had movement near its position. From all indications, the movement was probably enemy. That didn't mean that they knew the team was there, just that the likelihood that the team was about to make contact was very high.

Without having received a request from the team leader for extraction, Zummo made the announcement that that particular team leader was always spooky and told me to leave his team on the ground —no matter what. Then Zummo just walked out.

As the evening went on, the movement around the team began to escalate in frequency and appeared to be closing on the team. In the team leader's opinion, he was about to make contact.

I had checked as soon as I got the first call and found that the team was a light one—six strong—with a mission of watching a long canal for reported enemy sampan traffic. They were too light in combat strength and in a bad location to get in a rock-throwing contest at night.

The sounds kept up and he began reporting muffled voices. I told him to prepare to be extracted, but not to make a move yet. I then alerted the gunship pilots and the standby slicks and the C & C.

Mike Reitz came in to see what was happening and the leader of the gun team called me from the pilot's hootch to see if I needed him there. I told him that I probably needed him sitting in the seat of his gunship more than I needed him in the TOC.

Zummo came in while I was briefing Reitz and asked me what the hell was going on. I explained that I was getting the air package ready to pull the team in the event it made contact or was seriously compromised. Zummo started yelling, "Negative! Negative! Negative!" He then reminded me that he was commanding F Company and I wasn't.

I told him that I couldn't leave that team on the ground, six men strong, and not do something to back it up if the crap hit the fan. He waved his finger at me and told me that I was not to pull the team from its location under any circumstances. And then he disappeared again.

Reitz left but gave me a look that convinced me that he would be ready if I needed him.

About three in the morning the team called in again. They had seen enemy troops moving along the concealment offered by a thin tree line on a nearby paddy dike. They were sure the enemy patrol was trying to flank them.

I remembered what Bill Pfeiffer had drummed into our heads about moral courage and doing what was right and not just what was right for us. I was sure that I was asking for lots of trouble, but told the team leader to stand by for extraction once again.

Zummo overheard my instructions and came barreling into the TOC. He yelled and screamed and carried on and when he was through the only words I heard out of him were, "You're relieved! Get your shit and get out of my company."

My service in F Company had lasted not even four days and I had been fired. Being relieved in a combat assignment was something I had never heard of any officer surviving.

As I packed my gear into my rucksack and the single laundry bag I had brought with me from the rear I wondered what civilian life was going to be like. I was sure that Zummo would make a point that we had disagreed and crucify me.

Suddenly, the contact siren mounted on the roof went off. It was the signal for all in the compound that a team was under fire and for everyone to drop everything and stand by to help.

I figured that didn't apply to me since I no longer had a job in F Company.

Zummo exploded into the sleeping area of the building, still wearing his shorts and his hat and screamed at me. He wanted to know just what the hell did I think I was doing. I told him I was packing, just like he told me to and that I was leaving on the next thing headed east. He said the hell I was and that I better get my ass in the C & C and go out and pull that team before they got overrun.

I couldn't wait for a better time. As we flew out to the AO to pull the team I asked Mike Reitz what the hell the deal was with Zummo. "He's nuts," is all he said.

I asked if he was like that all the time. Mike shrugged and said that he'd never seen him any other way: Explosive, temperamental, and completely unpredictable. We were lining up to pick up the team under fire so there wasn't time for more conversation.

It was my first hot extraction and it was incredibly black outside the windscreen of the chopper. I looked at my watch and guessed it was still two hours until dawn. I had hoped that my first such flight would be in the daytime, when I could see better and have more of a sense of control over what was happening.

The team had taken two bursts of fire from the enemy element not a hundred meters away. The team leader had elected not to return fire in the event that the enemy was only conducting recon by fire to determine exactly where the American patrol was. After the first two bursts there had been nothing for almost a half an hour. But the team leader said that they could hear the movement continuing toward them up until the sound of the choppers drowned it out.

We decided upon a pickup zone to the rear of the patrol's position. They would pull back from the last known location of the enemy gunners and then give us a visual signal where they where so would could pick them up.

It seemed to take the patrol forever to crawl the fifty meters to their pickup point. The team leader held up a shielded strobe light, and Mike coordinated the touchdown of the pickup ship and the chase ship with the parallel firing passes of the two C-model gunships that were going to burn a wide strip of paddy dike up.

Mike put the C & C almost on top of the pickup ship and followed it down to the PZ, passing over its rotors as it lost all forward motion on touchdown. Mike pulled a hard left turn to pass back over the pickup and I saw the gunships spew streaks of flame out of the miniguns as they took turns rolling in on the target area.

The calm voices of the pilots were a contrast with the sounds of violence and powerful swishing of the chopper blades that could be heard in the background as they keyed their lip mikes.

I had not seen the team moving until I caught a frozen image of a running LRP in the red light of the rotating beacon on the pickup ship. The pickup ship rolled forward and pulled itself up out of the wet paddy.

The team leader's voice, raspy and out of breath, broke the silence on his net and said, "We're up. We're okay!"

That's all I needed to hear. I asked Mike if his ships were okay and he raised his left hand off the collective and waved it so I could see it out of the corner of my eye.

I then asked the lead gun pilot if he thought he had a target worth firing on any longer. He wasn't sure and asked for permission to go low and look around. I told him that I didn't want to be pulling a gun team out of the paddies on the same night and called him off.

Back at the TOC the team members drank a beer, ate some sandwiches sent over by the mess hall, and gave a good debriefing of what happened. As I took notes and asked more questions I suddenly noticed that everyone was in the room for the debriefing except Zummo. I was just as happy not to have him looking over my shoulder.

It was at that briefing that I realized that F Company was more unlike the Tiger Force than like it. The size of the unit was great in terms of redundancy and degree of support and speed of response. But the larger a unit like F Company the more the negatives show up.

A bit at that debriefing, but more so in the months to come, I discovered that the problem was one of height and width—for lack of a better description.

The "height" of the unit was that distance from the lowest-level private first class scout to the lieutenant colonel who commanded the company. Depending on how you count platoon sergeants and platoon leaders, that meant that the echelons in the chain of command numbered five. Five echelons making decisions and setting policy for that PFC are bound to create and reinforce feelings of mistreatment and reduced concern.

The "width" of F Company was evident in how the teams were divided up organizationally and operationally into greater separations between teams and between individuals.

In a regular rifle company, each PFC has a chance to compare notes with the other PFCs in his platoon and other platoons. It gives the soldier a chance to recalibrate his impressions by measuring them against the experiences of others. Rifle companies, for the most part, did everything together or at least in platoon strength.

Not so with F Company's LRP team members. Their lives were lived in a routine that was in sequence to the other teams and not concurrent with their schedules. When one team was in, the next was out. When one team was at one set of grid coordinates, other teams were at other locations. Opportunities to meet and discuss things at any great length were slim during standowns and the few other slow periods. But those chances to compare notes were complicated by the personnel turnover, the internal reassignments, and the heavy demand for sleep and personal needs. In short, rifle companies had plenty of time and opportunities to see, feel, and hear how others were treated in their own company.

In F Company there was more left unknown. The result was a drastic reduction in the sense of universal awareness than I had experienced in the Tiger Force. It was a rare incident that happened to one or some of the Tigers when every man didn't quickly know about it in accurate detail. What one of them knew, all of them knew. They felt like they all knew what was going on.

In F Company, there was so much compartmentalization because of the size of the unit and the lack of unified commitment that some of the problems with poor interpersonal communications, operational misunderstandings, simple petty jealousies, and bitching might have been eliminated if we had pulled heavy teams from the same platoon all the time. But the rotation schedule and the randomness of the ready status of teams did not permit this.

There was also a weak link in the effectiveness of the leadership brought on by the structure of the chain of command and the training options. In a regular line unit, the commitment of a platoon to combat under the control of a platoon sergeant who had upwards of fifteen to seventeen years service was not a problem. When he received instructions, in person or over a radio, from an inexperienced lieutenant or a staff officer on the battalion staff, he was able to act accordingly. He would take into account the needs of the unit, which were factored into the decisions being made and passed to him. He would understand the lack of experience of the lieutenants, too. He realized that the lieutenant, as most did, had plenty of responsibilities, some authority, but very little experience. That was not the lieutenant's fault and through the interaction of the two the lieutenant would eventually become experienced enough to command a company.

But in Vietnam in 1968, and in F Company, specialists and sergeants ran patrols. And even the occasional staff sergeant had nowhere near the grasp of how things worked as the platoon sergeant with sixteen years of experience. As a result, the receipt of instructions were often second guessed in a vacuum and/or resented by the inexperienced team leaders or team members who had very little information with which to form an attitude.

In a rifle squad there was no end to the conversations. In a long-range patrol team there was very little opportunity to talk in the field. So there was too often friction between the team members and the chain of command. Part of it was justified, most of it was unnecessary. All of it was regrettable.

The lieutenant problem was a particularly difficult one. Every long range patrol and Ranger unit in Vietnam tried to recruit members who had combat experience. And finding enough enlisted men and NCOs who had spent as much as a year in a combat job before volunteering was not difficult. Not so with lieutenants. It was rare to find a lieutenant who had spent significant time in the field who wasn't on the verge of making captain.

During the mid-Vietnam years, the required time to make captain dropped dramatically from previous years. By 1967, a new second lieutenant could count on spending a year at that rank and a year as a first lieutenant before making captain. During that two years it was common for the lieutenant to have spent as much as a year in the States in schools and his initial assignment before going to Vietnam. That meant that by the time a junior officer spent some time in a platoon in a rifle company, he was nearly ready to make captain by the time he arrived at a LRP or Ranger company.

Of course there were those who were not selected to make captain, but whatever reason kept them from being promoted was sufficient to make them unacceptable to the LRPs.

So the company-size LRP units were forced to accept lieutenants who had little or no combat experience. Making them patrol platoon leaders led to resentment from the men in the platoons who thought that the measure of everything was how much time a man had spent in bad-guy territory.

To train them, they would be sent out with patrols. This was a useful training vehicle for the lieutenant, but left the platoon unsupervised while the lieutenant was in the field and made the team members training aides. And most of the team members had no idea of the responsibilities of the platoon leaders when they were back in the base camps. The lack of proximity—team member to platoon leader—was fertile ground for grumbling.

In earlier wars, lieutenants were occasionally commissioned from the combat units and then it was more common for junior officers to be more experienced and older. Still, the lieutenants did a good job considering the squeeze they were in. Many of them have gone on to be general officers and captains of industry who owe so much of their success to the PFCs and specialist fours who broke them in.

Aside from these small problems of rumors out of proportion, and the natural tendency of the soldier to assume that no one knows or appreciates his situation and his burden, F Company was an effective and highly reliable combat resource.

The weeks that followed my fast start only picked up speed. And my relationship with Zummo went from shaky to unpredictable. There were times when he said little or nothing to me while I went about what I assumed was my job of training and committing the company's teams and other assets to accomplish the missions given us by II Field Force.

On other occasions he would get irritated with me over something that seemed quite trivial. But overall, he left me alone. After a couple of weeks I began to see him less and less. He made frequent trips to the rear—Long Binh or Bien Hoa—for no reason that he ever cared to specify. I would just find out from a radio operator or the operations sergeant or Mike Reitz that Colonel Zummo had scheduled a chopper to take him to the rear.

Sometimes he would remain in the rear. I found it very peculiar for a commander with an extensive Special Forces background to behave that way. But it was not my place to approve of his techniques. And while he was gone he was out of my hair. I was able to follow through on plans I had made and provide some continuity for the teams getting ready to insert, on the ground, and coming out. It was my opinion that there was so much uncertainty in their individual missions that the best way to help them survive was to eliminate as many variables as I could for them.

I can't explain why, but sometimes that effort seemed to be okay with Zummo and other times he felt I was being too soft on the teams. We had a fundamental difference in how things should operate in F Company but he was the lieutenant colonel commanding the outfit and I was the captain operations officer—a fact he reminded me of on several occasions.

When Zummo was forward, at Cu Chi, I never knew what he was planning to do. I would plan, brief, insert, extract, and debrief teams—unless he was around. And as often as not, he would tell me that he was going to pick up a team, or pick one up and move it.

As good luck would have it, he didn't do it often. But when he did step into the operations it often ended up with him arguing with the team leader and me. His arguments with the team leaders usually ended once they were on a chopper coming out of a hot or compromised position. With me, he often resorted to relieving me. He did it several times, only to reverse himself when contacts took place.

Several times I found myself repacking the same bags and unpacking them to go pull a team out of the AO when a contact was made.

His unpredictable style of leadership soon stopped being a consideration for me. We were pulled back from Cu Chi and returned to our base at Bien Hoa in order to operate in War Zone D.

Once we returned to Camp Lindsey-Lattin I just about never saw Zummo again. He stopped showing up in the TOC and stayed to himself in his room or office or out of the compound somewhere. He found different times to do routine things. When we were having regular meals, he was in his room. When I was briefing or debriefing a team, he was nowhere around.

After a few weeks of this, he pulled out of the compound for good one day, while I was out inserting and extracting teams. He never said so much as goodbye. He just left.

CHAPTER 25

·

The departure of Joe Zummo did not generate too much sadness in F Company. I wasn't there during the months when he had created a rift between himself and many within the company and all I know is what I experienced. And the coolness that surrounded him was unmistakable. Once I discovered it, my first selfish moment was thinking that I hoped that I never found myself in that kind of a situation. The troops don't have to love their commander, but respecting him and being sorry to see him leave would be a nice start.

What had happened between Zummo and the company was so much fast-moving water under a shaky bridge. I couldn't change the history and had to deal with what I found when I arrived. So I never gave much thought to Zummo and his leadership style as something I could have changed. I was too busy getting to know my job and getting a new routine worked out with Zummo's replacement, Major George Heckman.

Heckman was everything that Zummo wasn't. He was smart, pleasant, and above all, dedicated. From the first moment I met him I liked him and knew that I could count on him. He gave off the unmistakable signs of reliability and professionalism. He jumped into the job fast and never slowed down.

Since there was no discernable break in operations to allow much time to get acquainted, we got off on a business level and stayed there. I never found out how he got the job, where he came from, what his background was, or any other personal or professional details about him. He was a major, an Airborne-Ranger, and my new boss. That's all I needed to know for starters. The rest fell into place quite naturally.

George Heckman came to F Company ready to go to work. He knew what F Company could do and what it had to do it with. In very short order he set the tone of operations and training and stayed consistent. He was a generous and deliberate man, not given to anger or moodiness. I was very thankful for that.

In the months that followed Major Heckman's arrival, things that were lumpy smoothed out and our routines took on an even more professional tone.

He was a real hands-on kind of boss but not disposed to over-supervision. He would give me a job and let me do it. If I screwed it up, he told me. If I did it right, he told me that, too. While he was a quiet and private kind of boss, not given to dramatics, you knew what he wanted and communication happened without lots of discussion.

The division of labor was one of the first things that Heckman changed. He put much greater demands on the platoon leaders to take care of their patrols and make sure that they wanted for nothing in the operational or morale departments. He was not as focused on putting platoon leaders on the ground and set their priorities for them —training them for more responsibilities.

He split up the supervision of the operational aspects of the company between the two of us. Teams went in, made contact, and came out at all hours of the day—every day. There was no way one officer could handle all the inserts and extractions and also be up to speed on the details of all the patrols.

He would set his schedule around the demands on his time that took him away from the company. He handled virtually all of the contact with the G-3 at II Field Force, and he and I split all of the routine and emergency supervision of operations.

There were days when either one of us would get into a chopper at dawn and not walk away from it until near dawn the next morning. The hours were brutally long and the needs of each team were usually handled as if they were the only team on the ground.

The thing I remember most about George Heckman was his private concern for the troops. I don't think he knew that I was aware of it, but when it was late and I would be controlling the teams on the ground so he could get some sleep, I would find him awake. He would spend long hours studying reports and maps and asking questions of himself and others when he should have been getting some rest. He cared that every team went into the AO prepared and had every chance he could give them of being successful and coming back home in one piece.

After George Heckman's arrival the immediate problems of the company cleared to allow us to deal with the more important ones. We were often misused by the system that collected and analyzed our information.

I discovered that we were getting missions to send patrols into locations of suspected bunkers or tunnels or the like only to find out we had reported them earlier. It was something that the rapid turnover of officers created. Had Tom Meyer still been with the company, he would have recognized missions to check out certain grid coordinates as places the teams had been before. But enough time had to go by for me to have put a team in, reported up the chain what they had found, and then later get a mission related to that report.

An example would be a team discovering an abandoned string of bunkers in a tree line and reporting their location, description, and condition. Some months later we might get a mission to confirm the location of a series of bunkers reported to be at the same location.

I don't think that any of these relooks were ordered with any malice or carelessness. After I looked into it, I found that it was a product of the staff system and the fact that we were under the supervision of the Field Force G-3. Our reports were passed to the G-2, intelligence section, of the Field Force for evaluation.

All intelligence reports were graded as to the reliability of the source and the probability of their accuracy. In order to expand their information, the G-2 section would look for opportunities to cross check input. Where the ball got dropped was when the source—being us—was somehow disconnected from the report. Ultimately, someone in the G-2 section would ask the G-3 to try to verify a report. By the time the reports, summaries, and requests had passed from hand to hand and desk to desk, no one remembered that we were the original source. As such, we were the last resource that should have been tasked to cross check.

As far as I was concerned there was no reason for us to send a team back into a location to confirm what they had reported. The risk associated with the confirmation was just too high and the confirmation could easily be done by aerial recon, a maneuver unit in the area, or by using the ARVN or RF/PF[82] forces who routinely worked the area. Heckman put a stop to it in short order.

For a few months we were able to work together well and each subsequent insert of a team showed that the improvements and policy changes that George Heckman made in the company were working. The numbers of successful patrols mounted. The kill ratio was very good by anyone's standards, and the incidence of death, wounds, and

[82] Regional Forces/Popular Forces. The RF were South Vietnamese provincial forces formed as company-size militia units to guard strategic points within their respective provinces. The PF were local forces organized to defend the villages where they lived. Collectively called "ruff-puffs" by U.S. forces.

injuries in the company were low. The numbers pointed to good training and high morale.

I would be leaving out a very large factor if I didn't mention the
contribution and the day-to-day involvement of the chopper pilots and
crews. No matter how good a team was, if the chopper crews that put
them in, took them out, and supported them in contacts were screwed
up, then the team would suffer. Heckman also cultivated better working relationships with the air crews.

Mike Reitz was not my only champion of flight. The mission commander of the attack helicopter teams that supported us was to Cobra
gunships what Mike was to slicks. Joe Stroud was a captain, former
warrant officer pilot, and former enlisted crew member who lived and
breathed helicopters.

Joe was dedicated to making the gunship support he provided to F
Company as slick and as effective as it could be. He spent endless
hours with the company even when he wasn't on call to fly. He and
Mike Reitz became intimately familiar with the operations, plans, and
procedures of the company and it showed in their performance.

The contrast between the excessive crosstalk and explanatory trans-
missions that we needed between choppers and the Tiger Force and
the relative radio efficiency with Joe and Mike was evidence of their
teamwork.

Good pilots are always good news for LRPs. So the war stories
about Joe Stroud's and Mike Reitz's chopper crews spread fast. I've
not yet met a member of F Company who didn't have the ultimate
confidence in the chopper crews. They would take advice and help
from Mike and the slick pilots and would trust Joe's gunship fires
enough to walk them so close to their positions as to risk taking fire,
had their marksmanship been less accurate. They had confidence in
the slicks and guns and I did too. They never let me down. When they
promised to do something or be somewhere I could count on them.

And time after time we would go in and pick up teams under fire,
and I could always count on them not to be squeamish. They were
reliable and quick to commit themselves to dangerous options to help
the needs of the teams on the ground or another chopper crew.

Never before or since then have I ever had such a close and reliable
working relationship with chopper pilots and crews. Aside from the
personal dedication of those crews, I would say the remaining ingredi-
ent was their frequent contact with the company. The more we
worked together the better we were as a team.

George Heckman had seen this long before he came to F Company and he made every effort to include the pilots and crews in the company activities to make them feel welcomed and valued. It worked.

Many months before I arrived at Bien Hoa and joined F Company a series of decisions set in motion the ultimate demise of the company. The irony was that the success of the long-range patrol effort caused the breakup of F Company.

The good intelligence and impressive contact results of the existing long-range patrol companies and detachments set up a demand for more of the same. It also started the ball rolling in the redesignation of the LRP units to the WWII and Korean War title of Ranger companies. And while the decision to redesignate them as Ranger companies was extensively studied and considered—a source of new units was being sought.

Planners at Department of the Army had responded to the wishes of commanders in Vietnam to expand long range patrolling and add more units. They elected to go to the National Guard for what they couldn't generate out of the active army.

The Indiana National Guard had a long-range patrol company that could be activated, modified for Vietnam, and deployed. On paper it sounded easy. In reality it sent out a series of waves that seriously disrupted schools, units, and individual LRPs.

In the process of deploying Indiana's D Company, 151st Infantry the decision was made to insure the greatest chance of success by polishing off their training. Not ready to rely on the level of training that the LRP company had been able to conduct in its National Guard status with its part-time schedule, the army gave the members of the company the opportunity to go to the best army schools. Some who were not Ranger qualified attended Ranger school. Those not Airborne qualified went to Airborne school. And still others went down to Panama to attend the jungle warfare school.

After the National Guard company completed its added training it was sent to Vietnam. The problem arose because no one had given adequate thought to what would be done with them on arrival. They were a corps-level LRP company but the two corps-level headquarters already in Vietnam had their own companies.

There was some discussion about breaking up the National Guard company and sending its platoons to separate infantry brigades to create LRP detachments. But those conversations took place in ignorance of the severe restrictions that apply to National Guard units. The gaining unit, II Field Force, was not authorized to break up the National Guard company. Neither was it allowed to infuse regular

Army officer personnel into the vacancies that would surely occur as result of combat operations and routine losses.

The momentum of D Company stopped at Bien Hoa and we had to make room for them. Initially, we were to introduce the company to combat operations by conducting joint operations and supplementary in-country training.

Then, early in 1969, the decision came down to break up F Company and send its personnel and some equipment resources to the 5th Infantry Division's separate brigade and to the 82d Airborne Division. And since those new LRP units would be detachment/platoon-sized, there was no need for the more senior officers and NCOs from F Company.

George Heckman was given a loose command authority over the National Guard company. And I, already unhappy with the decision, got even worse news. I was told to be prepared to move to Long Binh for reassignment. The Field Force G-1 had me slotted to become the new G-3 briefing officer.

The thought of being the daily briefer for the Field Force still sends shivers up my back. I was not so young or naïve as to think that that reassignment would be an acceptable alternative to commanding a company in combat. There would come a day in the not too distant future when my course would be determined as much by where I had been as by what I had to offer the army.

I was already painfully aware of the fact that I still had not finished college. Hell, I hadn't even *started* it. I knew that spending the second half of my tour in Vietnam in the air-conditioned headquarters of Long Binh would be time wasted. I tried to get out of the job. I asked to be reassigned to any infantry division, hoping I could work my way into a job as a company commander. I was quickly reminded that my assignment would be determined by the Field Force G-1 and for the good of the command. And I would be best advised to stop making waves.

I was very disappointed at the turn of events and did what I could to help George Heckman get the old F Company ready to break up while getting D Company ready to replace them. Then at the last minute, the field phone rang in the TOC. It was for me. I picked it up and heard the familiar voice of a good friend calling on behalf of David Hackworth.

He had a simple question for me. *Did I want to command a rifle company for Hack?* It took me a split second to tell him, "Hell yes!" He explained that Hackworth was back in Vietnam and had been tapped to command a leg infantry battalion in the 9th Division that had fallen on hard times.

The chain of command had not been happy with the performance of the battalion, and at the time the division was looking for a replacement battalion commander, Hack was immediately sent to the 9th Division and, from what I heard, eagerly accepted the challenge. And somewhere along the line, he made a deal that would allow him to replace selected members of the battalion with officers and NCOs of his choice.

Hack put me on a list of officers and NCOs to track down and get reassigned to the new battalion.

I thought he might run into a stone wall with the folks who owned me at II Field Force.

Two days later I had orders to report to the 9th Infantry Division in the Mekong Delta.

I felt pretty bad about the entire handling of the F Company–D Company changeover. The troops in F Company had worked so hard at honing their skills and deserved better than they got. The big picture had landed on them and there was just no way out of the morass of legal restrictions and regulation limits that prevented the mistakes from being reversed. F Company had to give way for D Company to work in Vietnam and there were just no allowances for the needs and the desires of the troops who were displaced.

I was further irritated by how quickly the administrative side of the war forgot about F Company and the terrific soldiers who had served it. One of the last things I did before leaving F Company was to finish off a large number of recommendations for awards for soldiers, pilots, and crews I had personally witnessed performing deeds of bravery and heroism worthy of the awards. And there was no shortage of that in F Company.

To this day I have seen no evidence that any of those recommendations were ever processed. In the long run, it was the LRPs of F Company who were not recognized for their individual acts of remarkable courage and there is just no excuse for that.

And I was sorry to say goodbye to George Heckman and Peter Laisik as I left Bien Hoa for the 9th Division. I feel that their contribution was pushed aside by the focus on how to fix the poorly thought out decision to add a LRP company where one didn't fit.

CHAPTER 26

·

The Mekong Delta came as another surprise to me. I thought I'd been through some rough and hostile terrain, but I wasn't even close in my estimates of what to expect. But once there, I was focused on the problems of assuming command of a company that had not done particularly well in recent months and was sure to be filled with far less motivated soldiers than the ones I had become accustomed to, working with volunteers in Airborne and long-range patrol units.

The 4th Battalion, 39th Infantry, presented me with a number of new experiences that I was not prepared for. On arrival I was immediately given command of D Company. The 9th Division had been allowed, as had many other divisions in Vietnam, to expand into four rifle companies instead of the usual three. D Company had an authorized strength of six officers and 158 enlisted men. During my time with D Company the most I was able to take to the field was eighty-six men.

I had three officers, a first sergeant who was in such poor health that I had to leave him in the rear, and virtually all of my NCOs had less than three years of service. My executive officer, a terrifically talented and capable first lieutenant was named Roberson. He was so good that he was the rotating company commander. Every time we lost a company commander in the battalion Hack would put Roberson in command until a new captain could be found. So, in effect, I didn't even have him.

My initial anxieties about motivation and professionalism of the soldiers in D Company were unfounded. While I found them short on experience, a bit lacking in appearance and the gung-ho attitude of lifers, they were serious and reliable. They took orders well, followed through, and suffered the miseries of the war in the swamps and reed marshes of IV Corps like any career soldier.

They were faster to ask "why" than the volunteers I had been used to. But once they got the answer, they delivered. What they lacked in experience and career orientation they more than made up for in youthful exuberance.

After I got used to them and they to me, we got along fine and dealt with the problems unique to the demands of our area of operation.

My time in the company, and I was thrilled to get the chance to command it, was cut short by a booby trap. In only a matter of weeks after getting into the saddle with D Company, I was knocked out of my job.

We were in contact with a small enemy element and had been making headway at closing with them and stacking up enemy casualties. I found it a chore to keep the forward elements of my company from being channeled into a narrow front by the restrictive terrain. Parallel to our movement was a steep river bank on one side and deeply flooded rice paddies on the other. The narrow, frosting-like mud path that we slipped and slopped through was a tempting alternative to the exposed flanks.

I moved forward with the lead platoon, and though I know I should have been more deliberate with my route, I stepped off the cleared path just long enough to trip a wire. My radio operator and I hit the ankle-high wire at the same moment and saw what we had done just a thousandth of a second before the two-pound coffee can attached to it exploded.

The booby trap was just a can filled with explosives, rocks, glass, and ragged pieces of metal. The blast threw me up and flipped me end over end. I remember seeing the head-high bamboo from the top and then landed in the gooey mud—on my back.

At first I felt no pain. I had no idea what the extent of my wounds were because I was literally covered in mud so thick that I was unable to see where I had been hit. Not so with my radio operator. He took much of the blast in the back—at kidney level, and needed to be evacuated immediately.

The only medevac we could find was Hackworth's small, light observation helicopter. Hack came in right away and evacked my RTO and told me he'd be back for me. But I had no one to replace me. I had no other officer to turn the company over to and we were still in contact with the enemy.

After Hack left with my RTO in the back of the chopper I started to feel the pain. As soon as the stunned sensation of the blast wore off I was able to be sure that I had been hit in the legs and was losing blood pretty fast.

I continued to move the company forward and trusted my senior medic to take care of my wounds until Hack could find a replacement for me.

It seemed like forever, gauging by the pain and the blood, before Hack came back and told me to find a place for him to squeeze his chopper between the Nipa palms to evacuate me. I asked him who was going to replace me. He said that he was.

Foolishly, I asked why him. He explained very bluntly that there were no other officers available and wanted to know if I had any doubts about his abilities to still command a rifle company. I realized the stupidity of my question and shut up.

I was unable to walk far enough or fast enough to keep the evac chopper from being exposed to the continuing fire. And the path from me to the chopper was uncleared ground. Hack waved off the soldiers who were ready to carry. He jumped out of the chopper, walked quickly to my location, oblivious to the danger of booby traps and the constant firing, picked me up, and carried me back to the ship.

I couldn't get into the back of the chopper because of the inflatable plastic splint the medics had put on my worse leg. Hack stuffed what he could of me inside and banged on the door to let the pilot know to get out of there.

I won't forget looking down at him and my troops with the sinking feeling that I had blown my chance at commanding an infantry company. Hack looked up at me and gave me his uniquely sloppy salute, which clearly communicated that he hoped I'd be okay.

Things picked up speed as the chopper did. I had enough time to smoke a cigarette in the chopper before I was dumped off at the clearing station at the division hospital. Medics in green gowns fussed and fluttered around me, stripping me and cleaning the layers of mud to get to a point where they could inventory my wounds.

I had tubes and needles inserted in various places—all of them uncomfortable, and within the hour I was on an operating table. From what I could tell before drifting off, they were far more concerned with the large amount of blood that I had lost than with the extent of my wounds. All I really know is that they couldn't have knocked me out any more effectively with an elephant gun.

I woke up in a fog of confusion, nausea, and pain. Everything hurt and everything smelled. My throat felt as if I had been breathing sawdust and my limbs all hurt. The trauma of the blast had put me through some motions I was not used to and set me up for some very sore muscles and joints.

My arms were tied down to boards, tubes were filling me with a variety of liquids, and my legs were both raised and bandaged from the thighs to the toes. The dressings on my left leg were white and clean, but the right was stained in various places with large blots of yellow-orange and dark red that seeped from my wounds into the material. I was not happy to see the evidence of the wounds. But I had both feet and that was a relief.

My sense of pain was so screwed up by the drugs they were giving me that I was unable to attach any specific pain to any particular place. I just hurt everywhere.

The first voice I heard as I tried to clear my head was Hack's. He stood at the foot of my bed in the recovery room of the division hospital with his arm in a sling, leaning on crutches. During the night my company had been hit again and David was wounded twice repelling the attack. But neither of his wounds appeared to merit much of his attention. Instead, he wanted to know about me, how I felt and if I needed anything.

I tried to sound positive and told him that I was sure I would be back in no time and for him to hold the company for me. He explained to me that he had already talked to the doctors and that I was going to be evacuated. He said he wanted me to go. That if I stayed he was only going to get me killed. It was at that moment I realized just how deeply he remembered all the time we had spent on the ground together. And just how much he cared for all of the troops that he had commanded in combat. He was aggressive and determined on the battlefield. But I never felt that he was cavalier with our lives.

Still, I didn't want to go. But I was never given a choice.

The next morning I awoke with a terrible hangover from the anesthetic and the other concoctions that they had fed into my veins. They packed me up to move me to a field hospital at Can Tho, not too far away.

I dozed in and out on the short flight and was vaguely aware of the jostling as medics strapped me into a chopper and then pulled me out to wheel me into the new hospital.

Can Tho was a bright, airy world of concrete floors and medical green walls. I passed through a number of stations where medical personnel looked at my paperwork and passed me on to other personnel for them to do the same. It went on for an hour or so until I finally ended up in a ward—next to the nurses' station.

A lot happened around and near me. But no one seemed to want to take any time to talk to me. It was all very impersonal, and I was eager to have someone tell me that I would be okay and that I'd be back to my job with D Company in no time. But that just didn't happen. Nameless doctors whisked by my hospital bed and flipped open the cover of my aluminum chart. They read, absorbed the information, and occasionally made some notation on the chart. But none of them looked at me or my wounds. They would just flip the chart closed and walk away.

The nurses were a little more conversational. But they had no information. They'd come by, take my vital signs, make a note or two, change a bottle hanging above me or bags dangling below, smile, and smell wonderful. When I asked how I was doing and what would be happening with me, I was always told that the doctor would be by to tell me. And I would drift off again in some fog of medication.

By the end of the second day at Can Tho I was beginning to get irritated. Still, no matter how much I asked for some feedback, I got nothing. Sometime during that afternoon I awoke from another one of my drug-induced naps to find that someone had changed the dressings on my legs again without me knowing about it.

I was at once curious and worried about what was beneath the large and abundant gauze wraps that covered most of my right leg and some of my left. I asked. I got the same answer, "The doctor will explain it all when he makes his rounds."

By the end of my fourth day at Can Tho they had slowly backed off on the drugs and replaced the dressings with smaller and smaller ones. The impact of both was quickly evident. The lack of numbing drugs let me know exactly where the pain in my right leg was coming from and that I had very little pain in my left. I had no feeling in my lower right leg, not in the normal sense—just general pain. I was worried that when I touched my lower leg and foot that I couldn't feel it.

By then I had opened a dialogue with the nurses. I also discovered that the reason that they had said so little to me before was because I was so filled with painkillers it was like talking to a drunk. I didn't make much sense. They didn't have time. And I wouldn't have remembered most of what they had said anyway.

They told me that it was too soon to be worried and that the trauma could account for temporary loss of specific sensation. I listened to them and tried not to worry.

As my consciousness became less and less altered by the drugs, I became more aware of the things around me and the degree of damage reflected in that ward. Everyone was bandaged to different degrees. Some were missing limbs. Others were trussed in the grip of huge racks that held them together at different attitudes. It was all masked in the efforts most of the patients made to be jovial, partly for the morale of others but partly to convince themselves the horror that had brought them there was over. And part of it was to be positive and hopeful about how they would recover and adjust to the damage done to them.

One of the first things I noticed after the fog of the drugs left me to nights on my own was that none of us slept. Sure, the army turned the lights off. And there were those in the ward who were too drugged or drained to hold their eyes open. But for the rest of us—we dozed in and out of sleep and listened to how the others were handling it.

There was a young sergeant two beds down from me who had taken a considerable amount of shrapnel in a rocket attack at his base camp. In the daytime the doctors would come by and stick a huge hypodermic needle up under his lower ribs and draw off the fluid that kept collecting in and around his lungs. That was hard to watch, and left me with little to say to him to encourage him.

But it was his nights that are still vivid in my memory. The number of pieces of metal in his body were too many to remove. So some of them worked themselves to the surface, and with a little digging, he was able to get them out—one piece at a time. Late at night I would hear him groan and hold his breath while he gripped the jagged pieces of metal that kept him from sleeping. I would know he was successful when I would hear the clink of the fragment hitting the ashtray on his nightstand.

It was just over a week after my arrival at Can Tho that I finally got to see the extent of my wounds. They took the bandages off to remove the drain from my leg and to let it get some fresh air. The newly promoted doctor-major explained that if I had been hit with a frag or a bullet that the process I was going through would not be necessary. They would have cut away the damaged tissue and sewn me up. But since I was booby trapped there were extra steps that had to be taken. While I was in the 9th Division hospital they had taken what was essentially a couple of ragged round holes, between quarter and half-dollar size, and cut away everything to form a long, clean slot. The slot was almost six inches long and went completely through my leg— between the two bones in the lower leg.

As the doctor explained what had been done I was unprepared for the bizarre appearance of the wound once he unwrapped it. I had expected it to be sewn up. But it had been left open. That was because they assumed it was created by contaminated fragmentation and they feared infection. The puncture wounds that went through my leg had been cut back to clean the undamaged tissue. As the doctor pulled away the last piece of blood-soaked dressing I could *see through my leg to the floor below.* The slot was not just long—it was wide open. I could have dropped an envelope through it.

The doctor explained that the next step was to take me back into surgery to close the slot with the use of heavy-gauge wire sutures. So much tissue had been cut away that the wire was needed to hold the sides of the wound together while my body tried to replace the missing muscle and bone.

I asked him how long he thought it would be before I'd be back on my feet. I was really asking him if I would be *able* to get back on my feet. He simply shrugged and said to wait until we saw how the closure worked out.

The second surgery left me with another nausea-laced hangover. I felt like crap for another few days and as soon as I started to feel better I became eager to get it all behind me and get out of there.

The doctor came by and unwrapped the dressing covering the sutures. I was surprised at how much wire they had used to close up both sides of my leg. It was about then I began to feel the tightness that the wire created, but I didn't feel much pain. I asked the doctor how long it would be before I got normal sensation back. He avoided answering me and went on to the next bed.

A couple of days later I tried to nail the doctor about all of the questions I had. When was I getting out of bed? When would I be able to go back to duty? When would I be able to feel my lower leg again? He was irritated by my tone and told me that I'd be lucky to keep my leg.

The flip response caught me completely off guard . . . *lucky to keep my leg!* What the hell was he talking about?

He explained that there had been more nerve damage than they had initially thought. My self-protective response was that I'd be okay with *a little feeling loss.* He explained to me that there was a good chance that I could develop circulation problems that would dictate the amputation of my lower leg. I told him no goddamn way.

He tried to explain to me that they were doing lots of terrific things with prosthetic devices and that I would be able to get along fine with an artificial lower leg—since I would keep the knee joint.

I tried to explain to him that I was a twenty-five-year-old infantry company commander and that's what I did for a living. I would not be able to do that with a wooden leg!

He became angry with me second-guessing him and stormed off. In less than an hour a colonel—also a surgeon—arrived with the *Manual for Courts-Martial* and began reading me my rights from Article 31.[83]

He was furious with me for giving one of his doctors crap. I lost my temper and told him that if he was going to tell me about me losing my leg that I would give him the same crap. Somehow, he calmed us both down and told me that there was no chance of saving my leg in Can Tho if the damage was as extensive as he guessed it might be. I tried to tell him that I just had to get my old job back. It was a pretty veiled attempt at begging him not to let me lose my leg.

He said Walter Reed. I didn't argue any more.

I was shuffled through the casualty pipeline. First stop was Japan, where they waited until I could be taken off of some of the medications. After a couple of weeks there, I was off to the States on a large jet medevac flight.

Arriving at Andrews Air Force Base was strange. We were hustled off the aircraft and into waiting medical buses to be whisked away to Walter Reed Army Medical Center. I didn't find out until later that the reason was the Andrews AFB folks wanted to avoid the press. They had been sending film crews there to capture shots of casualties returning from Vietnam for the evening news. The sight of crippled soldiers was good B-roll film for the anchors.

I was very excited about getting to Walter Reed since I assumed that whatever was wrong with my leg would be resolved there. Like most Americans in the sixties, I had more confidence in the medical profession's capabilities than I should have had. The truth was that I really wanted to believe that they could fix me up and discharge me.

Walter Reed was an experience in itself. The hospital complex and outlying clinics was a massive factory for fixing broken soldiers. And its size took a toll on the personal touch. I was immediately turned into another number, another bed. I was put through an extensive physical exam and assigned to a bed in the surgical ward.

Then I waited. No one showed up to look at me or decide on treatment. Days went by and I complained to the only people I saw—student nurses. They all promised that they would pass on my pleas for attention.

Finally a doctor-captain came into my room and flipped through my

---

[83] Article 31 of the UCMJ prohibits compulsory self-incrimination, and the accused must be advised of his rights under it as a part of pretrial procedure.

files. He ordered some tests, issued some instructions, and said almost nothing to me directly. His prescription? We wait.

Wait for what? For some sign that the circulation was going to get better or worse. In the meantime, I was to undergo an uncomfortable series of injections to clear up a destructive and threatening intestinal parasite that I had picked up in Vietnam. He was more concerned with that than he was with the prospects of me having to lose a leg.

His abbreviated conversation and his brief visit left me with two problems: Wait for some sign, and decide what to tell my family. I had no choice but to wait and I didn't think there was any advantage in worrying my family. So I didn't give them the details of my prospects.

Weeks went by and I tried to determine what was happening in my leg. I had hopes that things would improve when they removed the wire sutures. The removal was very uncomfortable and the process didn't seem to change any sensations for me. My lower leg felt like the sensation we all have when we have slept on an arm and it goes to sleep. Or to be more precise, it was the prickly, dull sensation like when the feeling is coming back. It was almost as if I was wearing a knee sock filled with ginger ale. And it didn't change.

But my leg stayed warm, indicating satisfactory circulation. And my parasites finally cleared up—after a second series of shots.

Then one morning the doctor of few words came in and said, "Well, you're going to keep the leg." No foreplay—just the flat statement. He then turned and started to leave. I asked him about the sensation not returning. He said it probably never would and just left.

I was introduced to a particularly muscular woman major who headed a physical therapy section. She was as short with me as the doctor. She gave me exercises to do and got me on my feet. By then the whole bottom of my foot had curled under like a claw. My Achilles tendon had shortened considerably, and I was cautioned that I would be smart to take it slowly.

The first time I put my foot on the floor and tried to press my heel to the linoleum I realized the changes that I would have to make. PT was back in my vocabulary. My status changed to ambulatory and I was able to move around a bit. I was determined to get my leg back in working order, feeling or no feeling. So while I worked hard in the physical therapy room I worried about my future, immediate and long range. I kept leaving messages for the doctor, asking him when I could plan on being released. I was ignored.

I was very concerned about what the wound was going to mean for me as an infantryman. If the doctor made an issue of the effects of the wound I might well find myself grounded and out of the running for all the jobs that I aspired to as an infantry officer. I was not forgetting that I had been given a chance to command a rifle company and didn't last long on the job. Chances like that didn't come more than once for most captains. I was sure that I would have to figure out a way to make up for my lack of company command experience if I wanted to stay in the army. I wasn't out of the woods by a long shot.

Then one day a man who I would nominate for angel status in the infantry walked through my door. He was a stocky, cigar-smoking fireplug of a man who looked most uncomfortable in a civilian suit and tie. He stuck his hand out and introduced himself as Lieutenant Colonel Johnny Johnston. He told me that he was on his way to Fort Benning to assume command of an infantry battalion, and he wanted to know if I'd like to command one of his rifle companies for him.

I couldn't believe what I was hearing. *A second chance.* He asked me if I would be getting out of Walter Reed soon. He couldn't keep the job open for me too long, so I had better get to Benning ASAP.

His short and welcomed visit caused me to turn up the heat on my doctor. I sent enough messages through the staff and left notes at his office to piss him off. He came into my room and wanted to know just what my problem was. I told him that I wanted out of Walter Reed and that I wanted to go back to work.

It is worthy of note here that during the Vietnam years there were plenty of doctors on active duty who were neither career officers nor were they aware of what made us who were tick.

My doctor looked at my chart, told me that he thought he could put me on ninety days of convalescent leave and then another thirty days of regular leave on my way to my next assignment. I told him that I didn't want all that leave. I just wanted to go back to work.

He scribbled the name and office number of another doctor on a prescription pad and gave it to me. He wanted me to see the other doctor before he would check me out of Walter Reed.

I sat across the desk from the other doctor and he asked me weird questions that made little sense to me. Then the light went on—he was a shrink. I asked him why I was seeing a psychiatrist and he explained that in the three years he and my doctor had been in the army, neither one of them had ever seen a patient turn down paid leave.

I explained the situation to him and told him that if I sat on my ass I could lose my chance to command another company. He was completely baffled by my attitude but cleared me to leave anyway.

I was still one very sore infantryman when I left Walter Reed. But no one at Fort Benning was going to know about it. Not if I could help it.

The chance to command another rifle company propelled me to Fort Benning by the most direct route. The last thing I wanted was to get there late and find that Colonel Johnston had given the company to some other captain.

I was slotted against a vacancy in Company C, 1st of the 29th Infantry in the 197th Infantry Brigade. It was a leg rifle company in a leg battalion. But I didn't care. It was a TO&E company and I wanted the chance. Still, there was one minor problem. C Company had a secondary mission. Not only was it a regular rifle company with all of the normal missions, training and maintenance nightmares, it was also the Fort Benning Honor Guard Company.

It would be difficult enough commanding an honor guard company at any post. But Fort Benning was the doctrinal home of all things relating to the school of the soldier in general, and dismounted drill in particular. If you were going to be an honor guard company at Fort Benning, you had better make every move and issue every command by the book. In this case the book was the field manual. And command of an honor guard company would be difficult enough with both legs working properly.

I reported in and found myself in Colonel Johnston's office. He was every bit as engaging as I remembered him from our very short meeting at Walter Reed. He and I chatted for a while about what he expected from me and what I could expect from him, and I felt that I had to tell him that I was not yet one hundred percent. He pulled the fat cigar from his mouth, looked up at me from under his eyebrows and simply said, "Well, get that way. Take a week or two and practice."

I knew what he meant and we didn't need to discuss it any more. He wanted me to figure it out, work it out, and do the job. That night after work, I went to the Airborne track on main post and continued to work on getting my leg back into shape. It was in those moments of pain that I realized just how important the months of convalescent leave would have been to my recovery. I had lost a considerable amount of muscle tissue, and the ligaments and tendons in my leg were stiff as cables. I had to be able to loosen up, build up, and fake the sensation to execute the marching movements.

I ran and I exercised and I practiced. I practiced facing movements and marching in my quarters and in my office and on the parade field in front of Infantry Hall. I drove out to the training areas I had come to know on previous tours at Fort Benning and hollered out into the kudzu, developing my command voice. All the while, I hoped to be able to perform without anyone noticing the limp and the stiffness of my gait.

Like the murder boards on the instructional side of Fort Benning, I was scheduled to put my company through its paces for the brigade commander and the assistant commandant. Both the colonel and the brigadier general were old infantry soldiers and knew what they wanted to see. It was up to me to make them see it.

The company, the band, and an artillery salute battery formed on a parade field and I took my post in front of the neat, starched and polished ranks of soldiers as commander of troops. A mock reviewing stand held my inspectors and Colonel Johnston acted as the visiting dignitary.

I called the company to attention, executed a perfect about face and reported the honor guard ready for inspection. Colonel Johnston marched to a point in front of me and then we both trooped the line and reviewed the honor guard. Marching shoulder to shoulder, I could feel the encouragement that he was giving me. After he gave me some quiet and supportive comments, he returned to the reviewing stand and I led the honor guard in a pass in review. Every man in the formation treated it like it was a real review and made me look lots better than I was.

It went off without my making a fool of myself and I got the job.

What appeared to be a wonderful job for an infantry officer at a Stateside post didn't come without problems. While we spent much of our time staying combat ready, and some time putting on ceremonies for the post and visiting dignitaries, there were also some unpleasant duties. The war in Vietnam was raging. It was the autumn of 1969 and the casualties were coming home in bigger and bigger numbers. For those kids who gave their lives there waited a military funeral if their families wanted one.

That translated into C Company providing the funeral details to go to the surrounding towns, to give the dead soldiers the best burial honors we could.

The funeral details would have been tough enough under normal conditions, but we were smack in the middle of the South and the middle of the racial tensions that marked the sixties. It was not unusual for me to take or send a funeral detail to a small town only to get threatened by the families of the deceased. We had problems with the Ku Klux Klan and from simply bigoted survivors who had problems with the black soldiers as pall bearers. They refused to let them in their churches and funeral homes, and occasionally called their congressmen to complain bitterly.

These incidents made already unpleasant duties nearly unbearable. And the ugliness of racial hatred didn't end once we returned to the post. While I never had an incident within the company, the post was reflecting the frictions that were becoming commonplace outside the front gate. Soldiers were assaulting soldiers over matters of color, and as company grade officers we were often involved in maintaining order or serving in courts martials relating to those crimes.

It was only four years since my first trip to Fort Benning, but I was amazed at how quickly the rigid and regimented order of Fort Benning had changed into a fever pitch to support Vietnam and then to one of fear and violence reflecting the national race issue. None of us was happy to have to strap on loaded sidearms to keep the peace during many long, tense nights.

I was just getting myself back into shape physically, just getting comfortable with the pleasure of commanding a company like the honor guard and had just started night school to fight the college problem when Colonel Johnston called me into his office. His tone was down and uncharacteristic. He told me that he was going to have to make some changes in who was going to command C Company because of my performance.

I was stunned by his words. I stood in front of his desk listening to him set me up to be fired. He told me that I'd be relieved of command, effective that day. The only thing I could think to do was ask him why.

He smiled and told me that I might be good, but that I was not good enough to command two infantry companies at one time, and that I had been chosen to command Company A (Ranger), 75th Infantry (Airborne).

I could hardly believe what I was hearing. He was not relieving me for anything I had done wrong, but for what I must have done right. There was only one Airborne-Ranger company at Fort Benning and there had to be seven hundred available captains who would jump at the chance to command it. And I was picked to replace Tom Meyer—again—who was due for reassignment.

* * *

It was a coincidence that the Ranger Company was attached to the 1st Battalion, 29th Infantry. So my move from C Company to A Company would be pleasant and easy. I would still be working for Colonel Johnston and would only be moving a couple of buildings away from my job at C Company.

My being reassigned to command Fort Benning's Ranger company was a surprise beyond my wildest dream. I could think of no other company that I would want to command at that time. But I was happy just to have a chance to command C Company, and I knew that Tom was in the position and doing a good job at it.

For me, assuming command of A Company was like old home week. Many of the NCOs in the company had been in combat LRP and Ranger companies in Vietnam and I couldn't have been happier to have them on board.

The job was high visibility and very complex in its conflicting training and readiness missions. As with any units that were considered by some to be elite, the troops in A Company were under a microscope. Any move they made that was even a slim margin below the highest standards reflected badly on the company. And in any unit like a Ranger company there was high level of energy, bravado, and just plain boyish playfulness. That too came back to haunt me.

Those problems of exaggerated standards and heightened enthusiasm were to be expected. I had bailed plenty of LRPs and Airborne soldiers out of tight squeezes with MPs, senior NCOs and officers, and occasionally local police. It wouldn't have been a Ranger company without the occasional flaps.

What was most pleasant and liveable was still being under the wise and tempered eye of Johnny J. Johnston. He was a no-nonsense commander. But he understood soldiers and what made them tick. Not that there weren't some uncomfortable moments when he had to call me on the carpet for the behavior of some of my animated warriors. I remember most the fact that he didn't go ballistic when he received heat from his commander and his commander's commander. I know that he absorbed a lot of the heat for fights and pranks and stunts that my Rangers pulled.

My real day-to-day problems came from three different directions. As a resident company on Fort Benning post, I was saddled with some missions specific to Fort Benning. Those involved providing support troops to the infantry school to act in an aggressor role in tactical training. And the ability to mount convincing enemy operations to test the school's students was a simple matter with so many Vietnam-LRP veterans.

My second mission was to train the troops who were on orders to go to Vietnam. That mission required that I set up a small training group to provide Vietnam-specific training to make sure that soldiers leaving Fort Benning were ready for service in Vietnam.

Additionally, I received the mission of conducting riot-control training to keep the company ready for deployment to any one of the hot spots that dotted the American cities. Racial tensions had spilled over more than once into rioting and property damage. A Company had to be ready to move within a few hours' notice of any such incident.

While we were training others and training ourselves for missions created by Fort Benning and the 197th Brigade, I still had a company safe filled with missions for overseas deployment.

A Company (Ranger), 75th Infantry (Airborne) had evolved from D Company, 17th Infantry. Under that designation, it was charged with being organized, trained and equipped as a corps-level long-range patrol company. Its headquarters on deployment would be V Corps in Germany. That meant that the company's organizational equipment and individual gear had to be tailored for operations in the German countryside. It also meant a completely different way of communicating than most of us were used to.

A traditional, European-oriented, corps-level long-range patrol company had to be ready to work as far as a hundred and fifty miles forward of the main body of the allied forces. That rendered the standard FM voice radios useless for communicating vital information to the rear. Each team had to master CW—continuous wave—radios. That also meant that everyone in the company had to have from a passing to an expert level of proficiency in sending and receiving Morse code. All this on top of the local training requirements.

That tasking to be on call for Germany didn't go away when the company was redesignated as a Ranger company. Instead, it took on added contingencies to also be organized, equipped, and trained to deploy to Vietnam. In that configuration A Company had to be ready to deploy on short notice to Vietnam as a corps-level Ranger company.

That mission had almost nothing in common, training- and equipment-wise, with the other missions. The communications vans and other vehicles essential to operate along the Iron Curtain were fairly useless to us should we head for Vietnam.

We might have been able to avoid staying up to speed on some of the missions had the army relieved us of the requirement to stand repeated surprise inspections. The words IG (inspector general) and CMMI (command maintenance management inspection) had always kept company commanders awake at night. And that was for rifle companies with only one mission. But for a Ranger company with its elite status, that served to fan the flames of some jealousies among non-Airborne, non-Ranger inspectors. And that nightmare came in multiples. We had to stand inspections to determine our readiness in our role as a Benning-based and Vietnam- and Germany-bound Ranger company.

And while all this was happening, there were no real training or doctrinal precedents to lean on. The training, organization, and equipment of World War II and Korean War Ranger companies were outdated for us. We were cutting new trails as we came to them and had little in the way of a recent history to lean on.

I relied on Fort Benning's Ranger Department, the Pentagon's planners, Colonel Johnston, and the Rangers of A Company for help and guidance. All measured up even though they too were often going on gut instinct when it came to the training and development of the company.

We were even orphans. When the LRP companies in Vietnam and the States were redesignated as Ranger companies, there was no parent headquarters designated. That left A Company as the de facto holder and coordinator of things that might properly be handled by a battalion or regimental headquarters. Matters of lineage and heraldry were addressed to A Company. The problems of standardizing things between the companies arrived at our doorstep and questions about us from the rest of the army were plentiful.

I handled as much as I could, but quickly jumped at the suggestion to designate the director of the Ranger Department the honorary regimental commander. That gave me a chance to pass most of the ceremonial duties on to Colonel John Geraci, or as he was known by his Vietnam callsign—Mal Hombre.

I had known Colonel Geraci from Vietnam and was glad he was the Ranger Department director.

For the platoon leaders and NCOs, all this meant preparing and constantly checking the equipment and training of each man in the company in threes. And each soldier had Benning gear, Germany gear, and Vietnam gear. He also was trained for what he was doing and what he could be asked to do on different sides of the globe.

* * *

It was a constant problem, identifying the demands and requirements placed on the company by missions, policies, and regulations and making sure we were up to speed on each. At the same time we were trying to do that the army was going through tremendous change because of Vietnam, race, and drug problems. It was during these months I first heard and recognized the tongue-in-cheek saying that any army could react—it took a good army to overreact. And overreact we did.

Policies came pouring out of the Pentagon that put demands on the leadership in every company in the army to provide personal attention and counseling for a wide variety of reasons. And the counseling sessions had to be reduced to paper and reported to higher headquarters.

As company commanders we personally had to advise short-timers as to their reenlistment options. We personally had to conduct race-relations seminars and drug classes. The instructions were very specific. In earlier days the commanders could delegate plenty of such additional duties to lieutenants and senior company NCOs. But the Pentagon took away many of those options.

For me that meant that I had to squeeze more time out of an already crowded schedule. I made changes in my night-school classes to take only the latest of classes. It wasn't unusual for me to leave the company area around nine on the nights I had class to make it to a course that met from nine-thirty to eleven. Then I would go home and hit the books and still make it back to work for first call at five A.M.

I was feeling the pressure and the ante went up when the White House began announcing a schedule for the withdrawal of whole divisions from Vietnam. It translated to most of us as a sure prediction of a reduction in force that would follow. And a RIF meant that they would be cutting officers as readily as enlisted men. They would be using competitive criteria for retention. And the standards would revolve around professional development and potential.

To my own mind I was a bundle of potential. What I was concerned about was my lack of competitive credentials—I was not a regular army officer and I had not collected even a handful of college credits. I was still not sure if or where any paperwork existed which described the details of my wounds and the permanence of my losses.

All I knew how to do was put my head down and keep charging into brick walls. There was just no allowance or concern for what I needed careerwise. My job was my company command and not my career. I had more than enough on my plate to keep up with the multitude of requirements that filled the notebook tucked into my pocket. The days were too short and still the demands kept piling up.

* * *

And during this escalating pressure and backlog of demands on my time and the resources of the company, the outside influences on the army were trickling in at an alarming rate. The draft lottery was taking plenty of heat on the streets. The White House was a focal point of dissent. Racial incidents, demonstrations, and pressures were increasing in frequency and visibility. And handling antipolice, antigovernment, and general antiauthoritarian civil disorders was well beyond law enforcement's capacity. That meant that the Pentagon was up nights cranking out contingency plans for every conceivable flare-up. And nothing slowed those plans on their way to Fort Benning.

The Rangers in A Company took on all of the extra training and the strange array of possible missions with remarkable patience. Most of them had been to Vietnam. And they, as well as the ones who hadn't been there yet, were happier to be in a difficult duty assignment at Fort Benning than somewhere in Vietnam while the war was drawing down.

Discipline was never a problem in A Company. Any flaps that came up were usually outside the company and involved military personnel or civilians who somehow had a problem with the Rangers.

I recall a situation where I had a junior sergeant who was in trouble for having done what we were demanding he do—take care of the troops.

The problem occurred when a DR (delinquency report),[84] landed on my desk with a directive that I take disciplinary action on the sergeant. He had been stopped at the front gate to Fort Benning late one night with a car full of drunken Rangers.

He was sober but the others were having too much fun. The attention they drew to themselves caused the MPs to stop them and shake them down. The MPs checked passes and ID cards and insurance papers and vehicle registration and on and on. They finally decided that the sergeant was driving a car with mufflers that were too loud and cited him.

I investigated the incident and saw no reason to punish the man. The post provost marshal disagreed with me and again demanded, through channels, that the sergeant be punished. By that time I ended up in Colonel Johnston's office over the problem. He was unflappable.

[84] The name of the report military policemen submit to the provost marshal in cases of individual misconduct. It is forwarded to the commander of the soldier concerned for ultimate disposition.

He asked what the story was. I explained that I had been on the officers and NCOs in the Ranger company to make the lives and the welfare of their troops a high priority. I told each of them that I expected to see them find ways to look out for the troops.

The sergeant in question had been coming home from a movie downtown with his wife. As they approached the post he spotted four of his squad members driving erratically toward the post. He could tell they had been drinking and would surely get busted if they drove through the gate drunk and singing. He waved them over, let his wife drive his car home, and took the wheel of the drunken Ranger's car.

He had done his job and I had done mine. I called in the owner of the car and gave him two days to get the mufflers fixed or get the car off post. I saw no reason for the sergeant to be punished.

Colonel Johnston leaned back in his chair, blew cigar smoke toward the ceiling and simply said, "Ya did the right thing, son. Now let me handle the provost marshal." I never heard another thing about the incident. But rumors flew that someone from the provost marshal's office had made some remarks about us not being able to get away with that kind of behavior. I soon noticed MP sedans and jeeps in places where I hadn't seen them before.

Each morning when I left my quarters for work there would be an MP vehicle sitting at the end of my street. On the roadway to Kelly Hill, where the Ranger company was billeted, I would usually run across another, and there was frequently one at the company area.

The troops must have figured out that we were all under extra surveillance and acted like Rangers would act. I came out of my office a few days later and found a handmade license plate placard bolted to the front of my car. It was in Ranger red, black, and white colors and had a ranger scroll on it with the words: "Commanding Officer, A Company (Ranger), 75th Infantry (Airborne)."

By the end of the week, every POV in the company had its own plaque. After that, the presence of MP vehicles in our lives seemed to diminish.

We had won the cold war with the MPs. But the company was on its absolutely best behavior to deny them the chance to get the better of us.

With the drawdown underway in Vietnam, there seemed to be a slight reduction in the number of overseas orders arriving. More Ranger combat veterans were coming back to Fort Benning and filling the vacancies in A Company. And fewer of those in the job were getting orders to go back to Vietnam. That meant stability. When that happens in any unit the training level goes up, unit cohesion tightens, and esprit de corps rises.

And that's exactly what happened to A Company. It turned out to be a terrific assignment. Not much slack, but an infantry captain's dream job.

Across the board, proficiency scores went up. Reenlistments went up. Discipline problems went down. And the company began to get involved in other pursuits. Company personnel found the time to get into sports parachuting, intramural sports, post activities, and sponsoring events for the kids on post.

Our interaction with the Ranger Department increased as we provided more Rangers for doctrinal tests and studies. We also provided aggressors for several of their problems that needed a level of expertise that some of the other school support units didn't have. And we were permanent fixtures at Lawson Army Airfield. Rangers filled every available parachute to increase their Airborne proficiency. We were the only TO&E unit on post that was on parachute status and that was a plus for everyone. We were able to make qualifying parachute jumps several times a month. In many Airborne units they were lucky to get a jump every quarter. And in most Airborne units in Vietnam they had even suspended the quarterly qualification jumps.

It was a long day at A Company. But I could hardly wait to get there in the morning.

The Camelot period soon came to an end. The company was alerted for permanent movement to Fort Hood, Texas. The army had created a major test facility there called Project MASSTER (Mobile Army Sensor Systems Test, Evaluation and Review), a Pentagon effort to resolve some of the nagging questions that came out of Vietnam. It was there that the army found itself inadequate in surveillance, target acquisition, and nighttime operations. The hope was that by focusing on changes that needed to be made and the possibilities of using state-of-the-art technologies, the army could close the gap in target identification and acquisition.

Many years later the fruit of that effort was validated on the battlefields of the Persian Gulf.

But for A Company (Ranger) it meant major upheaval. While the instructions were for me to move the entire company and all its equipment to Fort Hood, that's not exactly what it meant. With the mission to move came the restrictions on who could go. Soldiers recently assigned to A Company were exempted from the move and went to other companies at Fort Benning. Some of the others who were soon to be reassigned to schools and overseas assignments were peeled away from the company in anticipation of those moves. That left the original company understrength in some positions and critically short in some key slots.

Additionally, Department of the Army augmented the company's authorized strength to allow for some modifications necessary to become the test project's aggressor element. So between the losses and the added unfilled authorizations, the company was well understrength for its upcoming job.

Then I was told that I would have to relinquish command of A Company because the army had me slated to attend the Infantry Officers' Advanced Course. The news was very disappointing. I wanted to stay with A Company, but was reminded that it was not up to me.

I said good-bye to A Company and was reassigned as the Battalion S-3 of the 1st of the 29th Infantry until my class began. The only good news was that it was a great job and I was still going to be working for Colonel Johnston.

All these years later it is so gratifying to see the legacy of A Company of the 75th in the current Ranger regiment, which now has three Ranger battalions. Their professionalism and expertise are widely known within the army and NATO for their successful involvement in Grenada, Panama, and the Persian Gulf. They are the best-trained and best-equipped infantry fighters in the Free World. And I enjoy the opportunities to meet today's Rangers. Five minutes with any one of them is a shot of confidence in today's army that can't be equalled.

My first few weeks as operations officer for the battalion reminded me of my first days around an operations section in the 101st. Back then, I never in my wildest dreams would have seen myself as S-3 of a battalion. But there I was and I was immediately convinced of my need to get to the Infantry Officers' Advanced Course, to master those skills needed for that job. I was not very good at the job and I'm sure that had I not been under the wise and tolerant eyes of Colonel Johnston I would have been canned.

I didn't even get a chance to settle into that job when a series of events completely changed my life. The first was a completely surprising announcement. The promotion list for major came out of the Pentagon and I was on it. Selected very early for promotion, I was astounded to learn that the army had picked me to promote to major —and this before my twenty-fifth birthday.

Colonel Johnston chuckled knowingly. I suspect that with his connections to infantry branch he had some early warning that I was going to make that list. He was generous in his support of my promotion and his congratulations.

I had hardly absorbed the announcement when I got a call from infantry branch telling me that I had also been selected for a special college program that they had found some money to fund. It was unlike the old Bootstrap Program that everyone was familiar with. In that program you had to gather almost all your college credits and they would send you to school for your last semester or two. It was hard to qualify for and hard to get into that program.

The new program, called the Officer Undergraduate Degree Program, was a selection process run from Department of the Army. Once selected, you were offered a full scholarship to college provided you could finish four years of college in two years. How you did it was up to you as long as you ended up with a fully accredited and appropriate degree. During that schooling the army would pay to move you, pay you your normal pay, and pay all the tuition and fees, and all you owed them on graduation was one more year on active duty. I jumped at the chance. My thinking was that even if I got out of the army to go to college on my own it would take me at least five years—working part time and going to classes.

I was completely panicked about trying to finish a four-year degree in two years, but I didn't tell infantry branch that. So I accepted and they told me to line up a college to accept me upon completion of the Infantry Officers' Advanced Course, which was six months long.

The good news didn't end there. While I was in the advanced course I received notification that I had been picked to receive a regular army commission. Regular army was a very difficult plum to get. It was given to graduates of the military academies and to distinguished military graduates of ROTC. But OCS graduates were commissioned in the army reserve and carried reserve commissions. Not being regular army was like not having tenure at a university. Again, I was thrilled with my good fortune.

CHAPTER 27

.

During the advanced course the army began to make sweeping changes. The pressures to do away with the draft were so great that the notion of a volunteer army was everywhere. The press began pursuing the Pentagon, and the Pentagon began floating trail balloons. Benning wasn't immune to efforts to explore the possibilities for making the army more attractive.

VOLAR, volunteer army, became a word that everyone at Fort Benning was talking about. The response to the concept was mostly negative. And while I was a member of a class of combat-experienced captains and majors, we expended plenty of energy discussing the subject on our breaks or over beers at the Infantry Bar. But the ball was in motion, and one way or the other the army was going to have to get along without the draft.

The decision to go to a volunteer force became very clear to me one day in the hallway of the infantry school. I was standing outside a classroom with a few other captains when a colonel on the school staff walked up. He stopped and looked at us—each sporting closely cropped Airborne haircuts, then blurted out, "Gentlemen, you hair is too short. Haven't you heard of VOLAR? Get with the program!" And then he walked off.

That day was the moment when I realized that the army was changing. It had been going on for some time. But I had been isolated in Airborne, LRP, and Ranger units for so long that I just didn't get it. I wasn't particularly opposed to the VOLAR concept. I just joined my peers in thinking that it just wouldn't work. I felt that the involvement of draftees was important and wise. I had not been let down by draftees on the battlefield and felt there would be problems losing them.

Was I ever wrong. The transition was lumpy and saw some tough times, but it has turned out to be one of the most successful efforts since World War II.

And for me, the early days of VOLAR were experienced away from my duty station. I left the advanced course before graduation in order to start college. And while I was on campus there wasn't an army post anywhere near. While I was going to school in Michigan, my headquarters was Fort Sam Houston, Texas.

I might have been more motivated to follow the progress of the volunteer army if I hadn't been so swamped with college. My life was suddenly void of uniforms and things military. I carried more than a full load and graduated with a full, four-year degree in history seventeen months later. And even though those months were packed with long hours and an accelerated curriculum, I loved every minute of it.

It was in college that I discovered that going earlier would have been wasted on me. Going when I did was just right. I waded in and appreciated what a gift I had been given and what a second chance I had in my grasp. My grades were top notch; I was accepted on campus without incident.

At the same time, I discovered that the soldier's view of the college student was every bit as distorted as the student's view of the soldier. I didn't find the draft-card burning, rabid antiwar activists. Not every student was an anarchist radical. They were normal kids with realistic anxieties about the draft and the Vietnam war. I could hardly blame them. I'd been there and I was going back there. Just before graduation I got alerted for Southeast Asia again.

One after another, units were coming out of Vietnam. It was the summer of 1972 and those maneuver units that remained in Vietnam were packing and had been nearly relieved of all combat commitments. Their basic missions were to protect themselves and other U.S. installations until they pulled out.

But that was not the end of the war or the expectations on the United States to support the efforts of the allies still fighting the communists. The South Vietnamese, Thais, Cambodians, and Laotians were all clamoring to get commitments from the U.S. to support, train, equip, and fund their anticommunist efforts. They were willing to take what they could get. But they didn't want us to leave, and they didn't want the massive supply of resources to end.

So as the maneuver units moved back to the States, the activities in Southeast Asia returned to something similar to the behind-the-scenes advisory efforts of 1961 to 1965. Training the allies to shoulder the burden of the war was the major effort, and providing them with the arms and equipment to do the job was the twin effort.

I reentered the war that had changed from direct combat to the training and support of the warriors. It came in the form of a phone call from infantry branch. They told me I was going back and that this time I would be wearing a green beret. I was sent to what until a few weeks before had been known as 46th Special Forces Company in Lop Buri, Thailand. But due to the increase in responsibilities it had been expanded and took on the less specific title of Special Forces Thailand.

I had come full circle. I remembered the green beret that one of those sergeants wore that day at Fort Dix. At the same time I thought that I could never see myself wearing one. And though I was not too thrilled to be leaving my family for still another unaccompanied overseas assignment, I was a lot happier going to a Special Forces assignment than so many other unpleasant jobs that I might have drawn.

Arriving in Thailand, I had great expectations about the expertise and professionalism of the men assigned to the unit. And within minutes of arrival at Lop Buri I was given command of my own A-Team. I had to absorb the good luck. I could easily have been given a staff job because I had already commanded four infantry companies.

Assuming command of the A detachment was filled with even more surprises. I fully expected to meet Special Forces soldiers with a wealth of combat and tactical training experience. And that's exactly what I found. But I also found them to be tired. They were by no means lazy or unprofessional. They were, instead, tired. Tired of the years and years they had spent in Vietnam, Laos, and Cambodia; tired of the missions they ran up and down the Ho Chi Minh Trail; tired of the dangerous nights they spent in North Vietnam; and tired of working so long and so hard trying to get the South Vietnamese motivated to fight their civil war.

I couldn't blame them. They were the last of the Americans left in Southeast Asia trying very hard to train the allies while they watched the antiwar movement in Washington dismantling what they had worked so long and hard to build.

They did their training and combat jobs out of Lop Buri with professionalism and dedication, but I could feel that their hearts were not in it. They were as professional as ever, keeping their personal disappointments separate from their duties as many of them planned for a different future.

The reduction in force was happening all around them. Officers and NCOs with extensive Special Forces experience, but little time in regular units, were let go. Younger officers who had limited Special Forces experience and little college were also asked to leave. And the old-timers talked of fishing boats and opening motels in Florida after the retirement.

They'd been worked hard and almost forgotten by the Pentagon. Many of them quietly left the Army and started new lives. But all of them had memories of better days.

The year in Thailand flew by for me, and I awaited my alert notification for reassignment to a Stateside job. I was expecting to go back to an Airborne or Ranger unit when I was surprised to find myself on the selection list for the Command and General Staff College at Fort Leavenworth. I thought that was years away and wasn't even aware of the remote possibility of being picked for such advanced schooling so early. The army was continuing to surprise and challenge me, and I stepped out of fatigues for the first time in my career and into class-A uniforms for classes.

My class was long on majors, lieutenant colonels, colonels and even a couple of allied brigadier generals. It was also the first time I had come in contact with what was known as "purple suiters," or officers assigned to joint staffs comprised of army, navy, air force, Marine, and allied members.

I was immediately as disoriented by the demands of the upper-level schooling as I had been in my first days in basic training.

The first and most surprising discovery at Fort Leavnworth was the complete sense of amnesia about Vietnam and the previous twelve years. Everything was oriented on war along the eastern borders of Germany, and all the training was tailored to that eventuality.

I hadn't thought about Germany and fighting Russians or East Germans since I was in Kaiserslautern and Mannheim. Suddenly, I was surrounded by officers who had it down cold. They knew the most minute details of the mechanized, armored communist threat that drove the curriculum. I quickly realized that I had some catching up to do.

The year was a complete change of focus for me. I had to forget what I had learned and start thinking bigger and looking toward the Fulda Gap in Germany. I had to master the intricacies and nuances of higher-level staff procedures, major unit logistical planning, and coordination and joint-service operational planning. It was a tall order for me but one without option. I had to get up to speed on a volunteer army with a European orientation, and stay there for the duration of the year-long course.

I busted the books, as we all did, and studied things that I hadn't even been aware of. Armor had been moved into the forefront of the doctrinal philosophies. No longer was it seen as a supporting arm to

help the infantry close with and destroy the enemy. It had replaced the
infantry as the principal player on the modern battlefield. The infantry's new mission was to protect the tanks to allow them to destroy
large enemy armored-mechanized forces attempting to sweep across
the north German plain.

Amphibious operations were as alien to me as were the classes in
transactional analysis and operations research. It was like a different
army and a different world for me. And most of my experience in
LRP, Ranger, and Special Forces units was not very useful to me as a
student. I was coming from a small-unit leader's point of view into a
world of divisions, corps and army groups.

I survived the year and met the requirements to graduate, only to
find that I had been selected to remain at Fort Leavenworth as a
member of the faculty. I was assigned to the tactics department, and
spent my summer taking still another course in instructor training and
learning the courses I was expected to teach.

But, like Fort Benning, there were lengthy murder boards to survive. The level of sharpshooting was elevated to a science at Leavenworth. The faculty knew every hot-shot question and comment that
cocky students could throw at instructors, and threw them at me.

Toward the end of the summer, and before the regular curriculum
began, I was called in by the department director. He was a bright and
energetic colonel who had just been selected for promotion to brigadier general. He told me that he was concerned that we were going
overboard on the European scenario and failing to retain that expertise we had developed in Vietnam. He wanted me to develop an elec-
tive course on special operations and become the principal instructor
of the course. He gave me a blank slate and free reign. I was happy to
get the job.

So for the next couple of years I taught "Infantry Battalion Operations in a European Scenario" from August to January, and I taught
"Special Operations" from January to June. Then during the summers
I was assigned to the instructor training committee to train the new
instructors.

Teaching Leavenworth faculty members how to teach at Leavenworth was far, far away from the timid basic trainee I had once been at
Fort Dix, New Jersey. And being an instructor in the world of the
modern battlefield was perfect for me.

Teaching special operations was a great job too. What I came to
understand during that time was that the students who took my class
had little understanding of what LRPs and Rangers did. I was teach-

ing it because I had spent my time with those special men while my students had been in more conventional units. If I had to be away from a troop assignment, that was as good as it got.

Leavenworth gave me a chance to catch my breath. At least that's what I thought was happening. The truth was that the entire country was shifting gears and the national mood was focusing on putting Vietnam behind us and distancing ourselves from foreign entanglements—especially those involving combat. The move to put Jimmy Carter, a peacemaker Democrat, in the White House offered promise of change that would heal what was traumatized in our nation.

For me the change was welcomed and uncomfortable at the same time. I felt a release of some of the pressures that had been born from being in combat assignments or at training bases where combat preparedness was the be-all and end-all of our daily efforts. Leavenworth was more of an ivy-covered academic environment with green uniforms. It was more introspective and more contemplative than any place I had ever been. We mused over matters of ethics, honor, responsibilities, and the future of the army.

In my personal life I was getting a second chance. My first marriage had become a casualty of the war, a casualty that I might have avoided. The long hours at work and the months away from home only exacerbated the simple lack of energy I brought to my marriage. I have to take all of the blame for its collapse and credit my wife for a level of maturity and class that it took me years to recognize and appreciate.

During those Leavenworth years I married again. That time, to a woman who was more adventurous than I could ever be. She was addicted to travel and discovery, and took jobs that would allow her to see the world. We met in Thailand, where she was teaching at the International School. We were married after my first year at Fort Leavenworth, and she was killed in a tragically senseless automobile accident on her way home from work one evening—two and a half years later.

I had hardly gotten over my own disappointment with the failure of my first marriage when a harsher chunk of reality slammed into me.

The army reacted as I might have expected—like a family. I was smothered with condolences, kind gestures, offers of all kinds, and the endless tiptoeing. People, soldiers too, treat widowers differently. They don't know how to let the loss creep out of the room or the conversation or any contact with the widower. I appreciated everyone's efforts and consideration, but there came a time when I wanted to scream: Please quit asking my secretary, "How's he doing?"

It was a small post with a smaller college faculty and everyone had a big heart. Still, I felt the whispering when I entered a room. I had become an oddity. Leavenworth had its share of bachelor majors—but I was not a bachelor. I was a widower.

After several months of trying very hard not to be rude to the large number of friends and co-workers who were trying so hard to be compassionate, I got a call from Washington. It was time for me to be reassigned. I had been at Leavenworth for four years and was ripe for a move.

During the mid-seventies the army had decided to optimize the resources of its officer corps by tasking each of us with a secondary military occupational specialty to complement our primary specialty. The theory was to spread out the good assignments and the bad. It was also supported by an argument that it would give the combat-arms officers an appreciation for the more mundane jobs that were none-theless essential to mission accomplishment. The argument had its merit, but those of us who were in combat-arms jobs saw it as little more than a chance to get home before dark, pull less field duty, and justify a funded graduate degree to enhance our skills.

Since my primary specialty was Special Forces, Airborne infantry, I was given a more administrative secondary specialty in Army Informa-tion. That was Pentagonese for public relations—community relations. Had I not been so preoccupied with my own problems I might have objected to the fact that no one bothered to ask me if I wanted to be enrolled in that specialty. I knew nothing about the Army Information program, was told that I had to pull a tour in my secondary specialty, sooner or later, and that I would learn on the job. I was expected to take the job cheerfully and just go with the flow.

I have to admit that I had little fight left in me, and accepted the assignment to the Los Angeles Public Affairs office without the slight-est idea what the job would entail. Thus, I left Leavenworth.

The most important thing that I learned during my last year there was that, above all, the army is a family. And when one member of the family is hurt they all grieve.

The job turned out to be necessary, but not for me. The army needed someone in Southern California to be able to represent the secretary of the army, but it hardly needed a colonel and two lieuten-ant colonels. I took advantage of the time there to rebuild the parts of my life that had been fairly well beaten up by the war, a divorce, and the death of a wife.

During those same years the already slow-moving, post—Vietnam army seemed to grind to a halt. Funds dried up, pay raises didn't happen, cost of living went up dramatically, and signs of interesting and challenging assignments were not showing up in my viewfinder. I had been promoted to lieutenant colonel and moved into upper-middle management. That meant a greater distance from the things I loved—soldiers—and nearer proximity to paperwork and staff duty.

It wasn't up to the army to change to suit my preferences, and I still felt good about the army that I had spent two decades in. But I wasn't convinced that I would be happy serving in one staff job after another with only an occasional and brief assignment to troop units. I had some decisions to make.

I was still in my thirties and thought that it was time to make a career change. I asked the army to find my replacement and draw up the papers for me to leave the army on the twentieth anniversary of the day I reported to Fort Dix, New Jersey.

I quietly signed out of the army, filled with vivid memories not as much of events as of people.

EPILOGUE

•

No American boy or girl should ever have to go to war to protect country and family. But reality continues to put young Americans in harm's way over and over again. We came out of Vietnam with the whisper of *never again* and still found ourselves in Iran, Beirut, Grenada, Panama, the Persian Gulf, Somalia, and Bosnia-Herzegovina.

And in every one of these deployments, the critical jobs that allowed the larger units to perform went to soldiers and sailors in special units. The same unselfish devotion to duty, that of the LRPs, Rangers, and Green Berets I was privileged to serve with, lives on today. There has never been a shortage of qualified and properly motivated American men and women to fill the slots long since vacated by the special men from the Vietnam years.

We can sleep better knowing that they are on the job, willing to take the risks, make the sacrifices, and meet the challenges, unmotivated by ego or glory.

A day doesn't go by when I don't remember the soldiers I served with and appreciate the influence they had on my life and my heart. They would never tell you themselves, but they were truly special men.